THE WESTERN
MEDITERRANEAN KINGDOMS
1200–1500

THE MEDIEVAL WORLD
Editor: David Bates

Already published

. . . . .

THE WESTERN MEDITERRANEAN KINGDOMS 1200–1500

The Struggle for Dominion

David Abulafia

Longman

An imprint of **Pearson Education**

Harlow, England · London · New York · Reading, Massachusetts · San Francisco
Toronto · Don Mills, Ontario · Sydney · Tokyo · Singapore · Hong Kong · Seoul
Taipei · Cape Town · Madrid · Mexico City · Amsterdam · Munich · Paris · Milan

Pearson Education Limited
Edinburgh Gate
Harlow
Essex CM20 2JE
United Kingdom

and Associated Companies throughout the world

© Addison Wesley Longman Limited 1997

The right of David Abulafia to be identified
as author of this Work has been asserted by
him in accordance with the Copyright,
Designs and Patents Act 1988.

First published 1997

ISBN   0 582 07821 0   CSD
        0 582 07820 2   PPR

British Library Cataloguing-in-Publication Data

A catalogue record for this book is
available from the British Library

Library of Congress Cataloging-in-Publication Data

Abulafia, David
The western Mediterranean kingdoms, 1200–1500 : the struggle for
dominion / David Abulafia.
p.   cm. — (The Medieval world)
Includes bibliographical references and index.
ISBN 0–582–07821–0 (hardcover). — ISBN 0–582–07820–2 (pbk.)
1. Western Mediterranean—History, Military.   2. Civilization,
Medieval.   3. Kings and rulers, Medieval—Biography.   4. Normans—
Western Mediterranean.   5. Royal houses—Europe, Western.
I. Title.   II. Series.
DE94.A38   1997
940'.09822—dc21   97–20258
                                                          CIP

10 9 8 7 6 5 4 3 2
04 03 02 01 00

Set by 35 in 11/12 pt Baskerville
Produced by Pearson Education Asia Pte Ltd.
Transferred to digital print on demand, 2002
Printed & Bound by Antony Rowe Ltd, Eastbourne

In memory of
R.C. Smail

The wisdom of man is to be found in his writings,
And the tip of his pen carries understanding,
So that with his pen as his staff he can ascend
As high as the sceptre in the hand of a king.
Samuel ibn Naghrila ha-Nagid,
vizier of Granada (993–1056)

CONTENTS

LIST OF MAPS

GENEALOGICAL TABLES

EDITOR'S PREFACE

David Abulafia's *Western Mediterranean Kingdoms* is a wide-ranging political narrative of the struggle for control of Sicily and southern Italy over the whole of the Later Middle Ages. Borrowing the phrase from a better known, but arguably no more important, conflict Dr Abulafia describes events in terms of a 'Two Hundred Years' War'. He skilfully integrates a panorama of the economic, cultural, religious and political considerations which absorbed the interest of all the great Mediterranean powers from the kingdom of Jerusalem of the thirteenth century in the East to the kingdoms of Aragon and Castile in the West, and which fatefully also sucked in the papacy and the kingdom of France. Crucially, the struggles are seen against the background of the internal tensions of the main participating kingdoms of Sicily and Aragon, and in the context of the fraught relations between Muslims and Christians and of economic rivalries which took in the entire Mediterranean.

The subject's origins lie in the conquest of southern Italy and Sicily by Normans in the eleventh century and their creation of the kingdom of Sicily in the twelfth. Sicily's geographical centrality within the Mediterranean world made it a legend for wealth and cultural diversity and attracted immigrants and adventurers throughout its history. Its acquisition by the Hohenstaufen at the end of the twelfth century placed it at the heart of the rivalry of Empire and Papacy and created the conditions which led eventually to its acquisition by Charles of Anjou, brother of King Louis IX of France. Charles's subsequent overthrow by Peter III of Aragon initiated the long conflict between Angevins and Aragonese for control which eventually merged into the so-called Italian

Wars of the late fifteenth and early sixteenth centuries. Over the whole of the period, the book is arranged around the reigns of the main participants, whose diplomatic manoeuverings and complex range of political interests are carefully analysed.

David Abulafia has published extensively on the history of the Mediterranean world from the eleventh to the sixteenth centuries. Well known for his recent life of the Emperor Frederick II of Hohenstaufen, he here brings together in accessible form the results of his extensive research and writings on numerous aspects of the Mediterranean world. Particularly impressive is his capacity to move assuredly around the complex linguistic and cultural and religious worlds of both medieval and modern Mediterraneans and that economic developments, especially large-scale changes, are placed in context of wider political developments. This book is an exceptionally welcome addition to the *Medieval World Series* because it takes on a large and complex subject on which there is no modern equivalent treatment, and because, in doing so, it casts light on a great range of the subjects which preoccupy political historians of the Later Middle Ages.

. . . . .

AUTHOR'S PREFACE

. . .

THE SICILIAN QUESTION:
A TWO HUNDRED YEARS' WAR

This book is concerned with events in Italy and Spain that
dominated the political consciousness of those who lived not
merely on the shores of those lands, but far afield in France,
the Low Countries, Greece, north Africa, occasionally even
Germany and England. The issue was control of either or
both of what would later be called the 'Two Sicilies': mainland southern Italy on the one hand, the island of Sicily
and its smaller neighbours such as Malta on the other. This
'Sicilian Question', apart from upsetting the affairs of the
English king Henry III in the mid-thirteenth century, was
one of those great perennial disputes that sucked popes,
emperors and French and Spanish princes into conflict from
the end of the twelfth century to the start of the sixteenth.
Between the foundation of the Kingdom of Sicily in 1130 and
the absorption of southern Italy by Ferdinand of Aragon in
1503, claims to rule the Sicilian kingdom, or the two separate Sicilian kingdoms after 1282, drew foreign forces into
Italy, moulded the factionalism of the Italian city-states, and
determined wider relationships linking Italy to the Balkans,
Africa and above all Spain. The entire Italian south – Sicily,
southern Italy and Sardinia – became the stamping ground
of Catalan-Aragonese armies sent by rulers of a fragmented
group of states in which central power was weak, and in
which the monarchy complained of a constant lack of money,
yet which achieved a remarkable series of conquests beginning with Majorca in 1229 and ending with Naples in 1442
and again 1503.

The history of Italy in this period cannot be written without paying attention to the Catalans and their ambitions. Or rather, it can be written without them, at the risk of producing what is really a history not of all Italy but of the major Italian republics in the north and centre, Florence, Venice, and so on. Unfortunately, too many histories of Italy have not been more than histories of those great centres. Put differently, the time has come when it is necessary, for lack of any such work, to write an outline of the political history of Italy looking at the country from the south upwards, from the perspective, that is, of by far the largest state, the south Italian kingdom. In view of the capital importance of this kingdom in economic and cultural developments, those aspects too must be considered, within a wider Italian framework. By the same token, the history of Spain in this period has generally been examined from the perspective of the kingdom of Castile which was, by the sixteenth century, clearly the dominant element in the emerging federation of Spanish kingdoms. Here an attempt is made to look at Spain's other face, that of Aragon-Catalonia, whose rulers, though much involved in Iberian affairs, looked increasingly outward towards the Mediterranean, across the Balearic islands to Sicily, Sardinia and Naples; and whose territories in the middle of the fifteenth century were half in Italy and half in Spain. The result is an overview of the political and economic changes taking place in the lands surrounding the western Mediterranean, not just the Italian and Spanish lands, but the territories in France and even Africa which were drawn into the political and economic web of the Crown of Aragon.

These two different perspectives, one on Spain, one on Italy, are intimately related through the power struggles that brought the Aragonese kings into Italian affairs, and are expressed through the long-lasting vendetta between the house of Barcelona and their rivals in Italy and the rest of the Mediterranean, the house of Anjou. In 1283 plans were laid for the duel between these two lines of kings to be settled permanently in single combat at Bordeaux. The duel itself did not take place; but a Two Hundred Years' War of Anjou and Aragon continued, with intermissions, to dominate the western, central and even at times eastern Mediterranean.

This book is the product of several years of thinking and writing about the western Mediterranean kingdoms in the period from the late twelfth century to the end of the fifteenth. While it seeks to draw together conclusions I have reached from several projects in the history of Sicily and southern Italy and of Catalonia-Aragon, it also seeks to work these results together into a coherent picture of the interaction between the Catalans and Italy, from the middle of the thirteenth century to the takeover of the Kingdom of Naples by Ferdinand II of Aragon at the start of the sixteenth century. It could be read as a study of the prelude to the Italian wars of the sixteenth century; or it could be read as a study of how trade and other business interests helped mould the policies of the most important Christian kings in the Mediterranean world. Since it appears in a series which contains a good many distinguished biographies, it has seemed a good idea to give the book a biographical framework, even if the number of rulers subjected to this treatment is quite large. The idea of 'parallel lives' goes back at least as far as Plutarch, and here the concept has been redeployed to show first of all how separate realms in Spain and Italy became entangled, at which point the kings of Aragon and of Sicily-Naples have distinct chapters to themselves; while subsequently, by the fifteenth century, the interweaving of interest has become so tight that the rival dynasties have been brought together in the same chapters. This has also, I hope, avoided unnecessary repetition in the last pages. There is no need any longer to defend the use of analytical biography or the writing of the history of 'high politics', which were long in disfavour, particularly among historians of the famous *Annales* school; even they have undergone a conversion of sorts in recent years. It is the contention of this book, and the experience of its author in observing the world, that events in the realm of high politics percolate down through society, and that any attempt to write history without attention to the decisions made at the top levels of government produces an immobile or static view of past societies which is indefensible. On the other hand, a good deal of attention is paid in this volume to economic developments (particularly trade) and to the encounter between religions in the Mediterranean, because these were issues that generated problems for governments and, in the case of economic factors, even determined what policies could be adopted; and, again, they filtered down to affect large numbers of the subjects of the kings who are the focus of this book, many of them Christians, but also, as will be seen, a good many Jews and Muslims with their own special preoccupations.

A feature of this book is the space devoted in the last section of each chapter to a review of what has been surveyed in greater detail in the chapter as a whole. This has been done with the intention of providing essential background to readers who have a particular interest in one or another period, theme or region, but who also need to be able to understand the wider setting. Thus someone with a special interest in (say) Robert the Wise and fourteenth-century Naples is invited to read the final section of each preceding chapter if time or patience precludes fuller attention to the earlier chapters.

The footnotes are intended to offer a sensible guide to the very variable literature which exists dealing with late medieval Sicily, southern Italy and the Catalan world. In some cases the items cited are simply a small selection of a much larger literature, for example on the trade of Barcelona; in other cases, such as the important reign of Robert of Naples, the literature seems hardly to have expanded during the twentieth century, with a few notable exceptions. I have attempted to be fairly generous in references to literature in English, but there are areas where deeper penetration is possible only with the help of the literature in Italian, French, Spanish and, increasingly, Catalan, which in recent years has recovered its honourable place among the languages of Europe. In the circumstances, it would not make sense to document each and every edition of the key primary sources, and, once again, I have borne in mind what is easily accessible, such as the Catalan chronicles, which do exist in English translation.

I am grateful to David Bates for his encouragement, his helpful criticism and his belief that the topic of this volume makes sense; to Andrew MacLennan for his patience and interest in the gradual unfolding of this project; to countless friends and colleagues in Sicily, Sardinia, southern Italy, Catalonia and other lands who have been so generous in providing me with copies of their own books and articles, to many of which I refer in the footnotes. Michael Jones and Cambridge University Press have kindly not objected to the fact that some material in Chapters 5 and 7 uses similar words to my contribution to the forthcoming volume of the *New Cambridge Medieval History* devoted to the fourteenth century. Anna Sapir Abulafia and my daughters Bianca and Rosa have been eminently agreeable audiences for the history of the Mediterranean. Over the years I have managed to visit a large proportion of the territories mentioned in this book, in Catalonia, Aragon, Majorca, southern France, southern Italy, Sicily, Sardinia, Corsica, Hungary, and even Albania during its long dark night of Stalinist-Maoist oppression; and much nearer home I have had to put up with the sight of the coat of arms of René of Anjou on a flag flying almost at the bottom of my garden, when the Queens' College eights are competing in the college bumps. My own college, Caius, has continued to provide a magnificent working environment and stimulating colleagues in medieval and modern history.

But it is to the memory of Dr R.C. ('Otto') Smail of Sidney Sussex College, Cambridge that I want to dedicate this book. Those who knew him will also know why he inspired such strong enthusiasm among his colleagues and pupils, as a superb lecturer, a rigorous scholar and an eminently agreeable companion.

David Abulafia
Gonville and Caius College, Cambridge
September 1996

PART I

THIRTEENTH-CENTURY CHALLENGES

Chapter 1

THE ORIGINS OF
THE SICILIAN KINGDOM

. . .

THE LURE OF THE SOUTH

The Norman Kingdom of Sicily and southern Italy, founded in 1130, is usually regarded as one of the strongest and as probably the wealthiest of the monarchies of twelfth-century Europe; as early as the thirteenth century, legislators and insurgents in the south of Italy appealed to the good old law of King William II (d. 1189) as the embodiment of wise government. The impression that the former Norman territories were a source of enormous wealth and military resources remained strong in the minds of late medieval conquerors such as the French invaders Charles of Anjou, who was crowned king of Sicily in 1266, and Charles VIII of Valois, who added the Neapolitan crown to that of France in 1494–95. 'A land flowing with milk and honey' had attracted the first Norman invaders in the eleventh century, to quote their biblically-conscious chroniclers; these writers were only the first to draw a comparison between the wealth of southern Italy and that of the ancient land of Israel, for Frederick II (d. 1250) is also supposed to have drawn a direct comparison, saying that his Sicilian kingdom would have provided a more luxurious home for the Children of Israel than had the Promised Land of Canaan. Such persistence in the historical sources that southern Italy was wealthy and flourishing raises two important questions: how far the reputation of southern Italy acted as a magnet for would-be conquerors; and how far this reputation was based in solid reality.

The great Italian liberal historian, Benedetto Croce, tried in 1924 to disentangle some of the contradictions presented by the history of southern Italy. Here was a region whose princes, lawyers and philosophers were held in the highest esteem by earlier writers; a kingdom which was seen as the precocious instigator of the ideal of an 'absolute secular and enlightened monarchy'.[1] Croce recalled the words of the Swiss historian of the Renaissance, Jacob Burckhardt: at the court of Frederick II, in thirteenth-century Naples, first appears the notion of the state and its government as 'a work of art'.[2] Yet Croce was keenly conscious that southern Italy had fallen far from this peak of glory, even supposing such past achievements were not mythical. What had been praised by Venetian merchants of the twelfth century as the realm of peace, free of brigands, in later centuries had an almost opposite reputation; and the efficient, impartial administrators of Norman and Hohenstaufen days gave way to venal, wayward government by the fifteenth century. Croce pointed to the lack of national unity in the south of Italy; there existed indeed one political entity, ruled from a capital at Naples, but under its control a great variety of regional interests – towns aspiring to autonomy, warlords trying to build great estates, and also geographical and ethnic diversity. Perhaps in the twelfth century there were some rulers who maintained a benign interest in the good government of the many peoples in their domain, but by the fourteenth century the princes and their bureaucracy stood much further from the population, separated to some degree by the powerful territorial and governmental claims of a large feudal baronage:

> no people, no nation came to birth; there was not even a name which fitted all the various stocks, for Sicilians, Apulians, Longobards, Neapolitans were all appellations of a purely local character; the burghers and the common people did not impose their will, and the feudal lords did so only in a highly anarchistic manner which did not further the good of the state . . . The parliaments, called together at long intervals, served only for the proclamation of laws or the levy of moneys to meet some

---

1. B. Croce, *History of the Kingdom of Naples*, ed. H.S. Hughes (Chicago, 1970), p. 11.
2. J. Burckhardt, *The Civilisation of the Renaissance in Italy*, ed. P. Burke (Harmondsworth, 1990), p. 12.

financial emergency; there is no record of either give-and-take
with the king or legal opposition to him.[3]

Croce wrote in a spirit of political idealism; but it remains
difficult to escape from some of the problems he posed:
above all, the decline from the well-articulated system of rule
historians have identified in Norman Sicily and southern
Italy, in the twelfth century, to the disorder of Angevin Italy
only two centuries later, when much of the Norman fabric
of government crumbled. So too the wealthy kings of the
twelfth century, whose display certainly aroused much envy,
were succeeded by relatively impoverished rulers who tided
over their financial problems by taking massive loans from
foreign bankers. Such contrasts are easily over-drawn, and
it should not be supposed that southern Italian kings lost
their well-established influence in Italian and Mediterranean
politics; they made many attempts to maintain past glories,
often on an ever greater scale. But to do so cost money; and,
amid the strains of government crises and rebellions, it was
less easy to live as a magnificent monarch in the thirteenth
than in the twelfth century.

When Croce talked of 'decline' he did not mean decline
in international significance: the rulers of southern Italy in
the thirteenth century were actively involved in imperial politics in Germany and northern Italy, even after the death of
Frederick II, in plans to reconquer the Empire of Constantinople, in crusades to recover the Kingdom of Jerusalem,
to establish and uphold supremacy in northern Italy, whether
in alliance with or as opponents of the papacy and its Guelf
allies. Frederick II issued his *Constitutions of Melfi* for the
kingdom of Sicily, but the law code glories in his titles of
Roman Emperor, king of Jerusalem, king of Arles. Charles
I of Anjou, when he died in 1285, bore among his titles
those of King of Jerusalem, King of Sicily, King of Albania,
Count of Provence, Count of Piedmont.[4] But it was to his
conquest of the Kingdom of Sicily and southern Italy that
Charles and his heirs owed much of their influence in the
Mediterranean. It is necessary to look at the origins and
resources of their south Italian state.

---

3. Croce, *Kingdom of Naples*, p. 18.
4. David Abulafia, *Frederick II. A medieval emperor* (London, 1988), p. 204.

· · ·
LAND AND PEOPLE

The lands the Normans and their successors conquered possessed neither geographical nor political unity. Long sea coasts provided the best means for moving from region to region. Large areas of southern Italy are mountainous and there are no extensive internal plateaux. Inland there are few important towns, though Melfi and Venosa were significant exceptions, as was the papal enclave of Benevento. The coasts are where the centres of settlement have always lain: the plain around Naples owes its fertility to the part benign, part destructive lava flows of Vesuvius. By 1300 Naples was one of the larger towns in Italy, much the most important focus of population in southern Italy; Palermo too was a large town by European standards, soaking up a significant part of the food supply of Sicily. Both may have had populations of very roughly 25,000; only a select few north Italian cities – notably Florence, Genoa, Milan and Venice – can have greatly exceeded this figure in the years around 1300. Down the coast of the Tyrrhenian Sea ancient merchant settlements at Gaeta, Amalfi, Salerno and other centres also contributed to the importance of this relatively small region. But rocky Calabria, the toe of Italy, was thinly settled and had no big coastal towns to rival the bay of Naples. On the east coast of southern Italy lay long, low plains, a source of wine, grain and olive oil, stretching from the Apennine foothills down to the sea; and along the sea existed a long line of towns, some of them famous as centres of shipping, especially pilgrim traffic: Bari, Barletta, Trani. Significant inland centres included Frederick II's administrative headquarters at Foggia, and the Muslim settlement at Lucera, itself a Byzantine foundation; in the early thirteenth century the hinterland of this region (known as the Capitanata) was emerging as a major source of good quality grain for the export market. The northernmost part of this coastline was, however, less well populated and bordered on the wild Abruzzi and Molise regions, the haunt of bears and wolves still. The thirteenth-century new town of L'Aquila, meaning 'the eagle', expressed the sensitive role of the region as a frontier defence zone. The papal town of Rieti stood not far off, and the authority of the bishops of Rieti actually straddled the frontier of the south Italian kingdom.[5] Finally, the island of Sicily, rich in grain-productive uplands, especially in the west of the island, still preserved even in the late Middle Ages some of the exotic character it had possessed as an Arabic island. The coastline was known for its luscious gardens; sugar-cane and other 'oriental' foodstuffs were grown in the Norman period, but were less visible under Frederick II: he tried to revive their production, but in reality it only recovered in the fifteenth century. In the north-east of Sicily, around Messina, the economy was more diverse, with extensive wine production and local textile industries.[6]

The conquerors of southern Italy were attracted more by the reputation of the lands they coveted than by exact knowledge of their condition. They knew that the rulers of Sicily and south Italy were exceptionally wealthy; they may have heard that the sources of wealth lay partly in taxes on trade, partly in the export of grain from royal estates, partly in the efficiency with which the royal government was able to collect the taxes it actually claimed. But it is more likely that would-be conquerors were attracted by the sight of Sicilian gold and silk or by news of the size of Palermo and Naples (and therefore, they might assume, their wealth) than by tales of sacks of grain. If they won their wars, it was through experience of government that they learned the realities of south Italian geography and resources.

The history of the late medieval Mediterranean was moulded in significant ways by events in the south of Italy during the eleventh and twelfth centuries. Before AD 1000, the south of Italy was divided many ways: there were local dynasties, who exercised authority over a primarily Latin Christian, Italian-speaking population in the small but wealthy commercial centres of Campania such as Amalfi and Gaeta, and in the Duchy of Naples; extensive tracts of the interior were under the control of princes descended from Lombard conquerors of the early Middle Ages; all these occasionally owed allegiance to the Byzantine emperor, far away in Constantinople, whose power was remote enough to prompt little

5. R. Brentano, *A new world in a small place. Church and religion in the diocese of Rieti, 1188–1378* (Berkeley/Los Angeles, 1994), pp. 83–5.
6. S.R. Epstein, *An island for itself. Economic development and social change in late medieval Sicily* (Cambridge, 1992).

worry about a serious recovery of Byzantine control in all of southern Italy.[7] Nevertheless, the south-east, Apulia, was controlled by Byzantine governors, as was occasionally the toe of Italy (Calabria), and both areas retained a substantial Greek-speaking population throughout the Middle Ages, although only tiny Greek remnants survive now.[8] Apulia and indeed virtually all south Italian towns were also home to a Jewish community that may have numbered 5 per cent of the overall population, and which was well integrated into wider society, being heavily engaged in textile production.[9]

In the island of Sicily, by contrast, there were many Greeks, maybe 40 per cent of the entire population around AD 1000, and significant numbers of Jews, but almost no Latins or 'Italians'; the majority was an Arabic-speaking population of Muslims, some of them descendants of the ancient population who had converted to Islam after the Muslim invasions of the ninth century, some descendants of Arabs and Berbers from north Africa, some very recent settlers from as far afield as Persia and Yemen, who took advantage of the island's prosperity astride the key trade routes of the Islamic world to take up residence in such great cities as Balarm (Palermo), more generally known to the Arabic-speakers as simply *Madinat Siqilliyah*, 'the city of Sicily'.

.   .   .

THE NORMAN STATE

The conquest of these areas by the Normans was not the result of a master plan to subdue the region and transform into into a single kingdom. The region would, indeed, for long retain its diversity in language, religion and social structure. The Norman conquest in the eleventh century reveals, rather, how a small group of foreign mercenaries who first arrived at the start of the century could make themselves so

---

7. The most recent major study of Lombard Italy is that of H. Taviani, *La principauté lombarde de Salerne, IXe–XI siècle*, 2 vols (Rome, 1991); see also B.M. Kreutz, *Before the Normans. Southern Italy in the ninth and tenth centuries* (Philadelphia, 1991); J. Gay, *L'Italie méridionale et l'Empire byzantin* (Paris, 1904).

8. V. von Falkenhausen, *Untersuchungen über die byzantinische Herrschaft in Süditalien vom 9. bis ins 11. Jahrhundert* (Wiesbaden, 1967).

9. N. Ferrorelli, *Gli Ebrei nell'Italia meridionale dall'età romana al secolo XVIII*, ed. F. Patroni Griffi (Naples, 1990).

valuable to the warring parties in southern Italy – Byzantine and Lombard – that they inserted themselves into the command structure as territorial lords rewarded for their sterling services. In time, under the leadership of Robert Guiscard (d. 1085) they acquired control of the Byzantine province of Apulia, and began to consolidate their hold on southern Italy; by the 1060s they felt able to respond to appeals from Sicily to help sort out factional strife on the island, seizing control of the island for themselves under the vigorous leadership of Robert Guiscard's brother Roger I, Great Count of Sicily. Guiscard, for his part, concentrated heavily on the defence of his interests in Apulia against the Byzantine emperor, whose rights in the area he had usurped; Guiscard led vigorous campaigns into the Balkans, attacking Durazzo (Dyrrachium) in what is now Albania and the Greek island of Corfu.[10]

At the start of the twelfth century there existed, in fact, three major Norman political units in the Italian south: Apulia and contiguous lands under the rule of Guiscard's heirs; Sicily and Calabria, notionally dependent on Apulia but flourishing under the rule of Roger I and his heirs; and a third statelet, the Principality of Capua, which lay under the rule of another group of Normans entirely. Having failed to secure the recognition of either the Byzantine emperor (not surprisingly) or the German emperor (who had his own powerful ambitions in Italy), Guiscard and Roger I built close ties to the third of the claimants to universal authority, the pope, who was glad to accept the vassalage of Robert Guiscard in 1059. The Normans proved unruly vassals, but they also provided valuable protection to the papacy at dangerous moments, such as Gregory VII's bitter quarrel with the German king Henry IV (though their hospitality to Gregory in 1084 was cruelly marred by the sacking of Rome at the same time). Later, without compromising the formal dependence of the count of Sicily on the Norman duke of Apulia, Pope Urban II in 1098 appears to have conferred special status on Roger I of Sicily, allowing him effective day-to-day control of the Church on the island, in the hope that the Normans would organise the first Latin Church structure on the island,

10. H. Taviani-Carozzi, *La terreur du monde. Robert Guiscard et la conquête normande en Italie* (Paris, 1996); see for the sources K.B. Wolf, *Making History. The Normans and their Historians in eleventh-century Italy* (Philadelphia, 1995).

and hold this frontier area against the danger of an Islamic resurgence.[11] The rights of the papacy in southern Italy and Sicily can thus be summarised as an acknowledged claim to sovereign papal authority over the entire area, which was a detached part of the Patrimony of St Peter administered on the pope's behalf by his Norman agents. Nonetheless, within this area the Norman ruler of Sicily retained special powers of control over the Church which in some respects counterbalanced the awkward fact of ruling what was technically part of a papal province. Moreover, neither the German nor the Greek emperor was especially willing to recognise that the pope possessed those rights over southern Italy and Sicily, which they continued to claim for themselves as integral (though lost) parts of the ancient Roman empire to which each laid his own claim. In other words, southern Italy and Sicily stood at the point where the two Roman empires, of East and West, lay closest to one another, and the rulers of the Italian South had to pursue delicate policies if they were to maintain their autonomy in the face of such powerful rivals. Papal claims to suzerainty were themselves of fundamental importance for the political history of the Sicilian realm.[12]

The weakness of the duchy of Apulia in the early twelfth century opened up for Roger II, count of Sicily, the opportunity to absorb the lands once conquered by his late uncle Robert Guiscard, and to unify the Norman domains, drawing in even the extremely reluctant princes of Capua. In 1130, taking advantage of a papal schism, Roger secured from Pope Anacletus II, who was desperate for his support, the grant of a crown, having already been begged by his barons, at his suggestion of course, to become their king. Thus it remained uncertain whether the pope or the assembly of barons was the constitutive agency, a problem complicated when a later pope dragged his heels over recognising Roger's son William as the new king after Roger died in 1154. Hereditary claims

11. S. Fodale, *Comes et legatus Siciliae* (Palermo, 1970); J. Deér, *Papsttum und Normannen* (Cologne, 1972), and the same author's handy source collection: *Die Papsttum und die süditalienischen Normannenstaaten, 1053–1212* (Göttingen, 1969); also H. Houben, *Tra Roma e Palermo. Aspetti e momenti del Mezzogiorno medioevale* (Galatina, 1989).

12. Deér, *Papsttum*, gives one possible view of how this relationship was expressed in the twelfth century.

were also an issue: the problem of whether the barons could over-ride the assumed rights of inheritance arose in 1189 when William II died and no one in Sicily was especially keen to accept as king the heir to the German throne, who was married to Roger II's daughter Constance of Hauteville. On this occasion, the pope and the barons were of one mind, fearful of the implications in allowing the German crown to dominate not just its homeland and northern Italy, but also southern Italy and Sicily. Such an accretion of power would spell the end of the autonomy of the papacy in central Italy.

Under Roger II and his heirs William the Bad and William the Good, the kings of Sicily adapted the existing Greek and Arab bureaucracies in Sicily and southern Italy, utilising skilled professional administrators, some native, some from abroad, and developing a multilingual administration that could address the needs of the monarchy and also communicate with the king's subjects.[13] Justice was effectively dispensed in far-flung provinces (parts of central Italy, the Abruzzi and Molise were brought definitively under Norman rule under Roger), and tensions between Muslims, Greeks and Latins were held in check, at least under Roger II. Under the two Williams, power shifted away from the bureaucrats, and the Latin baronage acquired growing influence at court; Muslim and even Greek administrators were pushed more to the margins; thousands of Italian settlers were lured into the kingdom, a policy that started as early as the rule of Roger I in Sicily.[14] What must be stressed is that the 'Norman kingdom of Sicily' was not particularly 'Norman', though there was a large scattering of Norman barons who intermarried with the local Lombard nobility in southern Italy. The administrative structure of the kingdom owed little to the Normans, except for local customs; the Normans certainly did not create a 'feudal structure', but melted into what was there already. Those who believe in a strong Norman identity tend to qualify their assertions (and this is some qualification!) by insisting that one major characteristic of Normans was their

13. H. Takayama, *The Administration of the Norman Kingdom of Sicily* (Leiden, 1993); E. Jamison, *Admiral Eugenius of Sicily. His life and work* (London, 1958).
14. David Abulafia, 'The end of Muslim Sicily', in James M. Powell, *Muslims under Latin rule, 1100–1300* (Princeton, 1990), pp. 101–33.

ability to assimilate rapidly into the surrounding society.[15] Memories of common Norman ancestry were revived in the late twelfth century to stimulate diplomatic relations with the English monarchy, which by then was not very Norman either. The ruling dynasty of Sicily was Norman by origin, but it is probably an exaggeration to say that Norman French was much spoken at court. Roger II had a north Italian mother, and he and his courtiers would have known Greek, Arabic and some Italian.

The magnificent Byzantine mosaics in the great churches of Palermo and Cefalù, the intricate Arab ceiling of the Palace Chapel in Palermo, the occasional multilingual inscription, the flurry of translation of ancient philosophic and scientific works from the original Greek, the fulsome poetry and scientific research of Muslim visitors to the royal court, all these have created in the minds of subsequent observers the gorgeous image of a 'kingdom in the sun', in which rare values of tolerance and mutual trust that transcended religious and ethnic boundaries were created, almost uniquely in twelfth-century Europe.[16] This image speaks more for the noble sentiments of those who have articulated it than it represents the full reality. Even at court, non-Latins were only able to enjoy a high degree of influence under Roger II, who was an able manipulator of his subjects, anxious to win the support of the Muslim majority in Sicily, for otherwise he could not hope to make his kingdom a reality. Roger also appreciated the administrative and cultural gifts that Greeks and Arabs could offer. Yet his aim, ultimately, was to manage to be a recognisably western-style king to his Latin subjects, a Byzantine-style *basileus* to his Greek subjects, a sultan to his Muslim subjects. His great achievement lay in this ability to be all things to all people, or rather the right thing to the right people.[17]

15. Here I side more with R.H.C. Davis, *The Normans and their myth* (London, 1976), than with D.C. Douglas, *The Norman achievement* (London, 1969), and *The Norman Fate* (London, 1976).
16. Thus Lord Norwich actually entitled the second volume of his engaging narrative history of Norman Sicily *The Kingdom in the Sun* (London, 1970); repr. as part 2 of *The Normans in Sicily* (London, 1992).
17. The meaning of many mosaics is elucidated by E. Borsook, *Messages in Mosaic. The royal programmes of Norman Sicily, 1130–1187* (Oxford, 1990).

Ambitious foreign adventures under the Normans pre-figured later expeditions by Sicilian rulers into Africa, the Balkans and elsewhere. Roger in the 1140s managed to gain control of several key towns on the facing shore of Africa, among them Tripoli and Mahdia, the terminus for the trans-Sahara gold routes. This 'kingdom of Africa' was lost by William the Bad; hence, in part, William's unpopularity.[18] The dream of dominating the facing shores of Africa did not go away in later centuries, as will become plain. But William II followed in the footsteps of both Robert Guiscard and Roger II in launching invasions of the Byzantine Empire. In a daring campaign in 1185 William the Good seized Durazzo and Thessalonika, and seemed poised to capture Constantinople.[19] Yet the massive Sicilian fleet rarely secured the victories that King William sought, off Alexandria and the Holy Land, or at Majorca, which was fruitlessly attacked in 1181–82. The prime success of the fleet was, rather, in creating a cordon sanitaire around the kingdom, but even then ambitious German kings, mindful of their own claim to rule the south of Italy, penetrated time and again into the region: Emperor Lothar faced Roger II, Frederick Barbarossa faced William I, finally Henry VI succeeded in conquering the south in 1194 on behalf of his Norman wife Constance.

Sea power was one of the great strengths of Norman Sicily, but there were other powerful contenders for mastery of Mediterranean waters, notably the fleets of the rising Christian republics of Genoa, Pisa and Venice. An important aspect of the history of the Norman kingdom is the gradual intrusion of the merchants from these cities into the economic life of Sicily and southern Italy, following treaties with the Norman kings which were intended to prevent the north Italian navies from joining the king's enemies.[20] Thus in 1156 a particularly generous privilege was granted to the Genoese, in order to dissuade them from alliances with the western and the Byzantine emperors, offering in addition tax exemptions and rights of access to the wheat, cotton

18. David Abulafia, 'The Norman Kingdom of Africa', *Anglo-Norman Studies*, 7 (1985), pp. 26–49.
19. C.M. Brand, *Byzantium confronts the West, 1180–1204* (Cambridge, MA, 1968).
20. David Abulafia, *The Two Italies. Economic relations between the Norman Kingdom of Sicily and the northern communes* (Cambridge, 1977).

and other goods produced in Sicily. This was the beginning of a slow process by which the trade of Norman Sicily was gradually redirected away from its traditional commercial partners in north Africa towards Latin Europe; the process was accompanied by the immigration of settlers from the area around Genoa. It was thus part of a wider process of latinisation which was taking place in Norman Sicily. Although the north Italian merchants did not obtain an iron grip on the economy of Sicily (indeed, the Genoese quarrelled with William I of Sicily within a few years of the treaty mentioned earlier), the acquisition of Sicilian wheat was of considerable importance to the cities of northern Italy, providing them with the means to grow still further in population and output. Throughout the central and late Middle Ages, the relationship between the north Italian merchants and the rulers of Sicily and southern Italy was of major importance in the economy and politics of the Mediterranean world. Some scholars have argued that this relationship had a major influence on the economic structures that developed within Sicily itself and other have played this down, but it is impossible to deny that this relationship had massive political and commercial repercussions in the city palaces and on the quaysides of the maritime cities of northern Italy.[21]

.   .   .

THE COMING OF THE HOHENSTAUFEN

Certain fundamental features of the Norman kingdom thus had a major impact on the thirteenth-century kingdom as well. In the first place, the kings of Sicily were papal vassals. The papacy learned increasingly to accept the advantages which a powerful kingdom lying to the south of Rome might offer. No longer pirate kings, the Normans became protectors of the Church; in the early 1190s King Tancred of Sicily won the support of Pope Celestine III when Barbarossa's fierce son, Henry VI of Hohenstaufen, launched his invasions of the Norman kingdom. For, just as the papacy hoped to benefit from the presence of a strong, friendly monarchy to the

21. For an attempt to steer between the views of Bresc and Epstein on this, see David Abulafia, *Commerce and Conquest in the Mediterranean, 1100–1500* (Aldershot, 1993), chapter 1.

south, Pope Celestine was well aware of the dangers he would face if the western emperor added not merely northern Italy but also Sicily and the south to his domain.

This, of course, was precisely what occurred when in 1189 King William the Good died young and childless; by normal law of succession the kingdom devolved upon Roger II's daughter Constance as sole legitimate survivor of the royal house. The difficulty was not Constance, but her husband Henry of Hohenstaufen, heir to Frederick Barbarossa's lands in Germany, Burgundy and Italy. The barons of the kingdom set Henry's claims aside in favour of an illegitimate grandson of Roger II, Tancred Count of Lecce. Henry, backed by German, Genoese and Pisan forces, invaded southern Italy, and in 1194, on his second attempt, all fell before him. The defences of the kingdom were less strong than its tradition of government.[22]

For Henry and Constance did not transform their kingdom into a different type of state. They showed themselves highly responsive to the existing traditions within government. They did not wish to integrate the kingdom into the empire, but rather to hold it apart from the empire as a personal dominion, a special source of financial and military strength. Henry VI planned expeditions certainly to Jerusalem and perhaps to Constantinople, and these expeditions were to be based primarily on the manpower resources and shipping of southern Italy. Henry saw himself as the crusading emperor who would redeem Jerusalem, lost by the Christians as recently as 1187, and establish the name of his revived Roman Empire from one end to another of Europe and the Mediterranean world. What impeded Henry's grandiose plans of Mediterranean empire was his sudden death (1197); Constance shortly before then gave birth to a son, Frederick (1194–1250), whose reign left a legacy of strife to the whole of Italy.

. . .

FREDERICK II

Frederick II has suffered at the hands of historians who have tried to separate him from his Norman predecessors,

22. P. Csendes, *Heinrich VI.* (Darmstadt, 1993); H. Toeche, *Heinrich VI.* (Leipzig, 1867).

and to elevate him to a special place as the enlightened despot of the thirteenth century. He has been deprived of his real credit as the rebuilder of the damaged edifice of Norman monarchy: a conservative reformer who made more uniform and more workable the system of government created by his grandfather Roger II.[23] In his youth the Norman kingdom was dominated by rapacious warlords and pirates: the German Markward von Anweiler in Palermo, the Genoese Alamanno da Costa and Enrico Pescatore in Syracuse and Malta. Yet, as a papal fief, the kingdom should have been protected by its overlord, Pope Innocent III.[24] After Constance died in 1198 Frederick of Sicily was his ward. Innocent did indeed try to control Markward and other despoilers, and he even threatened a crusade against Markward in 1198–99. The governmental machine was not destroyed, however, and it continued to produce the documents the boy king's subjects needed; if rapacious barons were to legitimise their seizures, it was as well to have a royal chancery which could issue charters of confirmation. In essence what happened was that the balance shifted away from the monarchy towards what had always been strong regional power expressed by the barons and warlords.

The recovery of royal power took time, partly because Frederick became involved in the winning of the German crown which his father Henry had held. For several years it was in Germany that he lived and sought to make his authority meaningful. Frederick's measures against his enemies in southern Italy only began seriously in 1220 on his return from the north, and were vigorously prosecuted once again from 1231. Among groups who were successfully repressed were the Muslims of Sicily, the vast majority of whom were deported to the remote Apulian stronghold of Lucera, where

23. David Abulafia, *Frederick II. A medieval emperor* (London, 1988), as against E. Kantorowicz, *Frederick the Second, 1194–1250*, transl. E.O. Lorimer (London, 1931), on which see David Abulafia, 'Kantorowicz and Frederick II', *History*, 62 (1977), pp. 193–210; A. Boureau, *Histoires d'un historien. Kantorowicz* (Paris, 1990). For the beginning of Frederick's career, see W. Stürner, *Friedrich II.*, vol. 1, *Die Königsherrschaft in Sizilien und Deutschland, 1194–1220* (Darmstadt, 1992).
24. T.C. van Cleve, *Markward von Anweiler and the Sicilian regency* (1937); David Abulafia, 'Henry Count of Malta and his Mediterranean activities', in *Medieval Malta*, ed. A.T. Luttrell (London, 1975), pp. 104–25.

they were cut off from easy contact with the Islamic world and yet could provide the emperor with soldiers and with artisans skilled in weapon manufacture.[25] The Genoese in Sicily and Malta were also successfully disciplined. Frederick was later harshly berated by the papacy for stripping the Church of lands acquired during his childhood; while he did not generally exempt the Church from his attempt to restore royal rights, he also took care to protect those of its interests which were demonstrably sound in law.[26] He was no worse than his contemporaries in making use of the revenues of empty sees; he was a patron of the south Italian Cistercians and had close links to the eminent Franciscan Elias of Cortona. Another way forward was the proclamation of royal rights as enshrined in the Roman law codes: the Justinianic concept of the king as God's representative on earth, who is appointed to judge and to correct the evil actions of men, themselves the result of man's first sin in the Garden of Eden, was enunciated resoundingly in Frederick's legislation for the Kingdom of Sicily in 1231. The *Constitutions of Melfi* which embody that legislation have perhaps to be seen as an idealised statement of royal rights, and many of their concerns, such as control of usury, reflect current preoccupations of the papal *curia*; but they provided a basis for further legislation by Frederick and the Angevins.[27]

In economic affairs Frederick built on the basis of Norman practice to extend royal rights over certain commodities, notably salt and silk production. Interest was shown in the improvement of port facilities in the *Regno*, with an eye on the financial proceeds; occasionally the crown stepped in to take advantage of grain shortages in Africa, banning private sales of grain to Tunis and enjoying vast profits (at least in 1239) from the export of Sicily's prime commodity. Attention was paid to the quality of the *Regno*'s coinage, with improvements

25. David Abulafia, 'Ethnic variety and its implications: Frederick II's relations with Jews and Muslims', in W. Tronzo, ed., *Intellectual life at the court of Frederick II Hohenstaufen* (Washington, DC, 1994), pp. 213–24.
26. H.J. Pybus, 'The Emperor Frederick II and the Sicilian Church', *Cambridge Historical Journal*, 3 (1929/30), pp. 134–63; see also J.M. Powell, 'Frederick II and the Church in the Kingdom of Sicily, 1220–40', *Church History*, 30 (1961), pp. 28–34 and 'Frederick II and the Church. A revisionist view', *Catholic Historical Review*, 44 (1962/3), pp. 487–97.
27. Abulafia, *Frederick II*, pp. 202–14.

in the silver coinage during the 1220s and the issue of a fine gold coin, the *augustalis*, in 1231; made most likely of African gold, this coin was also an advertisement for the revival of Frederick's authority throughout his realms, for it portrayed him as Roman emperor rather than as a regional king.[28]

One reason Frederick was able to enforce his will in southern Italy is that his authority extended far beyond the old Norman kingdom. As has been mentioned, a daring expedition to Germany brought him the German crown in 1218, and, in consequence, the crown of the western Roman Empire, which he received at Rome in 1220 from the hands of Pope Honorius III. After this vigorous defeat of Frederick's enemies in Germany, his enemies in southern Italy perhaps judged it best to submit to the new emperor in 1220. Certainly, many lost their lands, for Frederick took tight control of feudal inheritance in the south of Italy. Though possibly strengthened in southern Italy, Frederick was not permanently strengthened in Italy as a whole. Memories were now revived of the tactless behaviour of his grandfather Emperor Frederick I Barbarossa, who had caused great alarm in Northern Italy by his expeditions in the 1150s and 1160s; when a German emperor who was not merely Barbarossa's lineal descendant but king of Sicily and southern Italy also tried to visit the Lombard plain and to hold an imperial Diet at Cremona (1228), many northern towns resisted, fearing the loss of their autonomy to the emperor, to whom they were technically subject. The Milanese refused to be present at the Diet; they also blocked the mountain passes and prevented Frederick's German vassals from attending the Diet. Frederick insisted that the Lombards had nothing to fear: he was mainly planning to organise a crusade to recover the lost city of Jerusalem. Since he had taken the cross in 1218, on the occasion of his coronation in Germany, it was quite reasonable to bring together, after such lengthy delays, his German, Italian and Sicilian vassals. By no means all the Lombard towns wished to join the Milanese uprising against Frederick II, and even the papacy did not give vocal support

28. Abulafia, *Frederick II*, pp. 214–25; and at greater length, David Abulafia, 'La politica economica di Federico II', *Federico II e il mondo mediterraneo*, ed. P. Toubert and A. Paravicini Bagliani (Palermo, 1994), pp. 165–87.

to the Lombards as it had against Frederick II's German grandfather Frederick Barbarossa in the 1160s.[29]

The involvement of a south Italian king in Lombard politics was a post-Norman phenomenon, resulting from the fact that the king of Sicily was also Holy Roman Emperor. The Norman kings of Sicily had used bribes and commercial treaties to influence north Italian politics, and they had done this because they saw the Lombard towns as a buffer against the empire, when the empire threatened to assert ancient rights over southern Italy. But the Hohenstaufen kings of Sicily needed, of course, no buffer against themselves: the Lombard towns and the papal state were sandwiched between the German Kingdom in the north and the Kingdom of Arles or Burgundy in the west, with the Kingdom of Sicily to the south. It is not surprising that the Lombards attempted to separate north from south by attracting to their cause Frederick II's son Henry (VII), King of Germany and deputy for his father north of the Alps. But Henry's rebellion against his father only increased Frederick's bitterness.[30]

The papacy too was worried. In the 1220s there were bitter accusations against the newly powerful Frederick: he was said to have abandoned the cause of the crusade. (Later writers also pointed to the fact that he had a Muslim bodyguard, which was odd for a Christian emperor.) Gentle admonition under Honorius III (1216–27) gave way to stern reproof under Gregory IX (1227–41). The quarrel reached its peak when Frederick married the heiress to the Latin Kingdom of Jerusalem, ignoring her (supposedly for his harim girls) and, worse still, ignoring her influential father John of Brienne, who believed that he too had some claim to be regarded as king of Jersualem in right of his own late wife, Isabella's mother. The papacy was unsympathetic to the claim that Frederick was prevented from going on crusade by rebellions among the Muslims of Sicily, among the Lombards, and elsewhere. After one false start, he was excommunicated and in 1229 sailed east without papal blessing; he recovered the Holy City by negotiation; his presence in the Latin Kingdom of Jerusalem and in the Kingdom of Cyprus, an imperial fief, caused political chaos as rival factions grouped for and

29. Abulafia, *Frederick II*, pp. 229–41.
30. Ibid., pp. 292–3.

against him. Meanwhile a papal war was preached against the crusading emperor: his father-in-law reappeared to settle his grievances, leading a papal army into southern Italy and Sicily in 1229. Frederick returned swiftly from the Holy Land and suppressed the rebellion, beating back the invaders in total victory. Gregory IX, agreed to terms of peace at San Germano in 1231. Frederick characteristically did not try to push his own advantage too far in dealing with the papacy. He showed respect for the papal office: he sought as main advantage peace. Frederick's mollification of the pope made good sense: he needed a friend in his dealings with the Lombard towns. Gregory IX did use his good offices to send papal legates into northern Italy, but these legates felt less bound than Gregory to respect the interests of the merciful Frederick. They counselled the Lombards to end their rebellion, but they also insisted Frederick should impose no punishment, advice Frederick consistently ignored. He saw the rebels as traitors who by denying his authority, as constituted by Christ, were in effect heretics too.[31]

Frederick's position in Lombardy was greatly strengthened by his military victory at Cortenuova (1237). Controversy surrounded his alliances with local despots, such as the infamous Ezzelino da Romano, despot of Verona.[32] It was hardly surprising that Frederick accepted allies wherever he could find them, as in fact did the pope; it was something of a diplomatic achievement that he had so many friends in northern Italy. Nor were the Lombards free of taint: the free communes resisting the 'tyrant' emperor had among allies of their own the Este, another family of territorial lords from north-eastern Italy, whose rivalry with Ezzelino could be usefully exploited. The papacy used Frederick's opportunist alliance with these and other despots to brand him and his friends as heretics: Ezzelino certainly gave willing refuge to heretics in Lombardy, and, if it was a sin for Ezzelino to protect heretics, it was in papal eyes a sin for Frederick to

31. Abulafia, *Frederick II*, pp. 302–10.
32. The term 'despot' is not ideal; it is a pejorative description of a commonly accepted type of lordship. These figures were great lords, *signori*, and signorial government became the norm in the vast majority of Italian states by 1400. See D.M. Bueno de Mesquita, 'The place of despotism in Italian politics', in J.R. Hale, J.R.L. Highfield, B. Smalley, eds, *Europe in the late Middle Ages* (London, 1965), pp. 301–31.

protect those who protected heretics. Yet Frederick himself had passed extremely severe legislation against heretics in southern Italy, and pursued them actively in those areas of northern Italy where he possessed influence. The reality was that the emperor had been sucked into a destructive Lombard civil war, fought out by opposing armies who looked for succour to the pope, emperor or another saviour, such as Henry (VII) King of Germany.

The breakdown of relations with the papacy was clear after Cortenuova. In 1239 Gregory IX elevated the struggle to defend Rome against the Hohenstaufen into a crusade in defence of the relics of Sts Peter and Paul.[33] Thereafter battle was joined permanently, and not even the emperor's capture of a shipload of prelates sent to discuss his case, or a papal interregnum from 1241 to 1243, were able to force the disengagement of the parties. In 1245 Pope Innocent IV, elected after a long conclave which each faction had desperately sought to influence, turned against Frederick. He fled to Lyons and excommunicated the emperor. He declared Frederick deposed from his thrones. The grounds for doing so were that the emperor had despoiled the Sicilian Church, had consorted with Saracen infidels, had strayed far from Christian belief and practice; the emphasis in papal accusations was not, generally, on the threat Frederick posed in Lombardy and in central Italy. More particularly, the papacy made every effort to separate Sicily from Germany; from the time of Honorius III the question of a divided inheritance, with Sicily passing to one heir and Germany to another, stood prominently on the papal agenda. This was not necessarily something Frederick opposed; but he was not prepared to let an outside party determine the succession to his thrones.[34]

For the five years following his 'deposition' Frederick fought with some success to hold together his heritage: the lay nobility in Germany largely stood by him, and he retained much support among the Ghibellines of northern and central Italy. He was relentless in attempts to raise money in Sicily and southern Italy. He showed no mercy towards conspirators

---

33. David Abulafia, 'The Kingdom of Sicily and the origins of the political crusades', *Società, istituzioni, spiritualità. Studi in onore di Cinzio Violante*, 2 vols (Spoleto, 1994), vol. 1, pp. 65–77.
34. Abulafia, *Frederick II*, pp. 368–9.

sent, arguably with papal approval, to murder him. Yet he also showed a surprising willingness to come to terms with the pope; suggestions were in the air to the effect that he would retire to a life of crusading, for the sake of peace. But Frederick suddenly died of a fever at the end of 1250, when his prospects for holding the papacy at bay still seemed good. It was left to his sons to defend his reputation, which had been the constant target of bitter, often apocalyptic, papal propaganda casting him at worst as the Antichrist, come to persecute the Church in its last days before redemption.[35]

Nor were those who sought to destroy his power in Sicily simply adherents of papal policy. The emergence of internal opposition in the *Regno*, in which even his close adviser Piero della Vigna was supposedly implicated, served as a warning: heavy taxation and the repression of local liberties by a ruthless government at war with the papacy could, in fact, fail to achieve their objectives; instead of maintaining internal peace and strengthening royal finances, Frederick's policies in the late 1240s created new enemies and revived old memories of pre-Norman liberties. The papacy dangled in front of the townsmen of the Bay of Naples promises of urban liberties similar to those practised by the autonomous city-states of northern Italy. Such tensions were also part of Frederick's legacy to later conquerors of Sicily and the south.

Frederick II has acquired a powerful reputation as a cultural leader, which has been accepted very uncritically. He certainly had contact with Jewish and Muslim scholars, such as Judah ha-Cohen in Castile and ibn Sab'in in Ceuta. He was the patron of the great astrologer and physician Michael Scot, who had earlier been in papal service. On the other hand, Frederick's own entourage consisted predominantly of Christian scholars, and his contact with Islamic scholarship, unusual though it was, was achieved through the exchange of letters or during the visits of ambassadors. By the thirteenth century, the Spanish courts had become the major centres of contact between Christian, Jewish and Muslim scholars; but that of Frederick, itinerant through Italy, retained some

---

35. Yet some of this documentation must be treated with caution, as Peter Herde points out in 'Literary activities of the imperial and papal chanceries during the struggle between Frederick II and the papacy', in *Intellectual life at the court of Frederick II*, pp. 227–39.

echoes of the Norman past as a result of the emperor's fascination with ornithology, expressed in his famous tract on *The Art of Hunting with Birds*, which reveals an impressive knowledge of Aristotle and of Islamic authors. Frederick was no 'baptised sultan'. The development of courtly love lyrics, based closely on those of the Occitan troubadours but written in a formalised Italian vernacular, was one of the most lasting legacies of Frederick's cultural patronage. Spending on the fine arts had a strongly propagandist aspect, as can be seen in the surviving neo-classical sculptures of the Capua gateway, which proclaimed to those travelling into the *Regno* the pervasiveness of royal justice. But it was on the restoration of Norman castles such as Lagopesole or the building of palaces and hunting boxes in Lucera, Castel del Monte and elsewhere that funds were most often disbursed; little was built at royal expense for the Church, a point which perhaps unfairly reinforced the image of the emperor as its opponent.

· · ·

FREDERICK'S INHERITANCE IN ITALY

Frederick II's sons struggled to maintain their inheritance. Conrad IV, king of Germany and Sicily (1250–54) found it all but impossible to juggle his Sicilian and German duties, in the midst of rebellions on all sides; and it was only through the willing cooperation of his bastard brother, Manfred Prince of Taranto, that uprisings among the barons and townsmen of southern Italy were defeated. Conrad himself arrived in the south in 1252 and once again had to tackle resistance in Naples and the north-west of the kingdom. His success in bringing his opponents to their knees encouraged Conrad to appeal to his father's great foe Pope Innocent IV, and to attempt to have his royal title recognised by the technical overlord of the king of Sicily. But the pope was all the more afraid to see another German king sit upon the throne of Sicily; the long-felt need to separate the interests of the Hohenstaufen north of the Alps from their interests south of Rome naturally dominated papal thinking. Any other course of action risked a return to Frederick II's excessive accretion of power. Moreover, Conrad began to take an interest in northern Italy where, after all, his father's enemies still stood strong; his bastard brother Enzo, titular King of Sardinia, was actually held prisoner in Bologna. The papacy did not, however, lack a solution to the problem who should rule in southern Italy: within two years of Frederick's death the search was under way for a papal champion who could be installed on the Sicilian throne as a loyal vassal of the Holy See. The difficulty lay not in the idea; after all, the pope was overlord of southern Italy and could argue very well that it was for him to dispose of its crown. The real difficulty lay, rather, in finding a candidate both suitable and willing to replace the Hohenstaufen: a good soldier with handsome resources and a strong sense of duty to papal interests.

The papal search reached as far as England, where (for want of more prestigious candidates) King Henry III's little son Edmund was recruited to lead a papal expedition. Conrad IV died young, and for a few months in 1254 the papacy was actually able to send its own 'vicar', or representative into southern Italy, in the person of none other than Manfred of Hohenstaufen.[36] Innocent IV realised that Manfred was keen to exercise authority in the south and thought that he could utilise Manfred's enthusiasm on his own behalf. He did not wish to confer a crown on Manfred; indeed Conrad IV's infant son Conradin had a claim to Sicily which needed to be considered. Innocent actually confirmed Manfred's title as vicar and as Prince of Taranto, and came down to Naples to supervise the reorganisation of the kingdom: the creation at long last of free communes in Naples and other towns was to be one of the first acts in a revision of the Norman-Hohenstaufen system of central government. Within a few days Manfred summarily sundered his ties with Innocent, withdrawing to the Muslim stronghold of Lucera and defying papal anger and a papal army (December, 1254). His enthusiasm had indeed brought him hopes of a crown and of recovering his father's authority. The strength of papal resistance was sapped still further by the death of Innocent IV at the end of 1254 and the decision of his successor, Alexander IV, to concentrate on the alternative solution to the problem of Sicily: a return to the search for a papal champion. But the same year saw an agreement among the barons of Sicily and southern Italy to recognise as king

36. E. Pispisa, *Il regno di Manfredi. Proposte di interpretazione* (Messina, 1991).

neither Edmund nor Conradin but Manfred. The assumption that it was the barons – with perhaps a sprinkling of leading townsmen – who elected the king obviously contradicted the papal view that the ruler of Sicily was a papal vassal and must be confirmed in office or even chosen by the Holy See. It will be seen that the choice of a king by a 'parliament' of barons remained an important weapon to native Sicilians.

With Manfred the methods of rule and policies of Frederick II acquired new vigour. It seemed in the years around 1260 that Frederick's hopes had been redeemed. Within the kingdom, urban liberties were rapidly revoked. The port of Manfredonia, founded by him, was to remain an important centre of the grain trade of the Adriatic long after he died. Manfred took advantage of papal inanition north of Rome as well as in southern Italy. He could not hope to settle the internal rivalries of the north Italian towns, as past Hohenstaufen had dreamed of doing; he gave armed support to the pro-Hohenstaufen Ghibelline faction of Siena in 1260, when at the battle of Montaperti they and their Tuscan allies defeated a league of pro-papal Guelfs. As his authority in Italy grew, Manfred leaned increasingly towards the Ghibelline towns, claiming overlordship as far north as Alessandria in Piedmont. Although he could not match Frederick II, in the sense that he possessed no rights in Germany, he had effectively acquired the influence in central and northern Italy which his father had exercised. If anything, in fact, his influence was greater, because he had the backing of a solid Ghibelline grouping which took advantage of the weakness of the late thirteenth-century papacy to extend its network of alliances deep into Tuscany. Manfred, though a bastard, acquired the seal of respectability when his daughters made good marriages: that between his daughter Helena and Michael II, Despot of Epiros brought the Hohenstaufen as dowry the island of Corfu, as well as Durazzo, Avlona and Butrint on the Albanian coast.[37] Another daughter, Constance (carrying a venerable Hohenstaufen family name, redolent of empire) was betrothed in 1258 to the future King Peter III of Aragon. This marriage alliance was to rock the Mediterranean, and it is now necessary to look at the antecedents of Peter the Great in order to see why.

37. D.M. Nicol, *The Despotate of Epiros* (Oxford, 1958), pp. 166–82.

· · ·

CONCLUSION

The reigns of Frederick II and of Manfred proved clearly that the involvement of the ruler of southern Italy in the affairs of northern and central Italy was not simply an irrational obsession of the papacy. Whether or not the Hohenstaufen seriously proposed to absorb the papal lands in central Italy into their domains, the presence in Tuscany and Lombardy of factions which constantly appealed to Frederick and Manfred, or alternatively to the papacy, resulted in a succession of conflicts which no higher power seemed able to control. Each side was thus sucked into a struggle which in fact did little to serve its basic interests. The roots of the Guelf–Ghibelline rivalries certainly lay in internal issues, not so much concerned with major political questions but with the territorial and economic rivalries between aristocratic clans which traditionally governed the north Italian towns. Yet by looking for patrons in Rome or southern Italy, or even further afield, the faction leaders destabilised Italy and created an atmosphere of deep suspicion between pope and emperor. The potential for cooperation between the papacy and the Hohenstaufen had been revealed under Pope Honorius III in the years around 1220; the potential for a war of words was revealed when Gregory IX berated Frederick II for failing to fulfil such promises as his crusade vows, and this was the beginning of a propaganda war which became louder as the century progressed; the potential for armed conflict was shown in the Lombard war of the 1240s and the involvement of Manfred in the tortuous web of Tuscan politics.

The reputation of the Sicilian rulers as wealthy managers of a well-organised kingdom aroused as much fear as the image of Frederick or Manfred as 'baptised sultans', or, to use a more modern phrase, oriental despots. The papacy had an interest in the weakening of the centralised power structures within the *Regno*, as was shown by Innocent IV's encouragement to the south Italian towns to throw off the Hohenstaufen tyrants and to become free cities under papal suzerainty. In particular, the popes resented the enormous power of the Sicilian kings over their own subjects, when, after all, the king of Sicily held his own kingdom from the see of St Peter. If the pope could not control his greatest vassal, and if that vassal at times seemed poised to dominate all of Italy, the time had surely come to dispose of the Hohenstaufen entirely, and to grant the *Regno* to a more suitable ruler. The personal union of Germany and Sicily must never be repeated, particularly since the German king also exercised some sort of authority in Lombardy.

Finally, the forty years after 1220 confirmed that the ruler of southern Italy was not likely to avoid entanglements elsewhere in the Mediterranean: a marriage alliance with the house of Aragon, another one with the Greek rulers of the western Balkans. As under its Norman founders, the kingdom of Sicily looked outward in all directions.

Chapter 2

THE EMERGENCE
OF ARAGON-CATALONIA

· · ·

THE COMING TOGETHER OF ARAGON AND
CATALONIA

'The rise of Aragon' serves as a label both for the extraordinary success of the Catalan-Aragonese monarchy in asserting its authority far beyond the heartlands of Aragon and Catalonia in the course of the thirteenth century, and for the dynamic expansion of the major trade centres of the Catalan world, notably Barcelona and Ciutat de Mallorca, whose commerce reached way beyond the political boundaries of what is often called the Crown of Aragon (*Corona d'Aragó, Corona de Aragón*). This, indeed, has always been the central puzzle: how far the merchants led the monarchs in the conquest of much of the western Mediterranean, and how far the merchants followed in the wake of armed fleets whose aim was the glorification of the house of Barcelona or the vindication of its political claims. A question intimately connected with this is the degree to which the kings of Aragon conceived of the territories they acquired – the Balearics, Valencia, Sicily, Sardinia – as a coherent 'empire'. In the account that follows, the basic assumptions are that one can assume neither a close identity of interest between monarchy and merchants nor a single-minded purpose of creating a Mediterranean empire, at least before the mid-fourteenth century. Catalan writers of the time were accustomed to attribute the successes of their nation to Divine Providence. They were aware that the success of the Catalans seemed to have been achieved against the odds, and this was one way of expressing that view.[1]

'Aragon' is really a misnomer. The early history of highland Aragon and maritime Catalonia diverged significantly until the middle of the twelfth century; and even then the differences in language and economic structure remained – and still remain – permanent factors separating the two regions: Aragonese speech is part of the family of languages and dialects that includes standard Castilian Spanish; Catalan is a separate romance tongue much closer to the Provençal or 'Occitan' languages spoken in medieval southern France; Catalonia benefited from access to the sea, Aragon was landlocked. Indeed, Catalonia must be thought of as one part of a larger arc of territories stretching through what is now southern France as far as Provence, sharing many of the same cultural and political objectives. Most significantly, Aragon proper was by the early twelfth century a kingdom, though at that stage it was in a state of merger with neighbouring Navarre in the western Pyrenees, another factor that pulled its interests away from the Mediterranean and towards the Spanish interior; Catalonia was a collection of counties in which the count of Barcelona had by the twelfth century established a loose primacy that others, such as the counts of Urgell, could often choose to ignore.[2] Its rough boundaries spilled over the Pyrenees into the county of Roussillon and the northern part of Cerdagne, Catalan-speaking regions that were only definitively incorporated into France in the seventeenth century.[3] Aragon possessed a sizeable Muslim population, particularly after Islamic Saragossa (Zaragoza) was captured by King Alfonso the Battler in 1118; Catalonia had a very small one outside a few major centres on its

1. J.N. Hillgarth, *The problem of a Catalan Mediterranean Empire, 1229–1324* (English Historical Review Supplement no. 8, 1975); also J.N. Hillgarth, *The Spanish Kingdoms*, vol. 1, *1250–1410, Precarious balance* (Oxford, 1975); the work of J. Lee Shneidman, *The rise of the Aragonese-Catalan Empire, 1200–1350*, 2 vols (New York, 1970) has been justly criticised not merely for its many errors of fact but for a belief in the coherence of Catalan imperial ambitions, notably by Hillgarth.
2. T.N. Bisson, *The Medieval Crown of Aragon. A short history* (Oxford, 1986), for a reliable general overview of the antecedents.
3. P. Sahlins, *Boundaries. The making of France and Spain in the Pyrenees* (Berkeley/Los Angeles, 1989).

southern flank, such as Lleida (Lérida), though it possessed a significant Jewish community with close cultural links to Muslim Spain. Still, it is noticeable how much lighter is the imprint of Arabic speech on the Catalan language than it is on Spanish or Portuguese, reflecting the less intimate links between Christian and Muslim in medieval Catalonia.

In both areas early advances were made against Islam, which had dominated most of the Iberian peninsula since the Muslim invasion of 711. Barcelona shrugged off a Muslim governor at the very start of the ninth century, Girona even earlier, in 785. In this period, aid was extended to both the Catalans and the Aragonese by the Frankish ruler Charlemagne, who visited Spain on an expedition that brought few firm political results, but which was commemorated ever after in the legend of his faithful follower Roland, supposedly cut down at Roncesvalles in the Pyrenees by Muslim foes; in fact, the battle of Roncesvalles was an attack on his baggage train by Basque brigands. However, one political advantage that was gained from Charlemagne's intervention was the extension of Frankish overlordship over Catalonia, but not in any significant sense over Aragon; throughout the years up to 1258 the counts of Barcelona were technically dependent on the crown of France for their Catalan territories.[4] Yet it was more the absence of France than its presence that stimulated the counts into solving the region's problems on their own; Count Wilfred or Guifré the Hairy (879–97) acquired a large bloc of lands including Barcelona and Girona, and won repute as the patron of the restored see of Vic and of the great abbey of Ripoll. His reign was not all a success story; he died fighting the Muslims in Catalonia, and he did little to integrate his lands, which lay on both sides of the Pyrenees, into a coherent whole. This is hardly to be expected: notions of 'state-building' are not something for which one should bother to look in this period, even though later generations looked back to him as the founding father of the Catalan realm.

The early kingdom of Aragon achieved expansion more by settlement than by conquest; what began as a small Pyrenean

---

4. For the early history of the Spanish March, see R. Collins, 'Charles the Bald and Wifred the Hairy', in M. Gibson, J. Nelson, eds, *Charles the Bald. Court and Kingdom*, 2nd ed. (Aldershot, 1990), pp. 169–88.

county under strong Frankish influence grew to include Jaca, which took off as a major ecclesiastical centre, and then extended its influence gradually into the foothills around Huesca in the eleventh century. Ramiro I (1035–69) still did not describe himself as king, but only called himself, oddly, Ramiro 'as if king'. A royal title arrived when his son succeeded to the largely Basque kingdom of Navarre, and was simply perpetuated when Navarre and Aragon split again in the twelfth century. In both Catalonia and Aragon, the successes scored over Muslim rulers brought the superb dividend not of direct rule, but of tribute payments in Muslim gold; in the case of the city of Barcelona, such payments may have had a particularly stimulating effect on the economy.[5]

There is a current tendency to decry use of the term 'reconquest' to describe the process by which all of Spain gradually fell into the hands of Christian rulers between the Moorish invasion of 711 and the fall of Granada in 1492. Certainly, the Catalans and the Aragonese were just as capable of entering into alliances with Muslim warlords, especially in the turbulent eleventh century, as they were with Christian ones: the years around 1031 saw the disintegration of the once mighty Caliphate of Córdoba, and a squabble over the spoils that brought the mercenary captain El Cid to Valencia.[6] The petty Muslim kingdom of Saragossa was for a time closely allied to El Cid; the Aragonese, however, (not to mention their rivals, the rulers of León and Castile) had their eyes on it; in 1118 King Alfonso the Battler of Aragon-Navarre secured the city of Saragossa, which commanded the wide plains and fertile fields of the Ebro valley. The Aragonese had now definitively broken out of the Pyrenees, and had become a significant force within the politics of all the peninsula. They encouraged the Christians from Muslim Spain (the Mozarabs) to come and settle the newly conquered land on easy terms, alongside the Muslim peasants, many of whom remained *in situ* in subordinate

5. S. Bensch, *Barcelona and its rulers, 1096–1291* (Cambridge, 1995) is now the fundamental discussion of the city's emergence, after a 'false start' in the eleventh century.
6. For general accounts of the political ties between Muslim and Christian rulers, see R. Fletcher, *The Quest for El Cid* (London, 1988); R. Fletcher, *Moorish Spain* (London, 1992).

condition.[7] In the same period the Catalans made striking advances, taking Tarragona at the end of the eleventh century, though having to wait another quarter century before it was really secure; the defence of the region was the work of such diverse groups as Robert Burdet and his Norman knights, who established a Norman principality in the region, and Olguer or Oldeguer, archbishop of Tarragona in the 1120s.[8] Yet thus work would perhaps have proceeded much more slowly without the support of the papacy; this was the period in which the ideology of holy war against the infidel was being more clearly articulated. From the siege of Barbastro in 1063–64 to the Catalan and Pisan invasion of Majorca and Ibiza in 1113–15, the papacy began to formulate the spiritual rewards that were available to those who died for the faith, even to those who fought for it, within Spain. The First Crusade, launched in 1095, attracted the strong interest of Spanish knights; but the response of Pope Urban II was unequivocal: such work as the defence of Tarragona against the infidel earned the same merit as participation in the liberation of the Holy Land from the Muslims.[9]

The sense that the war in Spain was itself a holy struggle against unbelievers was thus something that arrived late, and that was in many respects a foreign import from the papacy and from foreign knights – Normans, Poitevins and others – who had come to earn their spurs on Iberian soil. Pushing south beyond Saragossa to Daroca, Calatayud and other Muslim centres, Alfonso the Battler showed an especially acute awareness of this dimension to the war in Spain; in his will of 1134 he left his kingdom (because he was childless) to the newly founded Order of Knights of the Temple, based in Jerusalem, to the Hospital of St John of Jerusalem, and to the canons of the church of the Holy Sepulchre in Jerusalem. It is generally conceded that there were sound enough political motives behind this act: he was afraid that his neighbour

7. C. Stalls, *Possessing the Land. Aragon's expansion into Islam's Ebro frontier under Alfonso the Battler, 1104–1134* (Leiden, 1995); also C. Laliena and P. Sénac, *Musulmans et Chrétiens dans le haut Moyen Âge: aux origines de la reconquête aragonaise* (Paris, 1991).
8. L. McCrank, 'Norman crusaders in the Catalan reconquest: Robert Burdet and the principality of Tarragona, 1129–55', *Journal of Medieval History*, 7 (1981), pp. 67–82.
9. J. Riley-Smith, *The Crusades. A short history* (London, 1987), p. 6.

Alfonso VII of Castile would lay claim to his lands, and he knew that by placing his realm in the hands of the Church he could probably avoid such an outcome.[10] The Hospitallers had not yet become the fully armed Military Order that was to evolve over the centuries into the Knights of St John and the Sovereign Military Order of Malta; the Templars were still few in number, though the Aragonese legacy increased their reputation enormously. The rulers of Aragon eventually found a different solution, which resulted in handsome compensation for the Templars, who emerged instead as a formidable fighting force guarding the southern frontiers of the Aragonese lands.[11] To resolve the succession crisis, not the only severe one in Aragon's history, Alfonso's brother, a monk, was brought out of seclusion to father a daughter; this child was betrothed to the count of Barcelona, Ramon Berenguer IV, whom she finally married in 1150. The Aragonese barons had, then, turned their backs on Castile and on Navarre, which resumed its separate existence as a remote Pyrenean kingdom.

Under Ramon Berenguer IV, who governed Aragon but did not himself take the royal title, Aragon and Catalonia continued in fact to take separate paths. In Catalonia, it was a bold enough step for the count to assume what has been called 'una autoritat supracomtal', in other words, primacy among the Catalan counts, through the issue of law codes such as the *Usatges de Barcelona*, where the count was assigned public authority in such matters as criminal jurisdiction and the minting of coinage.[12] Recognition of these claims was much slower to come than their assertion. Tighter management of the count's own lands coincided with increasing burdens on the peasantry; the golden age of light exactions, characteristic of many frontier societies in which every incentive was needed to attract settlers, was coming to its end at least in Catalonia. Comital taxation, expressed in the *bovatge*

---

10. E. Lourie, *Crusade and Colonisation. Muslims, Christians and Jews in medieval Aragon* (Aldershot, 1990), reprints several studies by Lourie of this problem.

11. A.J. Forey, *The Templars in the Corona de Aragón* (London/Durham, 1973); A.J. Forey, *The Military Orders from the twelfth to the early fourteenth centuries* (London, 1992), pp. 23–32.

12. D. Kagay, ed. and transl., *The Usatges of Barcelona. The fundamental law of Catalonia* (Philadelphia, 1994).

or 'cattle tax', which was in fact a general levy, aroused constant opposition; but even for the ruler to try to impose it was some indication of his growing stature as first among equals within the Catalan domains. Taxation was also the issue that tended to unite the barons of both Catalonia and Aragon against their master; paradoxically, it was by offending them with his tax demands that the ruler created among them solidarity, and even if this solidarity – expressed in early *Corts* or parliaments (as early, in fact, as 1164 at Saragossa, a little later in Catalonia) – set the barons against the prince, it still had a crucial role in creating a sense of political community.[13] The fragmented, early feudal world of tenth- and eleventh-century Catalonia and Aragon was giving way to a new order in which the central political issue was the degree to which the barons as a whole might be able to rein in the count of Barcelona and king of Aragon. Traditionally, medieval rulers escaped from such preoccupations by presenting themselves as successful war-leaders, even though the financial outlay that this necessitated often pushed them back into the arms of the barons.

Thus by 1200 the territories coexisted in a personal union. Alfonso II of Aragon (I of Catalonia[14]), who came to the throne as a child in 1162, pursued a vigorous policy of southward expansion into Moorish territory, agreeing in the treaty of Cazorla (1179) to let Castile absorb Murcia in southeastern Spain in due course, but setting Aragonese-Catalan sights on the more accessible Muslim statelet of Valencia, closer to home. On the other hand, Alfonso faced more immediate challenges in southern France, in defence of important family interests. Here the Aragonese asserted their authority in the imperial county of Provence, whose line of local counts, themselves of Catalan origin, faced extinction in 1166; Alfonso gathered up the county into his own hands, taking the title 'marquis of Provence' in 1185, though after his death it was once again separated from his core territories in Aragon-Catalonia. Until the mid-thirteenth century,

13. Bisson, *Medieval Crown of Aragon*, pp. 50, 80.
14. Considerable confusion can result from the differences in the numbering of the kings of Aragon and of the counts of Barcelona or Catalonia. In this text the Aragonese rather than the Catalan numbering has been adopted throughout; it tends to run one higher than the Catalan system, so that Peter the Ceremonious in the fourteenth century is Pedro IV de Aragón but Pere III de Catalunya.

Provence – even under its cadet dynasty of Catalan-Aragonese counts – maintained close, though at times contentious, relations with its big brother further west; its technical overlord was not the king of France but the Holy Roman Emperor, wearing his crown as the barely effective ruler of the kingdom of Burgundy or Arles. On the other hand, attempts by the kings of Aragon to create a bridge linking their Catalan territories through southern France to Provence encountered stiff opposition among the warring factions in Languedoc: counts of Toulouse, viscounts of Carcassonne, counts of Foix, not to mention external forces such as the English king, in his capacity as overlord of Gascony to the north. It is noticeable that at this stage the least influential of all the kings with claims in this region was the king of France, whose authority in Languedoc was little more real than it was in Catalonia. What mattered was that a king was close by, as the rulers of Catalonia and of Gascony were: that is, the kings of Aragon and of England. Southern French lords moved in and out of the Catalan-Aragonese political net, while the strains of internal strife were felt in the uncontrolled spread of popular heresy, notably the dualist Cathar faith, and in the ravages of mercenary bands.[15] Despite a long history of Catalan involvement in Languedoc, Alfonso met little permanent success in the lands between Provence and Catalonia, and yet the issue of Aragonese rights in Languedoc was for long remembered.

. . .

PETER II IN SOUTHERN FRANCE

It was in Languedoc that King Peter II (1196–1213) in fact faced his greatest difficulties. His wife Maria was heiress of Montpellier, one of the two richest and largest towns (with Toulouse) in the region, a major centre of international trade and industry; and this acquisition strengthened considerably Catalan-Aragonese influence in the region, as did the marriage of his sister to the Count of Toulouse.[16] Yet it was the fractious disunity of the southern French barons that

15. Hillgarth, *Problem*, pp. 13–14. Brief accounts of Aragonese interests in southern France appear in all good histories of the Albigensian crusade, e.g. J. Sumption, *The Albigensian Crusade* (London, 1978), pp. 22–3, 97–8.
16. J. Baumel, *Histoire d'une seigneurie du Midi de la France*, vols 1–2 (Montpellier, 1969–71).

posed the greatest problem. In 1209, the arrival of northern armies under Simon de Montfort, with the public aim of suppressing the Cathar heretics and their supporters (*fautores*) brought Peter directly into the Albigensian wars in defence of his dispossessed vassals. Peter was not seeking to defend the Cathars, whom he had vigorously persecuted in Catalonia; he was on good terms with Pope Innocent III, who crowned him king at Corneto near Rome in 1204. (Close links to the papacy were useful in guaranteeing his Aragonese kingdom against encroachment by its Spanish neighbours.) Initial attempts at accommodation with Simon turned into all-out war, with the unhappy result of the death in battle of the king of Aragon, at Muret, near Toulouse, in 1213. This event is often seen as the fatal check to Aragonese aims in southern France, but other evidence gives the lie to this assumption: the new king, James, remained in and near the Aragonese possession of Montpellier during much of his long minority, and a cadet line of Aragonese counts still held sway in Provence until the 1240s.

Peter's importance also lies in his successful joint defence of Christian Spain against the resurgent power of the Almohad Berbers, whose fundamentalist brand of Islam had taken north Africa and much of Spain by storm in the mid-twelfth century. The battle of Las Navas de Tolosa (1212) brought him glory and also indicated that the Almohads had lost the momentum which had earlier carried them to such stunning successes in the past.[17] The way south now lay open to the emergence of petty Muslim kingdoms, some loosely under Almohad obedience, but not, of themselves, able to pose a serious challenge to the Christian monarchs. Nor was Peter's struggle against the Muslims solely defensive. He initiated plans for a crusade against the Muslim kingdom of Mayurqa (Majorca), recently brought under the Almohad banner; these plans laid the groundwork for his son's ambitions in the same waters.

Peter's reign is important too because it reveals ever greater financial pressures on the rulers of Catalonia. T.N. Bisson's study of the fiscal documentation of this period indicates that the count-king's finances began to go into the red under Peter II, under the strain of internal conflicts, such as the endless struggles with the barons over the

17. Fletcher, *Moorish Spain*, pp. 124–5.

application of the count's law (the *Usatges de Barcelona*), and over the ruler's rights of taxation. By 1205 the barons were able to force Peter to keep the coinage stable, to abandon the much disliked *bovatge* tax, and to consult them on the appointment of the comital vicars who were generally lesser knights beholden to the count of Barcelona. The count's own claims had been expressed in the *Liber feudorum maior* ('great book of fiefs') of 1194.[18] Yet it is important to distinguish the rights the count-king claimed, and those he could actually exercise; in many respects he remained within Catalonia merely the greatest star in a galaxy of counts, and territories on the edges of Catalonia such as Roussillon and Urgell moved in and out of the count-king's direct purview well into the thirteenth century; the lesser counts did not necessarily enjoy antagonistic relations with the count of Barcelona, often in fact functioning as regional judges. While care was taken to ensure that the ruler could live of his own, by 1200 this did not guarantee him the autonomy he craved, and Peter's reign saw a growing dependence on the Templars as royal creditors; they were becoming known for their financial expertise, which originated in the need to hold funds and transmit them in due course to their headquarters in the Holy Land. Peter also made extensive use of Jewish financial advisers who were able to anticipate his income and manage his budget; many of his financial documents carry signatures in Hebrew by his Jewish officials. Despite such efforts, Catalonia, and, *pari passu*, Aragon, remained loose confederations which themselves made up the two elements in a super-confederation whose only real bond was the person of the count-king himself. In other words, the count-kings had ambitions; but there were also powerful brakes on those ambitions.

. . .

JAMES THE CONQUEROR IN MAJORCA

James I (1213–76) transformed the character of the monarchy. His birth was widely viewed as a miracle, not least because of the cordial loathing of Peter II for Maria of Montpellier; but the true miracle was the survival of Peter II's bloodline. Others such as the Aragonese count of Provence

---

18. T.N. Bisson, *Fiscal accounts of Catalonia under the early Count-Kings (1151–1213)*, 2 vols (Berkeley/Los Angeles, 1984), especially vol. 1, pp. 118–19.

would have been glad to assert a right to James's crown; yet a semblance of unity was maintained, expressed most notably in the general *cort* at Lleida (Lérida) in Summer, 1214, at which the king's leading Aragonese and Catalan subjects were pressed to swear fealty to a monarch whom many of them were actively trying to deprive of his lands, revenues and rights.[19] As during the Sicilian minority of James's contemporary Frederick II, the great lords realised that they could benefit from protestations of loyalty to a king who was really helpless to stand in their way. Over the next few years it seems that royal revenues began slowly to recover, thanks in significant measure to the hard work of the crown's Templar financiers, but thanks too to renewed confidence in the possibility of asking for taxes, as for example at assemblies in Huesca (1221) and Daroca (1223). Deft manipulation of the Catalan coinage by King James, which T.N. Bisson has analysed, brought the crown a profit of 25 per cent in replacing the old coinage.[20] More importantly still, compacts were made with the greater lords in Catalonia, such as Guillem Cabrera in Urgell, and lands pledged by Peter II in Catalonia and Aragon were gradually recovered. This would have been impossible without the support of powerful allies, notably Guillem de Montcada and the count of Roussillon, Nunyo Sanç, though even such close advisers all too easily became locked in conflict among themselves, apparently over trivial issues of honour. Yet James was rising to an age in which he could make his own political judgments. In 1228 he set his sights on Urgell, whose heiress, Aurembiaix, he had promised to defend; he won back Urgell with a brief and successful campaign which culminated in a secret contract of concubinage between James and Aurembiaix. It would be wrong to assume that James had quelled internal opposition; but at this point it became reasonable for him to set his sights on conquests beyond the borders of his realms.

James's first attempt to establish himself as a crusading leader against the Moors only excited the antipathy of the Aragonese lords, who were unimpressed by expensive failure at the walls of Peñiscola (1225–26). If anything, his poor

19. Bisson, *Medieval Crown of Aragon*, pp. 57, 59.
20. T.N. Bisson, 'Coinages of Barcelona' and other studies gathered together in his *Medieval France and its Pyrenean neighbours. Studies in early institutional history* (London, 1989).

experience there suggested that a successful campaign against the Moors could re-establish royal authority more successfully than any number of *corts*. In the chronicle usually regarded as James's autobiography the king states that a primary aim of the campaign against Majorca was the reassertion of royal authority.[21] A king who could win glory in battle, conquer Moorish lands and serve God on crusade would be able to transcend the political tensions that had occupied his minority. In the concubinage agreement with Aurembiaix, of 1228, reference was made *en passant* to the king's plan to conquer Majorca. Yet it is plain that this was an old ambition of Catalonia's rulers: in 1113–15 Count Ramon Berenguer III had joined with the Pisans in a victorious invasion of Majorca and Ibiza; and the re-establishment of Muslim power in the islands was followed by decades of internecine strife which made Muslim Mayurqa seem very vulnerable. Moreover, the situation of the Balearics astride the Catalan and Provençal trade routes was a source of inconvenience, since Muslim pirates preyed on Christian shipping. Not for nothing had a succession of Italian fleets attacked Majorca throughout the twelfth century in the hope of repeating the earlier Pisan success, and it has been seen that Peter II harboured plans of his own for an invasion. The problem for the counts of Barcelona had always been the lack of a native fleet, which had led Ramon Berenguer to rely on the Pisans.[22] By the 1220s Catalan shipping from Tarragona and Barcelona had become more firmly established in the western Mediterranean, and the king was now able to plan a war from which the Genoese and Pisans (in any case friendly to the Muslim ruler of Mayurqa) were excluded. Even so, he relied heavily on Provençal naval contingents, and on the help of Montpellier, to supplement Catalan resources. With their help, Majorca City, the modern Palma, was besieged and taken by the end of 1229.[23] The rest of the island did not capitulate at

21. *Chronicle of James I king of Aragon*, transl. J. Forster, 2 vols (London, 1883), pp. 98–104. This is an antiquated translation, and editions of the Catalan original are widespread, the handiest being part one of F. Soldevila, *Les quatre grans cròniques* (Barcelona, 1971).

22. G.B. Doxey, 'Christian attempts to conquer the Balearic islands, 1015–1229', Cambridge University Ph.D. thesis, 1991.

23. F. Fernández-Armesto, *Before Columbus. Exploration and colonisation from the Mediterranean to the Atlantic, 1229–1492* (London, 1987), pp. 13–18.

once, and a further visit by James, now entitled also 'king of Majorca', was necessary before the Muslim opposition was flushed out of the mountainous *cordillera*, and before Minorca accepted tributary status in 1231, subject to guarantees of the right to practise Islam. The conquest of Ibiza was to be the work of the see of Tarragona in conjunction with the count of Roussillon and Prince Pedro of Portugal, in 1235, and was essentially a private expedition licensed by James.[24] Pedro of Portugal was also entrusted with the government of Majorca, but he spent little time on the island; the lack of intensive government intervention perhaps helps explain the extraordinary mushroom growth of the Catalan trading community in Majorca, which was unfettered by heavy taxes or complex regulations.

The invasion of the Balearics provides early clues to James's attitude to the Spanish Muslims who were to fall under his authority in increasing numbers in subsequent decades. Rapid submission resulted, as in Minorca, in the offering of a surrender treaty guaranteeing the virtual autonomy of the subject territory, except for the right to conduct an independent foreign policy.[25] Resistance resulted in a higher price: those Majorcan Muslims who failed to accept James as king faced loss of their lands and property, even enslavement. The result was that Majorca gradually lost its Islamic identity; indeed, the island was repopulated by Catalan, Provençal and Italian settlers, including Jews from Spain, Languedoc and north Africa. There is no hard evidence that the Muslims of Majorca even had their own community organisation or *aljama*, as did the Jews, during the thirteenth century; even the evidence for mosques is murky. The island was heavily catalanised in speech, religion and personnel. A few Mozarabs survived from pre-conquest days, and these arabised Christians sometimes prospered under the new régime. But many old Muslim communities were shattered in pieces, often resettled on newly carved up estates, in the hands of such absentee overseas lords as the count of Roussillon; the Order of the Temple acquired handsome estates, which – to papal alarm – were partly repopulated

24. Fernández-Armesto, *Before Columbus*, pp. 31–3.
25. David Abulafia, *A Mediterranean Emporium. The Catalan Kingdom of Majorca* (Cambridge, 1994), pp. 56–74.

with mainland Muslims in view of an apparent shortage of native manpower.[26]

The conquest of the Balearic islands is often seen as the moment when the outlook of the Catalan-Aragonese monarchy shifted decisively from southern France towards the Mediterranean frontier with Islam. In fact, the major consequences of the invasion of Majorca were, if anything, a strengthening of ties to the southern French and Provençal cities, which were rewarded with houses and commercial privileges in Majorca City, in gratitude for their crucial role in the conquest. Nunyo Sanç, count of Roussillon, also acquired extensive properties in Majorca City. As well, the Balearic Islands would later enjoy a political union with the southern French territories of the Crown of Aragon, of some significance in the bitter War of the Vespers (1282–1302). Nor did James I try to impose direct authority on his new kingdom, entrusting it to Pedro of Portugal who had in any case married James's former mistress Aurembiaix, acquired a title to the county of Urgell, and was now only too happy to relinquish Urgell in exchange for lifelong rights in Majorca which, as has been seen, he never did much to activate. At a stroke, James had a viceroy to govern Majorca on his behalf (after a fashion), and he had also gained control of the county that lay sandwiched between Old Catalonia and the highlands of Aragon, and that gave access to strategically valuable areas of the Pyrenees. Arguably, then, it was almost as much for Urgell as for Majorca that James had launched his invasion. Only gradually did James respond to the absence of interest shown by Pedro of Portugal in his Majorcan domain, developing instead a plan to grant Majorca to his second surviving son, also named James.

. . .

JAMES THE CONQUEROR IN VALENCIA

The difficulty was that the conquest of Majorca had been the work of James's Catalan and southern French subjects and allies, but there was no obvious benefit for the Aragonese

26. Abulafia, *Mediterranean Emporium*, pp. 56–60; Lourie, *Crusade and Colonisation*, essays nos v, vi, vii; T. Glick, *From Muslim fortress to Christian castle. Social and cultural change in medieval Spain* (Manchester, 1995), pp. 132–4.

barons, who complained, rather, of raids from Muslim Valencia into their lands, and who were anxious to take advantage of the instability within the kingdom of Valencia. Valencia was one remnant of a now fragmented Almohad empire, and within its borders there were already, on the eve of the Catalan-Aragonese invasion, large areas that owed no loyalty to the ruler Abu Zayd.[27] One warlord managed to carve out a statelet of his own which even embraced Valencia City. Because Abu Zayd was still master of the north, it is hardly surprising that he looked for support against his southern foes to his northern neighbour, James of Aragon. The alliance of Muslim and Christian against Muslim was a well established routine in Spanish diplomacy. In the end, Abu Zayd's desperation or gratitude reached the point where he had himself baptised.

A combination of clever diplomacy and border skirmishes brought James several key castles on the Valencian frontier, notably Peñiscola (1233), while the fall of Burriana the same year offered an indication of the fate that would befall those who resisted: expulsion and resettlement by Catalans and Aragonese. The conquest of the north was not difficult, especially in view of Abu Zayd's handsome concessions of major strongpoints. But, by contrast with the Majorcan war, which was over quickly, the conquest of central and southern Valencia proceeded at a snail's pace until 1245, with fundraising (at a *Cortes* in Monzón), the grant of a crusade tithe, appeals for help to reluctant Catalan shipowners, and the installation of an Aragonese garrison above Valencia on the Hill of the Onion, *Puig de Cebolla*. When Valencia City surrendered in September 1238, the Muslims had to pay the price for their resistance: the Muslims were exiled to a Moorish quarter (*morería*) in the suburbs but there was no significant pillaging, and the town became the focus for settlement by Catalans. Indeed, the presence of Catalans steered the kingdom of Valencia away from Aragonese baronial domination; Catalan law became prevalent, and so did Catalan speech. Yet this mainland kingdom was far harder to tame than the compact Balearic islands; Muslim lands, Murcia and Granada, lay to the south, and Catalan settlement was far thinner than

---

27. P. Guichard, *Les musulmans de Valence et la reconquête, XIe–XIIIe siècles*, 2 vols (Damascus, 1990–91).

in Majorca.[28] The result was that James never really managed to impose his authority over all Valencia; as late as the 1270s he had to send his son Peter to recover royal authority in the region. Nor did James take the title 'king of Valencia' quite as readily as he did that of Majorca; his original conception may thus have been of a Muslim tributary state, still ruled by his client Abu Zayd, only the northern edges of which were to be incorporated in the kingdom of Aragon. In 1236 James began to call himself 'king of Valencia', and in 1239 he moved away from prevailing Aragonese customs by issuing a territorial lawcode or *Furs* for Valencia which closely reflected Catalan usage.

Valencia was not, to the same degree as Majorca, another New Catalonia. In the north, there were significant pockets of Christian settlement, such as the lands of Blasco d'Alagó around Morella, or the city of Burriana, and there were extensive grants of lands to those masters of frontier management, the Military Orders. The Muslim population was largely undisturbed, and the inhabitants of Chivert seem to have enjoyed similar privileges to those granted earlier to the Minorcans. The small territory of Crevillent on the edge of the Castilian sphere of influence managed to survive until the start of the fourteenth century as a neutralised enclave often friendly to Aragon.[29] The Muslims of the Uxó valley were granted a charter in 1250 assuring them that they could retain their marriage customs, instruct their children in the Koran, travel freely, appoint their own judges, even prevent Christians from taking up residence among them; the price of this very favourable privilege was a tax of one-eighth.[30] The major area where regranting of lands by a *ripartiment* or

28. Fundamental are the many studies by R.I. Burns of the conquest of Valencia, among which may be singled out: *The Crusader Kingdom of Valencia. Reconstruction on a thirteenth-century frontier*, 2 vols (Cambridge, MA, 1967); *Islam under the Crusaders. Colonial survival in the thirteenth-century Kingdom of Valencia* (Princeton, NJ, 1974); *Medieval Colonialism. Postcrusade exploitation of Islamic Valencia* (Princeton, NJ, 1975); *Muslims, Christians and Jews in the Crusader Kingdom of Valencia. Societies in symbiosis* (Cambridge, 1984).
29. P. Guichard, 'Un seigneur musulman dans l'Espagne chrétienne: le ra'is de Crevillente (1243–1318), *Mélanges de la Casa de Velázquez*, 9 (1973), pp. 283–334; L.P. Harvey, *Islamic Spain, 1250 to 1500* (Chicago, 1991), pp. 42–4.
30. Guichard, *Les musulmans*, vol. 2, pp. 264–5.

division of the conquered territories occurred was Valencia City and its fertile agricultural hinterland or *horta*, in which the citizens of several northern towns such as Jaca, Saragossa and Montpellier received handsome rights, with Barcelona able to claim one-fifth of the urban property in Valencia City and one-sixth of the *horta*, and with Montpellier able to claim mastery of a goodly chunk of the town too. The aim was not simply to offer the Catalans good trading opportunities, but to create a sizeable Christian Catalan business community within the capital itself, while the Jews too received a substantial area for themselves in the city. The map of Valencia became a miniature map of James's realms, as men of Huesca, Roussillon and even of Pyrenean lands beyond James's frontiers were granted the right to carve out their own suburbs or city streets. In the south, a scattering of Christian lordships emerged, but there were few expulsions and even fewer massacres during the conquest; Christian lords thus found themselves, as at Chiva, charged with a Muslim population; the further south one travelled, the more obvious it became that the Aragonese had barely neutralised this area, which therefore retained its potential for revolt. The most dramatic revolt, certainly, was that of al-Azraq (1247–48), but even in the 1270s the greater part of Valencia was still of uncertain loyalty.

Potentially Valencia was an enormous financial asset, as Robert I. Burns has shown in a series of studies of the tax regime under James I.[31] One additional conquest, Xàtiva (Játiva), which fell in 1244, was particularly important because its paper factories provided James with the means to keep voluminous governmental records.[32] Valencia City itself was able to furnish the king with revenues from Muslim bath-houses, bakeries, butcheries, brothels; with poll-taxes charged on Muslims and Jews; with taxes on market place transactions and on trade through the port, which grew in importance partly as a result of the fall of Majorca; Catalan merchants, Muslims and Mozarab Christians maintained a constant flow of trade between James's two conquests within three years of

---

31. Burns, *Medieval Colonialism; Islam under the Crusaders*, etc.; Hillgarth, *Problem*, p. 7.
32. R.I. Burns, *Diplomatarium of the Crusader Kingdom of Valencia*, vol. 1, *Society and Documentation in Crusader Valencia* (Princeton, NJ, 1985), pp. 151–81.

the fall of Valencia. To a large extent, the monarchy simply perpetuated existing Arab administration, more obviously in Valencia than in Majorca; James had become the Christian king of a Muslim society, one which would retain a sizeable Moorish population right through to 1610. Yet it was also a society which could never cohere: the Christian minority came to form a small ruling elite, and cross-cultural fertilisation was impeded by what have been seen as fundamental psychological barriers: the audible contrast between Arabic-speaking Muslim and predominantly Catalan-speaking Christians; the visible contrast between Gothic church-tower and Islamic minaret, that between clean-shaven pork-eating Christian and bearded Jew or Muslim bound by dietary laws and subject to the maximum possible degree to their own separate courts of law.[33] For the Muslims, demoralisation was expressed in the gradual exodus of the traditional Valencian leadership, imams and noblemen, to north-west Africa or to Granada, strengthening the Islamic identity of the last Muslim state in Spain, but weakening the powers of resistance of those who remained, the *mudéjares*, a Spanish word of Arabic derivation which originally connoted domestic animals. It is thus not really surprising that significant numbers of conversions occurred here, as also in Majorca; for instance a large group in Valencia City in 1275. Moreover, there is still some uncertainty about the ability of the old Muslim elite to survive the upheavals of conquest, rebellion and reconquest which marked the reign of James I.[34]

James had title (of sorts) to Valencia under past agreements with the king of Castile to carve up Moorish Spain between themselves; more difficult was the question of Murcia further to the south, which had been assigned in these agreements variously to Aragon and to Castile. After the fall of Valencia James possessed a frontier with Murcia, which, however, was from 1243 a Muslim tributary of Castile. Alacant (Alicante) was willing to accept Aragonese lordship (1240), but James indicated that he could not take the city under his wing without denying Castile its legitimate rights.

33. R.I. Burns, 'Muslims in the thirteenth-century realms of Aragon: interaction and reaction', in J.M. Powell, ed., *Muslims under Latin rule* (Princeton, NJ, 1990), pp. 57–102, especially pp. 76–8.
34. Guichard, *Les musulmans*, vol. 2, pp. 476–7.

Despite occasional tension on the Valencian-Murcian borders between James I and Alfonso X of Castile, the king of Aragon was anxious to foster good relations with Alfonso, to the extent of responding vigorously to Alfonso's appeal for aid against the rebellious Murcians. The conquest of Murcia in 1264–65, funded by the Catalans alone in view of Aragonese hostility to Alfonso X, was a textbook exercise in the submission of Muslim territory, even to the extent of taking care not immediately to dispossess the Banu Hud who had ruled there by Castilian leave, and who for another dozen years were able to exercise limited authority as 'kings of the Moors of Murcia'. The invasion was followed by extensive Catalan colonisation in an area which, nonetheless, James had no intention of holding permanently. In Murcia City nearly half of all known settlers at this time arrived from Aragon-Catalonia, less than one-fifth from Castile, whose own population had already been drained southwards to Seville and Córdoba in the 1230s and 1240s. James had conquered Murcia for Alfonso, and to Alfonso he delivered it. The advantage he could hope to gain was the closure of easy access to southern Valencia by Muslim troublemakers from Nasrid Granada; the conquest of Murcia was also an act in the gradual subjugation of Valencia.[35]

· · ·

JAMES THE CONQUEROR AND FRANCE

James's successes in the south have to be set against a less successful record in the north. On the death of James's uncle Nunyo Sanç, Roussillon reverted to the king, helping James to consolidate his influence in the Pyrenees. Yet despite a viable claim to Navarre, James lost out there to the count of Champagne (1243), and later to the royal house of France (1274), with the long-term result that a spur of French-dominated territory stuck into Spain.[36] The crucial issue was the definition of the relationship between France and Catalonia: the rights of the counts of Barcelona in southern France and Provence, and the historic, though now barely audible, rights of the house of Capet in Catalonia itself.

35. Harvey, *Islamic Spain*, pp. 44–8.
36. Hillgarth, *Problem*, p. 13.

James's first major attempt to recover influence in the region was checked after the death of the last Aragonese count of Provence in 1243, and the winning of the hand of the sucessful heiress by the French prince Charles of Anjou in 1246; even though disputes about the Provençal succession rumbled on, and even though Charles was still suppressing rebels (in this case in Marseilles) as late as 1263, the house of Aragon had suffered the first of several blows at the hands of the ambitious Angevin. Opportunities for an Aragonese recovery in Languedoc were similarly closed when Alphonse of Poitiers acquired the title to the county of Toulouse. The French monarchy began to show its hand on the coast of southern France, not far from Montpellier, when the stagnant waters of the abbey of Psalmodi were developed as Aigues-Mortes ('Dead Waters') the first French royal port on the Mediterranean; the intention was not simply, as often supposed, to provide a departure station for Louis IX's substantial crusade of 1248, but also to strangle Montpellier, which stood a little way inland and lacked good outports of its own.[37] It was time to count up what was left of an Aragonese dominion in southern France, and to negotiate with the French monarchy over it.

The Treaty of Corbeil of 1258 offered real advantages to both France and Aragon. The French renounced entirely their sovereignty over the Catalan lands from Roussillon southwards, drawing a line north of Perpignan which was to serve for centuries as the southern border of France. In exchange, James withdrew his claims to territories in southern France (and, simultaneously, any remaining rights in Provence). There was no real mention of rights over Montpellier, however, which was retained as an Aragonese lordship, and which was not in any case held directly from the king of France but from a small-time local bishop. (The Aragonese lieutenant in Montpellier was in fact one of James's emissaries at Corbeil, and it is only with reference to this figure that the city appears in the final documents.) The treaty was not a defeat for James, but even so his heir Peter the Great was eventually to try to overturn it. Links to southern France remained intimate, and the king of Aragon

37. G. Jehel, *Aigues-Mortes, un port pour un roi. Les Capétiens et la Méditerranée* (Roanne, 1985).

registered his presence by, for instance, endowing the Cistercian abbey of Valmagne near Montpellier with gifts.[38]

Marriage alliances with the French were seen as another way of putting an end to centuries of discord over southern France. Less easy to manage was the relationship between the house of Aragon and the cadet French line of Anjou. Everywhere James trod Charles of Anjou seemed to be in the way. After acquiring Provence he set his sights on Italian politics: more of this shortly. In 1267 James I was working hard to secure Sardinia for his second surviving son, James of Majorca; the pope, in whose gift the island supposedly lay, demurred, but within two years Charles's son Philip had been proclaimed king of Sardinia by die-hard Guelfs at Sassari.[39] In 1267–69, James tried to persuade the pope that he should be granted a crusade privilege for an expedition to the East; the pope actively discouraged the expedition, which was rapidly scattered by Mediterranean storms. Although one apparent reason for the lack of papal support was James's immoral private life, it was becoming clear that papal sympathies lay entirely in another direction: in 1270, Charles became involved in, indeed perhaps helped plan, Louis IX's disastrous crusade to Tunis, which was already becoming a major base for Catalan merchants, mercenaries and missionaries, and a source of tribute for the king of Aragon.[40]

Throughout his reign James grappled with the problem of the succession. He thought of separating Aragon from Catalonia, or Valencia from both of those territories. In the end the question was resolved by the survival of only two legitimate heirs, Peter and James, the former of whom was in 1262 promised the mainland territories south of the Pyrenees, and the latter of whom would be allowed to establish a cadet kingdom, fully independent of Peter's realms, in the Balearics, Roussillon and Cerdagne, and who was also to receive the remaining lordships on French territory, Montpellier and the

38. *Layettes du Trésor des Chartes*, vol. 3, ed. J. de Laborde, Paris, 1875, docs 4399, 4400, 4411–12, 4434–5; *Chronicle of San Juan de la Peña*, transl. L. Nelson (Philadelphia, 1991), p. 71; J. Richard, *Saint Louis*, transl. S. Lloyd (Cambridge, 1992), pp. 204–5; Abulafia, *Mediterranean Emporium*, pp. 38–9.
39. Abulafia, *Mediterranean Emporium*, pp. 235–45.
40. J. Le Goff, *Saint Louis* (Paris, 1996), pp. 290–7, playing down the role of Charles of Anjou.

remote viscountcy of Carlat. Arguably this division reflected the wish to create two entities each of which would combine ancient territories such as Roussillon or Old Catalonia with newly conquered lands; intentionally or otherwise, the linkage of Majorca to lands on the French side of the Pyrenees emphasised the partly southern French character of the Majorcan kingdom. But Peter was furious at the proposal. Even on his deathbed James was adjuring his sons to live in amity, proud of his ability to provide for both of them; and partitions of this sort were a traditional feature of Spanish royal inheritances since time immemorial. But he was deluding himself.[41]

Disagreements between Peter and James of Majorca were not the only clouds to overshadow the last years of James the Conqueror. Issues such as control of Urgell became once again controversial; there were rebellious Catalan and Aragonese barons with whom to contend; there was a bitter dispute between Peter and his half-brother Fernan Sanç; Valencia became more and more restive. Peter's legacy was thus a troubled one.

James offers to view some intriguing paradoxes. He was capable of threatening to clear Valencia entirely of the Muslims when they stood in his way; but he was also astute in the offer of surrender arrangements that secured many of the vital interests of the conquered communities. James on one occasion received some Muslim emissaries from Murcia by offering them a traditional Arab feast of *halal* meat in a traditional Arab tent, addressing them privately (through his Jewish dragoman) to the effect that he and his ancestors had always sought to foster the Muslim communities in all their realms, 'just as well as if they were in a Saracen land'; only if Muslims failed to submit, he said, was it his habit to take their land and repeople it with Christians. This is a fair account, from his own presumed autobiography, of his philosophy of *convivencia*, of the coexistence in peace of Christian, Muslim and Jew. He understood the need for good diplomatic relations with the north African rulers in whose lands his Catalan subjects traded, but was desperately anxious to be seen in the Christian world as a great crusading hero and

41. Abulafia, *Mediterranean Emporium*, pp. 9–10, 44–5; see James's Book of Deeds, cap. 563, in Soldevila, *Quatre grans cròniques*.

as a hammer of heretics. In his relations with the Jews, there is a similar ambivalence. James was a keen supporter of the acerbic friar Ramon de Penyafort, who directed his campaigns against Jews, Muslims and usurers, all of whom existed in embarrassing plenty in James's realms. The king who in 1263 presided over the damaging confrontation between the Girona rabbi Nahmanides and the zealous friar Paul the Christian, a convert from Judaism, on the subject of whether the Messiah had come, extended his protection to his Jewish subjects, rapidly revoking the requirement that they should listen to conversionist sermons, and he licensed ample Jewish settlement in Majorca.[12] His private life, replete with a succession of mistresses, and his brutish treatment of churchmen for whom he conceived a dislike (such as the confessor who lost his tongue for revealing what he had heard), only made him more aware of his need to placate God by serving Him in war, and only made the pope more aware of his moral turpitude. Twice excommunicated, he took more easily his loss of the Church's favour than did his contemporary Frederick II; but then he was not also emperor and was not engaged in war with the papacy's allies. The truth was, as Catalan chroniclers emphasised, that under James thousands of masses were now being recited in lands that had once resounded (and actually still did so) to the call of the muezzin.

. . .

THE RISE OF BARCELONA

The most startling development under James I was, arguably, the emergence of Barcelona as a major port, whose merchants were able to compete with those of Genoa and Tuscany not merely in the western Mediterranean but even as far afield as Alexandria and Constantinople. There are many possible explanations: the town's role as a capital city, attracting to itself not just trade but tribute from Muslim borderlands, populated by a mixed business community of

42. J. Cohen, *The friars and the Jews* (Ithaca, NY, 1982); but cf. R. Chazan, *Daggers of Faith. Thirteenth-century Christian missionizing and Jewish response* (Berkeley/Los Angeles, 1989), which is a preferable interpretation of the evolution of anti-Jewish sentiment; also R. Chazan, *Barcelona and Beyond. The disputation of 1263 and its aftermath* (Berkeley/Los Angeles, 1992).

Jews and Christians, combining financial services to the count-king with involvement in commerce, urban investments, shipbuilding, dyeshops and so on. Yet the town was not in an outstandingly propitious situation, for it stood some way from the key markets of al-Andalus (Muslim Spain), and yet was cut off from the major trans-European trade routes by the Pyrenees.[43] In any case, there were significant competitors within the Catalan world: it is no coincidence that Pere Martell, merchant and shipowner of Barcelona, was based in Tarragona when he offered the king and his court a feast at which plans were laid for the invasion of Majorca. Tarragona merchants appear often in the early Catalan commercial records, as do those of Tortosa; after 1229, Majorca City rapidly became another prime centre of Catalan trade, acting in many respects as a twin of Barcelona in the opening up of African markets. The question is thus not simply that of the expansion of Barcelona, but the growing trade of Catalonia, backed up by the textile centres of the interior, notably Lleida, and by the financial support of bankers from Girona and elsewhere.

Another perspective is to look at Barcelona's links with southern France. Just as historians have underestimated the persistence of James's southern French policy, so they have not always done justice to a link that fed Barcelona's trade in its early days: Montpellier, Marseilles, and eventually Perpignan exploited their ease of access to the international cloth traffic passing from Flanders towards the Mediterranean; Barcelona tapped into this trade route, finishing off northern cloths in its dyeshops and then redistributing them, particularly towards Muslim Spain, the Maghrib and Sicily, which itself was a significant source of raw cotton for the developing Catalan industries, and of grain for the expanding cities of Barcelona and Majorca.[44] In league with the southern French and Provençal ports Barcelona acquired its first privilege for trade in the Holy Land, in 1190; in league with them and the king Barcelona invaded Majorca. Especially important was an understanding with the Genoese and Pisans, who

43. F. Fernández-Armesto, *Barcelona. 1000 years of a city's past* (London, 1991) is rich in reflections about the city's emergence.
44. David Abulafia, 'Catalan merchants and the western Mediterranean, 1236–1300: studies in the notarial acts of Barcelona and Sicily', *Viator: medieval and Renaissance Studies*, 16 (1985), pp. 209–42.

assumed automatic rights of priority in the Balearics and in north Africa. It was an act of inspiration not to punish the Italians for their support for the Muslim king of Mayurqa, but to offer them a renewal and extension of trading rights. Though the Italians were discouraged from making use of the port of Barcelona, and Italian bankers were repeatedly chased out of Barcelona and Majorca, there was valuable cooperation in the funding of trading expeditions to north Africa, and both Catalans and Italians were active in the grain trade out of Sicily, often in partnership.

Barcelona was not like the Italian cities in one important respect. It never achieved true autonomy. But instead it gained an equally important advantage, the involvement of the king in its affairs, for the king himself invested in trade and owned ships.[15] What the king sought was 'a just balance between royal authority and local autonomy'. By the end of his reign the *Consell de Cent*, the Council of One Hundred, had been granted day-to-day control of the city's affairs, while other towns such as Perpignan and Montpellier also possessed privileges guaranteeing internal self-government. At the same time the king had his own representatives in Barcelona, such as the royal *batlle* or bailiff, and could to some extent rely on the support of the greater patrician families such as the Grony and the de Banyeres, who were able to help in the collection of port revenues or were active in the exploitation of overseas markets. The king gave active encouragement to new initiatives such as the minting of the *doblench* coins as early as 1222, and of the *tern* coins in 1258, the latter minted from one-quarter pure silver, and much cited thereafter as a standard currency in the Catalan realms.[16] Another important factor in the rise of Barcelona was its reputation for shipping skills; here, the acquisition of Majorca was arguably of crucial importance, for intensive links to the Balearics could only be maintained by the development of impressive skills in all-year-round navigation. (Indeed, it was Majorca which was to become a distinguished centre of maritime cartography.)[17] By 1284, evidence shows that shipping was

45. Bensch, *Barcelona and its rulers*, *passim*, for the role of the Crown.
46. Bisson, *Medieval Crown of Aragon*, p. 61.
47. There is a big literature on Catalan cartography, e.g. Y.K. Fall, *L'Afrique à la naissance de la cartographie moderne. Les cartes majorquines, 14ème–15ème siècles* (Paris, 1985); Abulafia, *Mediterranean Emporium*, pp. 204–8.

regularly leaving Majorca in the depths of winter bound often for north Africa; the mainstay of the merchant fleet was the smallish *leny* (literally, 'wood'), but the growing demand for grain from Sicily and elsewhere encouraged diversification towards big, slow roundships. Further signs of navigational sophistication were visible by 1281, when Majorcan ships were able to reach England alongside Genoese vessels.[48] Finally, there is the evidence of the maritime law codes of the Catalan world, best known from the fifteenth-century versions of the Valencian *Consulate of the Sea* code, which incorporates thirteenth-century material: evidence for growing business, and the growing need to regulate it by the standardisation of norms.[49]

Looking into the future, the years after the invasion of Sicily were to see a gradual strengthening of the already notable Catalan trading presence there and in nearby Tunis; access to the markets of Alexandria and Constantinople was also much eased once Palermo and Messina were centres of Catalan trade. Improved access to Sicilian grain was a great bonus for the swollen population of Barcelona and Majorca City, the more so as Barcelona itself became an increasingly important centre of woollen cloth production after 1300, while Majorca City may have accounted for as much as half of the population of an island that had perforce to live mainly by trade rather than agriculture. Here one beneficiary was the king of Majorca, who drew considerable revenue from the island's trade taxes. The greater safety of the waters around Gibraltar made feasible regular sailings not just to Flanders and England in search of wool and cloth, but down the ocean coast of Morocco: Barcelona, Majorca and Valencia became important links in a chain of routes linking Italy, Seville and the Atlantic shores.

The hand of the Aragonese monarchy in the success of Barcelona is most clearly visible in the development of overseas consulates, primarily in north Africa, the function of which was to represent the commercial interests of the Catalan merchants as well as the political interests of the

48. Abulafia, *Mediterranean Emporium*, pp. 188–93.
49. The most recent translation is that by S. Jados, *The Consulate of the Sea and other documents* (Alabama, 1975), though it fails to explain what the real issues are; see also *The Black Book of the Admiralty* (Rolls Series), vol. 3.

crown. In the mid-thirteenth century, both the city of Barcelona and the monarchy asserted the right to appoint consuls; in the long term, it was the king who retained greater influence, even drawing under the wing of his consul Catalan merchants from cities other than Barcelona, notably Majorca. By the 1250s Tunis had its own Catalan *fonduk* or warehouse; many fonduks also contained offices for the consul, accommodation for visiting merchants, a chaplain, even a bakery. James I actively promoted the foundation of new fonduks, sending Raymond de Conches, who hailed from Montpellier, to Alexandria in 1262 to negotiate for its foundation; later, Guillem de Montcada became consul there, the carrier of a surname of unusual distinction, a man whose trading links to the court of the king of Tunis are also documented. Relations with Muslim rulers remained delicate: Raymond de Conches had to go to Alexandria a second time in 1264 when it became clear that Catalan goods were being seized; he was to threaten the sultan with licensed piracy against his ships. Force as well as diplomacy was the only way to protect Catalan interests overseas. But the king expected revenue from his consulates. In 1259 James I was outraged to hear that his consuls in Tunis were paying a rent estimated at one-third of what the fonduk could actually support; the rent was summarily tripled. In 1274 James sent an envoy to Tunis to find out why two years of rent had failed to arrive. The monarchy correctly identified in the consulates a major source of revenue which might enable the king to emancipate himself from excessive dependence on internal taxation of his Spanish lands.[50]

Here James was obliged to turn to the *Corts* and *Cortes* in search of grants of *bovatge* and *monedatge*, the former of which was in danger of becoming a regular general tax. Catalonia, Aragon and eventually Valencia possessed their own assemblies, which were often enlarged to include representatives of the towns. The *Corts* did not yet possess the influence that they were to acquire under later kings, and James seems

---

50. A.B. Hibbert, 'Catalan Consulates in the thirteenth century', *Cambridge Historical Journal*, 9 (1949), pp. 352–8; C.E. Dufourcq, *L'Espagne catalane et le Maghrib aux XIIIe et XIVe siècles* (Paris, 1966), pp. 133–56, 311–36; C.E. Dufourcq, 'Les consulats de Tunis et de Bougie au temps de Jacques le Conquérant', *Anuario de estudios medievales*, 3 (1966), pp. 469–79.

to have become disenchanted with them, calling fewer *Corts* together towards the end of his reign. There was no simple linear development towards the 'pactist' monarchy of the late fourteenth century. Indeed, James relied less on the *Corts* as his own finances became slightly firmer; the count's Peace proclaimed early in his reign in Catalonia provided a framework for James's vicars to extend their authority into the localities, so that – as with his contemporaries in France and England – the ruler's justice was increasingly experienced by all his subjects.[51] Financial administration benefited from the expertise of Jewish advisers such as Aaron ibn Yahya or Abinafia, who acted as tax collectors on James's behalf in Valencia; even in the Catalan and Aragonese towns there were plenty of Jewish bailiffs looking after royal lands and rights.[52] Finally, the fall of Xàtiva secured for the crown vast supplies of paper, and this provided the basis for a vast expansion of record keeping; greater efficiency was one of the keys to greater accountability.

The reign of James the Conqueror thus saw not merely ambitious expansion into the Balearics and Valencia but, no less importantly, an expansion in government and trade which helped to sustain a monarchy constantly looking for resources with which to pay for its grandiose projects. Aragon had arrived on the world stage.

. . .

CONCLUSION

The central dilemma for historians looking at the emergence of the Crown of Aragon as a major force in the medieval Mediterranean has always been the relative balance between the commercial interests of Barcelona and the other Catalan trading centres, and the political ambitions of the count-kings, which evidently extended beyond the Catalan-Aragonese patrimony to encompass parts of Muslim Spain, much of what is now southern France and also the islands of the western Mediterranean. Political expansion was itself fuelled by the constant search for adequate sources of income, and it was this that made the partnership between

51. Bisson, *Medieval Crown of Aragon*, pp. 72–82.
52. Burns, *Medieval Colonialism*, pp. 270–91.

the crown and the Catalan merchants so advantageous to both sides; the consulates in north Africa are the supreme example of an institution which was created both to serve the day-to-day needs of the Catalan traders and to meet the fiscal requirements of a monarchy that sought to emancipate itself from excessive dependence on the parliaments of its realms. It has been seen that the economic expansion that this engendered was rather different in character from that of the major Italian ports such as Genoa, where it was precisely the lack of royal interference that enabled economic take-off to occur. In essence, trade followed the flag, and the flag did not follow trade.

The Aragonese kings were products of the chivalric culture of the thirteenth century, a culture which had laid deep roots in south-western France where they still had significant interests, notably the major city of Montpellier. Such a cultural environment stimulated an emphasis on the recovery of the rights that their family historically possessed: Aragonese rights in Provence, which were snatched from them by the French prince Charles, count of Anjou; rights in Sicily, which belonged to the wife of King Peter III, Constance, granddaughter of Frederick II. It was the battle for recognition of just rights, rather than the defence of trade, which dominated the policy of the Aragonese kings towards their Christian neighbours. Looking in the other direction, the chivalric heritage of James I was expressed in his role as champion of Christendom against the Moors, and the conquest of Muslim Majorca in 1229 brought him fame and the reputation he needed to quell dissident Catalan barons at home. Less successful was the invasion of Valencia which, however, did offer the chance to develop new sources of income; it was at least potentially extremely lucrative. But these conquests also posed the problem of how to exercise Christian kingship in a society where many (in Valencia most) of the population was Muslim or Jewish. The question of the subject religions was to become an important aspect of public policy in Mediterranean Spain during the late Middle Ages.

Chapter 3

THE RISE AND FALL OF CHARLES OF ANJOU

. . .

THE SEARCH FOR A CHAMPION

As early as 1252 the papacy had explored the possibility of securing the services of Charles, Count of Anjou, brother of King Louis IX, as leader of an invasion of southern Italy, in order to displace the hated Hohenstaufen. As count of Provence from the 1240s, Charles had access to considerable financial resources; but first he needed to subdue opposition in the county (notably that of Marseilles, which last revolted in 1263).[1] His success in Provence meant that even the lords of those parts of Italy closest to Provence, such as the count of Saluzzo, began to acknowledge Charles as overlord. Not merely had he acquired, after fifteen years of intensive work, a wealthy Mediterranean domain; he had also begun to take careful notice of events inside Italy, entering the same arena as his future rival King Manfred.

Charles appears to have been driven by an acute ambition for power; and yet he saw himself also as God's agent, sent to scourge the unfaithful. He could be ruthless to his enemies: he hanged members of the greatest families of Marseilles who opposed his rule. Yet he was also capable of practical generosity: the community of Marseilles was granted some commercial privileges by him, despite its past disloyalty. A Genoese poet remarked that he was 'greedy even when he was not a count, and became doubly so as king'; other poets, even if in his pay, were far more positive. Not surprisingly,

---

1. For the early phase of Charles's career, see P. Herde, *Karl I. von Anjou* (Stuttgart, 1979); Italian version: 'Carlo I d'Angiò', *Dizionario biografico italiano*, s.v.; also S. Runciman, *The Sicilian Vespers. A history of the Mediterranean world in the thirteenth century* (Cambridge, 1958).

then, the Sicilian patriot of the nineteenth century, Michele Amari, found ample grounds for a hostile portrait; and yet French historians since then have sometimes shown a sneaking regard for one who created an 'empire français' in the Mediterranean.[2] A thirteenth-century Italian sculptor, Arnolfo di Cambio, portrayed Charles with a stern, bleak expression which was perhaps intended to convey a sense of remote majesty rather than of remoteness of character. Like Frederick II, he was a man of many moods.

Despite attempts by Manfred to win papal sympathy for proposed crusades, and despite indecision – or more likely clashes of opinion – at the papal court, Charles was eventually adopted as papal champion; the promise of annual tribute amounting to 10,000 Sicilian ounces of gold suggests that the pope gave way to financial as well as political temptations. Charles was forbidden to lay any claim to the imperial lands or titles in Italy, nor even in the lands of the Church, for there were understandable fears that he would become another Frederick, ruling both northern and southern Italy, and squeezing the papal lands in central Italy. Charles won the prize of papal assurance that a crusade would be preached and funds levied on his behalf in France and Provence, and the signs are that he took his duties as a crusader against the faithless Manfred very seriously.[3] Speeches attributed to him before his victories at Benevento and Tagliacozzo make plain his insistence that he was fighting sin on behalf of the Holy Church.[4]

Charles's military plans were well under way in 1265. He negotiated terms with Lombard towns and Italian lords through whose lands he proposed to take his anti-Hohenstaufen crusaders. He saw that his Sicilian campaign could not succeed in the face of opposition within northern Italy. Given Manfred's influence in the north, he needed strong

2. M. Amari, *History of the War of the Sicilian Vespers*, 3 vols (London, 1850); a more favourable view is in L. Cadier, *Essai sur l'administration du Royaume angevin de Sicile* (Paris, 1891); references here are to the new Italian edn prepared by F. Giunta, *L'amministrazione della Sicilia angioina* (Palermo, 1974).
3. N. Housley, *The Italian Crusades. The papal-Angevin alliance and the Crusades against Christian lay powers, 1254–1343* (Oxford, 1982), pp. 18–19, 33–4, 68–9, 98–9, 166.
4. Housley, *Italian Crusades*, p. 166.

allies there, despite his promise not to hold formal office in the region. Despite the failure of the crusade tax to produce all the funds he needed, he was able to put together a large composite force of French, Provençal and Italian knights. Many undoubtedly came in the hope of office in the kingdom to be conquered; others were recruited out of a sense of knightly virtue or, like the Italian participants, because they were committed to the papal and Guelf cause.

Charles crossed the frontier on 3 February; on 26 February 1266 Manfred's army was put to rout and Manfred himself killed, after fighting with characteristic courage.[5] Thus Charles found himself, rapidly and with ease, master of the kingdom. He knew that his victory was all the greater since the native opposition had lost in the battle not merely its king but very many of its lesser leaders. Few barons tried to hold out against him in the mountains; and he, for his part, wisely showed mercy to past opponents. He did not yet try to displace existing bureaucrats; indeed, he saw clearly that their help was essential if he were ever to gather the funds that were his due in a kingdom whose style of government was more elaborate and more efficient than those of either France or the county of Provence. He appointed several French and Provençal companions to high office, gradually intruding them into the existing administration; as in Provence, he sought to ensure that the highest echelons of administration would be staffed by subjects from his other lands. But he was not yet as generous as his followers must have hoped in grants of land: partly to try to win a degree of support from existing barons; partly, perhaps, because the royal domain was so obviously a major source of royal revenue that he could not easily afford to alienate his own lands. Innovations in government were surprisingly few: the use of French in some documents, particularly those addressed to Anjou-Maine; there were some new ordinances for old offices. Charles's decision, for instance, to call together an assembly of justiciars and financial officers, to examine appeals against them, is a clearly audible echo of the judicial provisions of Frederick II over thirty years earlier.[6]

5. W. Hagemann, A. Zazo, *La battaglia di Benevento* (Benevento, 1967), *in toto*.
6. Cadier, *Amministrazione*, pp. 79–145.

There were further dividends. His conquest of the south brought him enthusiastic support from a wide range of Italian towns, and when the representatives of the Lombard Guelf communes came to a great conference at Milan in 1266, there were Angevin observers there too, who were much in evidence. It was going to be difficult to avoid northern entanglements, even if Charles took no official title in northern Italy. And yet after the death of Manfred the north Italian Ghibellines did not delay in finding a substitute patron. Conradin, that infant son of Conrad IV whom Manfred had unceremoniously displaced from the throne of Sicily, emerged as an urgently desired political hope. First fugitives from southern Italy, then the Tuscan Ghibellines, called on him – aged a mere fourteen years – to come to Italy and to achieve for the Hohenstaufen cause what Charles had achieved on the papal behalf.[7]

At the start of 1267 the pope could see no alternative to asking Charles to intervene in Tuscany. Pope Clement IV allowed him to hold office for up to three years: the post of *podestà*, governor, had already been offered by the citizens of Prato and Pistoia, two significant towns near Florence. Yet it was difficult to see where to resist Conradin most vigorously. As the boy claimant entered Italy the native nobles of southern Italy began to agitate in Charles's rear. Sicily rose in revolt for the first time in Charles's reign. A mixed force which even included Berbers sent by the king of Tunis seized control of most of the island, except the two main towns of Palermo and Messina.[8] On the mainland of southern Italy another small army under Henry, prince of Castile, was active against Charles, on whose side Henry had in fact fought at Benevento. Disillusioned with Charles, who had not in his view shown him sufficient generosity, Henry was made Captain-General of the Ghibellines in Tuscany.

A hearty welcome at Ghibelline Pisa encouraged Conradin to march southwards to claim his inheritance. Charles of Anjou was forced to hurry south to try to quash at least some opposition before Conradin crossed the frontiers of the Kingdom of Sicily. From the siege of the rebellious Muslim colony at Lucera, Charles went to meet Conradin just inside the borders of the kingdom, near the village of Tagliacozzo.

7. Runciman, *Sicilian Vespers*, pp. 118–20.
8. Ibid., p. 121.

The battle hung in the balance, and the slaughter was enormous, but in the end the Angevins triumphed.[9] Conradin escaped but was taken prisoner. There followed in southern Italy months of merciless repression of the king's enemies. The victory of Tagliacozzo strengthened Charles not merely against the Ghibellines and against Hohenstaufen sympathisers in the south; the victory made him seem irresistible in all of Italy. Conradin's execution, after a show trial, brutally sealed Charles's success.

Charles I needed only to apply relatively light pressure after Tagliacozzo to find his position in northern Italy greatly strengthened. The citizens of Rome re-elected him Senator, an office he had held in 1263, with indecent haste: they had actually fêted Conradin shortly before the battle. Charles installed his own 'vicar' as governor of Rome and introduced important innovations in the administration of the city; building programmes also advanced Charles's stature among the Romans, and Arnolfo di Cambio's life size statue of the king was made in recognition of Charles's good government. Elsewhere in Italy his touch was even lighter: he did not intrude his own men into the government of the Guelf cities, but simply placed over these towns a vicar-general responsible for defending his interests and those of the Church. Diplomacy brought him valuable victories too: the Genoese, for instance, made peace with him as ruler of lands to which they greatly needed commercial access; the Sienese, after a brief decade of Ghibelline ascendancy, found themselves the victims of a Guelf coup and had in future to live under a Florentine-Angevin shadow.[10] But even Siena did not suffer from continuous direct interference. Charles reserved to himself the choice of the *podestà* from a short-list of four candidates presented to him by the Sienese. He had learned by example or by intuition the extreme danger of trying to fiddle with the free government of the autonomous communes.[11] Édouard

9. Runciman, *Sicilian Vespers*, pp. 127–32: Runciman at his best.
10. G. Caro, *Genova e la supremazia sul Mediterraneo* (Italian translation of *Genua und die Mächte der Mittelmeer*, Halle, 1895–99; 2 vols, Genoa, 1974), vol. 1, pp. 143–57, 170–8, 192, 207–27, for all aspects of Charles's troubled relationship with Genoa.
11. D.P. Waley, *Siena and the Sienese in the thirteenth century* (Cambridge, 1991), pp. 114–18; J. Hook, *Siena. A city and its history* (London, 1979), p. 12; also W. Bowsky, *A Medieval Commune. Siena under the Nine, 1287–1355* (Berkeley/Los Angeles, 1981), for longer term developments.

Jordan pointed out that even his financial demands on the north Italian cities were relatively moderate compared to those of the Hohenstaufen; nonetheless, it was clear testimony of his great power that he could demand and receive war levies without serious opposition in either Lombardy or Tuscany.[12] By the winter of 1269–70 he had been accepted as lord of the Lombard towns. In Piedmont too his power climaxed: the old financial centre of Asti was defeated in battle and brought to heel.[13] With the extension of his control over all Piedmont Charles's power consisted of an almost continuous line of territories from the banks of the Rhône through the Alps to Lombardy, Tuscany, Rome and Sicily. He even entered a bid to have his younger son Philip chosen as king of Sardinia (1267); the pope was not disposed to make this grant, in the face of competing bids from Prince James of Majorca and Henry of Castile, but Philip was elected nonetheless (to no obvious effect other than Aragonese irritation) by the island's pro-Guelf factions in 1269.[14] Charles's power was at its height; vacancies in the papacy (1268–71) and an interregnum in Germany (to 1273) left him free to expand his interests unhindered.

. . .

A MEDITERRANEAN EMPIRE IN THE MAKING

Charles's Norman predecessors had often aspired to extend their rule beyond the lands they had won in Italy to the coasts of Africa and the Balkans. Many have argued that Charles sought a Mediterranean empire for himself, and that the Norman heritage of Balkan and African wars stimulated his grandiose, even megalomaniac, plans. Such an interpretation needs to be given more depth: an interest in Balkan politics was part of his immediate inheritance as king of Sicily, and in certain respects he followed the initiative of Manfred. Manfred's alliance with the Despot of Epiros left Charles with a claim to the dowry of Manfred's daughter in southern

---

12. É. Jordan, *Les origines de la domination angevine en Italie* (Paris, 1909; repr. in 2 vols, New York, 1960), vol. 2, pp. 556, 586, 609–11.
13. É. Léonard, *Les Angevins de Naples* (Paris, 1954); Italian edn, *Gli Angioini di Napoli* (Milan, 1967), pp. 110–11.
14. David Abulafia, *A Mediterranean Emporium. The Catalan Kingdom of Majorca* (Cambridge, 1994), pp. 242–3.

Albania, and in 1271 he took advantage of the despot's death to seize control of Durazzo, the principal port in the lands he claimed. The next year he appears in a document with the title 'King of Albania', a totally new title which reflected new realities in the Balkans: the descent towards Durazzo and the Adriatic coast of increasing numbers of native Albanian hillsmen, whose chieftains recognised Charles's claim to rule.[15] Control of this region may have been seen as a step towards creating a *cordon sanitaire* around southern Italy and Sicily, comprising a ring of lands in Albania, Tunisia and Sardinia. Charles pursued an energetic policy of military expansion in Albania: he garrisoned Durazzo and occupied or built castles along the main roads into the mountainous interior at Berat, Kruja and other strategic positions. Durazzo was already weakened by a recent earthquake; famine and agitation inside the city broke his hold on Durazzo, but he had a capable vicar-general there, and administrative orders from Naples reveal how strenuous were the efforts he made to provision this key town.[16] The Kingdom of Albania was, certainly, a shadowy entity whose main signs of existence lay in a series of Angevin strong-points. It is likely that Charles saw Albania as a jumping-off point for more ambitious expansion in the Balkans, towards the heartlands of the Byzantine empire itself. For another of Manfred's legacies was a plan to use Sicilian resources to recover Constantinople for the Latins.

After its fall to the armies of the Fourth Crusade and to the navies of Venice in 1204, Constantinople had become the seat of an impecunious Latin emperor whose lands were mostly disputed by rival Greek and Latin warlords.[17] The most successful of these, Michael VIII Palaiologos, recaptured Constantinople for the Greeks in 1261, with Genoese aid.[18]

---

15. Dr Pëllumb Xhufi of the Institute of History, University of Tirana, informs me that in fact this title was only utilised on a single occasion. See P. Xhufi, 'Shqiptarët përballë anzhuinëve (1267–1285)', *Studime Historike* (1987), pp. 199–222 [with French summary]; D.M. Nicol, 'The relations of Charles of Anjou with Nikephoros of Epiros', *Byzantinische Forschungen*, 4 (1972), pp. 170–94.

16. A. Ducellier, *La façade maritime de l'Albanie au Moyen Age. Durazzo et Valona du XIe au XVe siècle* (Thessalonika, 1981), pp. 230–320.

17. J. Longnon, *L'Empire latin de Constantinople* (Paris, 1949).

18. D.J. Geanakoplos, *Michael VIII Palaeologus and the West, 1258–1282* (Cambridge, MA, 1959), pp. 92–115.

In 1267, before Conradin's threat was yet real, Charles negotiated an agreement with the deposed Latin emperor of Constantinople, Baldwin II de Courtenay; in return for military aid against the Greeks, Charles would receive extensive rights in Achaia (the Peloponnese) and the Aegean islands, plus a marriage-alliance between his own daughter and Baldwin's son Philip. Were Philip to die without heirs, the imperial title would revert to the Angevin dynasty. Throughout the 1270s there were small campaigns in the Balkans as the armies of Emperor Michael VIII and other princes tried to hold back the allies of the Angevins: a siege of Durazzo in 1274; nibbling attacks on the Aegean islands claimed by Charles or other western lords; a crushing defeat for Charles at Berat in Albania in 1281. But Charles's plan of a single, massive, consolidated campaign which would take the Angevins to the walls of Constantinople was delayed less by these manoeuvres in the Balkans and Aegean than by papal insistence that there might be another way to deal with the Greeks of Constantinople. Charles might indeed seek to return a 'legitimate' and Latin Christian dynasty to its throne in the east; but the papacy began to negotiate with the Palaiologoi, in the hope that the Greek Church could be brought under Latin supervision by peaceful means. Michael Palaiologos began serious negotiations for the reunion of the eastern and western Churches, between which the gulf had only been growing greater since the schism of 1054. Undoubtedly Michael saw that his prime hope of preventing an Angevin attack lay in compliance to the overlord of Charles, the pope. In 1274, under the enthusiastic patronage of Pope Gregory X, the Council of Lyons accepted the profession of faith of Michael VIII and of the Greek Church. Gregory was full of hope now that Greeks and Latins would combine in a crusade to resist the Turks and recover the lost city of Jerusalem.[19]

For Charles, the conquest of Constantinople was only part of a wider eastern policy whose ultimate purpose was a successful crusade. He had his own credentials as a crusader. In 1270 he had been a leading participant in the Tunis crusade of St Louis: indeed, he is often accused of having pressed his brother to send the crusade to North Africa to prosecute

19. Geanakoplos, *Michael VIII*, pp. 258–79.

his own interests, rather than to Egypt and the Holy Land where it was more greatly needed. Charles certainly had grievances when he joined the Tunis crusade: the emir of Tunis had summarily suspended payment of the traditional tribute paid to Frederick II. Moreover, there had been Tunisian participants in the Sicilian uprising of 1268. But neither he nor those close to Louis IX could control the pious king's deeply-felt desire to take up the cross. Certainly, Charles arrived late at Tunis, in the heat of August, to find that St Louis had fallen ill and died when the siege of Tunis was barely under way. Charles, if anyone, reaped the benefits of this disastrous crusade: by the time the Christian army withdrew, the emir had promised tribute to Charles and the re-establishment of commercial privileges for his subjects.[20] A further factor of some importance was the involvement of the Catalans in Tunis: an important base of Catalan trade, Tunis was forging dangerously close links with the Aragonese, whose interests were constantly colliding with Charles's, whether in Provence, Sardinia, southern Italy, Africa or the Levant.[21]

The Tunis crusade only highlighted the difficulties of the prime object of many crusades: the Kingdom of Jerusalem was deeply divided; among other problems, the right to the throne was in dispute between the king of Cyprus and Maria of Antioch, a descendant of the royal line of Jerusalem. Although the barons of the kingdom awarded the crown to Hugh of Cyprus in 1269, Maria made practical use of her claims and sold her title to Charles of Anjou (1274).[22] And Charles tried to give substance to the title: he gained papal approval; he sent Roger of Sanseverino from southern Italy to Acre with an Angevin fleet, and for a few years Acre was an Angevin stronghold. Little else was done. Nevertheless, the title 'King of Jerusalem and Sicily' was henceforth carried with great pride by the rulers of Naples, even when they had lost both Jerusalem and Sicily; associations with the crusading movement continued to shape Angevin policy in Italy and the Mediterranean, but constant distractions nearer home meant

20. J. Le Goff, *Saint Louis* (Paris, 1996), pp. 290–7.
21. See chapter 2, pp. 47–8, on the rise of Aragon for further analysis of this clash of interests.
22. J. Riley-Smith, *The Feudal Nobility and the Kingdom of Jerusalem, 1174–1277* (London, 1973), pp. 225–7, outlining clearly the great difficulties Charles's agents in the East faced.

that they were unable to save the kingdom of Jerusalem from extinction at the hands of the Egyptians in 1291. Charles had conquered Sicily by means of a crusade, and he never ceased to take crusading seriously; his Balkan wars themselves were part of a grander strategy which would supposedly culminate in the Christian recovery of Jerusalem.

. . .

TROUBLE AT HOME

Charles was not left free to concentrate on his eastern Mediterranean projects. The north Italian towns were not all in Guelf hands; his successes were arousing some alarm among those who were content to see him rule in southern Italy but not to see him emerge as the imperial substitute in northern Italy. Partly these changes reflect the instability of the town governments, too: the Genoese, for instance, broke with Charles when a Ghibelline faction took power in 1270 and Charles gave active help to their exiled Guelf opponents.[23] And there were signs that the free communes resented some of the financial impositions of the Angevins: the inhabitants of Asti rapidly grew restive, and by 1273 they were involved in a secret Ghibelline alliance which brought together several north-west Italian cities and lords.[24] A further reason for Charles's loss of influence was the awareness of Pope Gregory X that the long proposed limitations on Angevin power in the former imperial lands of northern Italy had never seriously been enforced. Gregory recognised Rudolf of Habsburg as King of the Romans (1274); he invited Rudolf to travel to Rome for the imperial coronation. But Rudolf not unnaturally attracted the loyalty of the Ghibellines in northern Italy, and Gregory X openly encouraged all the Lombards to act graciously towards the King of the Romans. Gregory tried hard to show himself as peacemaker in northern Italy; thus he suggested to Rudolf that he formally grant Charles of Anjou the county of Piedmont as a fief, while intimating secretly that he thought this would be a disastrous act of generosity.[25] The reality was that Rudolf and Charles remained deeply suspicious of one another.

23. Léonard, *Angioini*, pp. 135–7, 141–2.
24. Ibid., pp. 142–5.
25. Runciman, *Sicilian Vespers*, p. 167.

The pontificate of Gregory X was marked by the extension of papal authority into the hills and plains of Romagna, the northernmost part of the emerging papal state. At the time of his death (1276) Gregory was beginning to see that he might need Angevin aid if he were to hold Romagna in the face of competitors for control of so prosperous a region. His eventual successor, Nicholas III (1277–80), found himself obliged to pursue this course even though he compromised many of his policies by close attention to the interests of his own Orsini family. The vigorous defence of the north of Italy might appear to signify that it was there that Charles of Anjou faced the greatest risk to his power. But even Sicily, after stern repression, had not been entirely quietened. A new pope, Martin IV (1281–85), a Frenchman, moved closer to Charles and abandoned some of Nicholas III's reservations in accepting an Angevin alliance. Where Nicholas had insisted Charles resign as Roman Senator, Martin encouraged his re-election. Where Nicholas tried to bring peace and compromise to Florence and other troubled Tuscan towns (1279), Martin gave support to the Guelfs.[26] In Romagna there were rebellions against the Church, too. The most obvious sign that Martin had abandoned his predecessor's reserve lay in his approval of Charles's oriental projects. Martin brought together Charles and the Venetians in a definite plan to invade the Greek empire, agreed upon in July 1281. The fleet was due to sail in April 1282. It never did so. At the hour of Vespers on 30 March 1282 some Angevin soldiers insulted a young Sicilian wife at the Church of Santo Spirito on the edge of Palermo. A struggle broke out, blood was drawn, and the cry went up: '*Moranu li Francisi*', 'Death to the French!' The French garrison in Palermo was slaughtered and the revolt spread in a few weeks throughout the island of Sicily, until even the arsenal city of Messina was in rebel hands (28 April 1282).[27] The Angevins had lost Sicily, the very land from which they drew their most important title and resources. Who were the rebels and what did they want?

26. An attempt to settle the rabid internal strife of Florence was made in 1279, when Cardinal Latino, a relative of Pope Nicholas, visited the city and made imaginative proposals for constitutional reforms which, had they succeeded, would have reduced Charles of Anjou's capacity to intervene in the city's affairs: G. Salvemini, *Magnati e Popolani a Firenze dal 1280 al 1295*, ed. E. Sestan (Milan, 1974), p. 5.
27. Runciman, *Sicilian Vespers*, pp. 237–9.

Both questions are surprisingly difficult to answer, because it is not clear that the manner in which the Angevins lost control of Sicily was the manner all the rebels had in mind. At the height of the rebellion the representatives of the Sicilian towns and nobility appealed to the pope for protection: they wished to place Sicily under his authority, as a free community or communities; some towns certainly hoped to acquire similar status to that of the cities of northern Italy, as free communes under a rather remote sovereign authority. Although they cannot have had any illusions about papal sympathy for Charles, the cities were surely aware of recent precedent, when Innocent IV had encouraged them to break with the Hohenstaufen and claim their independence under papal suzerainty. Yet Pope Martin IV rebuffed this approach decisively. Certainly the rebels wished to drive out the French and Provençal administrators who had levied taxes with such efficiency. But their system of government was essentially that of the Hohenstaufen, and the grievances of 1282 echo uncannily the grievances against Frederick II in the last years of his reign. Some rebels, too, suffered at Angevin hands when the revolt of 1267–68 was suppressed: lands were confiscated, leaders of the revolt were exiled. One of the exiles, Giovanni da Procida, became very active in the courts of the Mediterranean, and it is sometimes, but not very convincingly, argued that he was the 'arch-conspirator' in a secret alliance keeping the Greek Emperor Michael Palaiologos in touch with events in the western and central Mediterranean.[28]

The accusation that Charles's government was repressive enough to engender a popular revolt has not always found favour with French historians. Léon Cadier was right to stress the Norman-Hohenstaufen heritage of Angevin government, but the fact of this heritage does not mean that government was prosecuted with tact.[29] The cry 'Death to the French' is itself revealing: Charles did rely heavily on administrators from outside Sicily and southern Italy. The French and Provençaux perhaps held first place, especially among the justiciars appointed after the rebellion in favour of Conradin; but there were increasing numbers of Tuscans

---

28. Runciman, *Sicilian Vespers*, pp. 313–18; H. Wieruszowski, *Politics and Culture in medieval Spain and Italy* (Rome, 1971), pp. 223–78, 309–14.
29. Cadier, *Amministrazione della Sicilia angioina* (Palermo, 1974).

too, and a number of Amalfitans – whose families had served the Hohenstaufen – retained high office in Sicily, and it will be necessary to return to this influential group shortly. Added to this, the intrusion after 1268 of French-born knights into south Italian fiefs created a new aristocracy with new bonds to the king, though in Sicily itself this group was in fact less prominent. In 1282 Charles, with a papal legate, tried to bring the rebels back under his control by a promise that abuses by royal officers would be severely punished. This was nothing but an admission that such abuses occurred. He had reconvened the Hohenstaufen assembly of justiciars at the beginning of his reign, to check complaints and abuses; but by 1282 many officials had been replaced and he himself was preoccupied with projects in northern Italy and the east. Under pressure of those war needs he expected to realise the income he felt was his due; as it was, he was indebted to foreign bankers. And his financial problems may just as easily have been accentuated by venal bureaucrats as alleviated by over-diligent ones.

Transformations in the social structure of Sicily help explain why the Vespers occurred.[30] Large numbers of north Italian settlers had trickled into Sicily to fill the vacuum left by the disappearance of the Muslim population, uprooted after its own lengthy rebellion against Frederick II; in the towns, merchant communities developed who consisted of Tuscans, Genoese and other Sicilianised northerners, and there were significant settlements of Latins in the interior, often benefiting from handsome privileges of tax exemption; for example, the 'Lombard' inhabitants of Randazzo, on the slopes of Etna, had been granted special rights of exemption as far back as Norman times.[31] Charles of Anjou did not simply rule the descendants of the Arab and Greek subjects

---

30. The latest study of the social structure of Sicily in this period is the impressive book of L. Catalioto, *Terre, baroni e città in Sicilia nell'età di Carlo I d'Angiò* (Messina, 1995).

31. David Abulafia, 'The End of Muslim Sicily', in J.M. Powell, ed., *Muslims under Latin rule, 1100–1300* (Princeton, NJ, 1990), pp. 105–33; David Abulafia, 'The Crown and the economy under Roger II and his successors', *Dumbarton Oaks Papers*, 37 (1983), 11–13; H. Bresc, 'La formazione del popolo siciliano', *Tre millenni di storia linguistica della Sicilia. Atti del Convegno della Società italiana de Glottologia* (Pisa, 1985), pp. 243–65; repr. in H. Bresc, *Politique et société en Sicile, XIIe–XVe siècles* (Aldershot, 1990).

of the Norman kings, but a Latin island in which Greeks and Jews were a small minority and Muslims were non-existent; the clearest sign of the transformation is perhaps the spread of forms of Italian vernacular which in some regions betrayed close links to the dialects spoken in Liguria and other parts of northern Italy. The linguistic evidence suggests that towns and villages in the north of Italy effectively targeted areas of Sicily, which were settled by many thousands of colonists, a process still continuing in the Angevin period. Evidence from southern Italy shows us the process at work: close to Lucera, Charles appears to have settled a group of Franco-Provençal farmers, whose descendants are still in place; the idea was to replace the local Muslim population with Christian settlers, just as had been happening in Sicily. In Malta too the Latinisation of the island appears to have been completed around this time.[32] Particularly worth stressing, however, is the existence of large numbers of settlers from the north and central Italian towns in the major Sicilian cities. Boccaccio's famous story of Lisabetta and the pot of basil takes place in Messina, in the house of three brothers whose father had migrated from San Gimignano in Tuscany; and their employee, who fell fatally in love with Lisabetta, is Lorenzo from Pisa.[33] Such figures mirror those who can be found in the documents: a Messinese document of 1239 describes the real estate of the daughter of a merchant from Lucca, bordering the street of the Pisans and the possessions of some Amalfitans, another mercantile community which struck deep roots in Messina.[34] Messina was the prime example, a city which had been given new life by its settlers from the mainland; but Palermo too was being renewed in population, by Genoese, Pisans, Catalans and many others.[35] Within the Sicilian towns, this new population may well have developed expectations about rights to self-government which were

32. David Abulafia, 'Monarchs and minorities in the medieval Mediterranean c.1300: Lucera and its analogues', in P. Diehl and S. Waugh, eds, *Christendom and its discontents. Exclusion, persecution and rebellion, 1000-1500* (Cambridge, 1996), pp. 237-9.
33. Giovanni Boccaccio, *Decameron*, Day 4, story 5.
34. L.R. Ménager, *Les Actes latins de S. Maria di Messina (1103-1250)* (Palermo, 1963), doc. 20, pp. 150-8.
35. For Messina see David Abulafia, 'The merchants of Messina: Levant trade and domestic economy', *Papers of the British School at Rome*, 54 (1986), pp. 196-212.

based on a north Italian model with which they were already in many cases very familiar.[36]

For Henri Bresc, the Vespers demonstrate that out of this new population of Latin and Latinised Sicilians had emerged a genuine 'sicilitude' [Sicilianness]; he speaks of 'une nation sicilienne', with a political consciousness of its own, distinct from the population of mainland southern Italy.[37] The revolt was, it is true, an island revolt, and the more extensive mainland territories did not rise up against the crown on the same scale, though there were disturbances even in Naples itself. This is often explained by the greater generosity of the crown towards the mainland cities, many of which benefited from royal programmes of harbour building, including even the inappropriately named port of Manfredonia. Royal neglect of Sicily can also be measured in the lack of visits by Charles to the island, except during the Tunis crusade; it is possible that Charles was convinced the Sicilians were his enemies long before 1282, and that the rebellion in favour of Conradin, which had been well supported in the island, led him to show more favours elsewhere.

The loss of status of Palermo, once a royal capital, was gradual, but the shift in the centre of gravity of the kingdom from island to mainland had begun under Frederick II, who had based himself increasingly at Foggia and Lucera in south-eastern Italy. By Charles of Anjou's time Palermo had even lost its function as the coronation capital of the kingdom, and damage to the city's economic life is likely to have resulted; the very fact that Palermo was no longer the centre of government meant a loss of direct access to the king's patronage which disadvantaged the petty nobility and the urban elite, accustomed to the benefits of royal favours in land grants and the right to tax farms. Still, it cannot be stressed enough that these changes were long-term ones, which were not simply the result of Charles's own policy decisions.

36. See now Catalioto, *Terre*, pp. 179–249.
37. H. Bresc, '1282: classes sociales et révolution nationale', *XI Congresso di Storia della Corona d'Aragona: La Società mediterranea all'epoca del Vespro. VII Centenario del Vespro Siciliano*, 4 vols (Palermo, 1983–84), vol. 2, pp. 241–58; repr. in H. Bresc, *Politique et société en Sicile, XIIe–XVe siècles* (Aldershot, 1990); W. Percy, 'The earliest revolution against the "Modern State": direct taxation in medieval Sicily and the Vespers', *Italian Quarterly*, 22 (1981), pp. 69–83.

Indeed, some of Charles's actions, such as the harbour building programme, have roots in Hohenstaufen ordinances, for here as in so many other areas the Angevins simply reiterated the policies of their predecessors. On the other hand, Bresc has assumed a degree of political consciousness, and an ability to organise themselves politically, which seems unlikely among the free farmers and other groups whom he places at the centre of the 'nation sicilienne'. For the roots of the rebellion lay not among the Lombards of the countryside and of the smaller towns, but among the Sicilian elites: the local nobles, led by such figures as Alaimo da Lentini, the wealthier merchants and lawyers of Palermo. A closer definition of the major participants in the rebellion is essential. The fact certainly remains that it began with an outrage committed by a French soldier against a young married Sicilian woman, and continued with what was apparently a leaderless popular uprising. Whether or not a major feature was Sicilian 'nationalism', precocious in the history of Europe, the hatred for the French garrisons is abundantly clear. And yet Bresc insists that the focus of the revolt was not and could not really be the French masters of the island, for they were physically remote, and there were rather few French feudatories holding land in Sicily itself. Indeed, one of the French landholders, Ugo Talac, who was established near Mazara, himself joined the rebellion against Charles I.[38]

Bresc has pointed to a particular dimension of Angevin government in Sicily which does deserve attention: the presence of a significant number of administrators drawn from the mainland, whom he characterises as the 'Amalfitans', since several came from the Costa Amalfitana, the Bay of Naples and adjoining areas.[39] For Bresc, the Vespers were as much or more 'les Vêpres anti-amalfitaines' as they were a revolt against the French. And one has only to look at the close collaboration between such figures as the turncoat Joscelin de Marra, a high official under Manfred and then under Charles I, to see how well trained administrators, products of the schools at Capua and of the nascent University of

---

38. Bresc, '1282', p. 246.
39. On this group, see N. Kamp, 'Von Kämmerer zum Sekreten: Wirtschaftsreformen und Finanzverwaltung im staufischen Königreich Sizilien', in J. Fleckenstein, ed., *Probleme um Friedrich II.* (Sigmaringen, 1974); Bresc, '1282', pp. 250–2.

Naples, ensured a smooth transition from the Hohenstaufen to the Angevin regime. Although French barons were often appointed over their heads, it was the 'Amalfitans' who actually understood the workings of the system; even so, this did not prevent (and possibly made easier) extortionate exactions and a tendency for civil servants to line their own pockets. While accepting the importance of Bresc's insight, we must also bear in mind the simple fact that the 'Amalfitans' were not a phenomenon of Charles's reign alone. It was already clear under Frederick II that this group of officials, led by the redoutable Rufolo family, had carved out a place at the core of the administrative machine; Sicilian *secreti* after 1250 included Federico Trara from Scala near Amalfi, Pietro Capuano of Amalfi and Matteo and Giacomo Rufolo. Where once the leaders of Amalfi, Ravello and neighbouring towns had been distinguished for their expertise in international trade, now government service became a great speciality of the elite. Federico Trara served Hohenstaufen and Angevins alike. After 1278 the hold of the 'Amalfitans' was confirmed, with the arrival of one Rufolo (Matteo) as *secreto* and another as his deputy. What we see, in fact, is a shift in emphasis: occasional Sicilian administrators such as Enrico Abbate of Trapani disappeared from the island government by 1265, and the hegemony of the mainlanders became increasingly secure.[40] And yet it seems that it was impossible to rely solely on the Amalfitans. At the heart of the *secrezia* there persisted a small but significant group of islanders, including Palmieri Abbate and Alaimo da Lentini, leaders of the subsequent rebellion, as well as Matteo Riso, who was to show loyalty to Charles I from his base in Messina. Bresc thus stresses that already several years before the Vespers a power struggle within the provincial administration of Sicily was under way; he sees this as a social conflict between a petty nobility, sometimes harking back to Norman origins, and what we might term the *noblesse de robe* represented by the 'Amalfitans'. As he says, the difficulty the 'Amalfitans' faced was that they came to be blamed by both sides: they were thrown out by the revolutionaries, while Charles I made them into scapegoats for the complaints against misgovernment that were in the

---

40. Bresc, '1282', pp. 250–1; cf. Runciman, *Sicilian Vespers*, pp. 227–8, 246–55, 274–6, for Alaimo's career.

air once the rebellion broke out, so that some in fact passed over to the Catalan-Aragonese camp after all.[41] Once again it is clear that the Vespers were not simply a revolt against the French, but a rebellion directed at a whole tradition of tight-fisted government, going back at least to the years when an embattled Frederick II charged his administrators with the maximisation of his income from the *Regno*. In fact, the level of the *collecta* gathered in Sicily under Charles I seems to have been generally no higher than that charged by Frederick II, with a few exceptions (notably 30,000 ounces of gold in 1272), though there was room for more complaint in other areas, such as that of monetary policy. The presence of administrative officials from the mainland in Sicily may indeed have sharpened the sense among Sicilian nobles and townsmen that the island was seen as no more than a source of grain and gold with which to pay for Charles's foreign escapades; on the other hand, there was a well-established tradition of avoiding the use of local men in administration, which was already being practised by Frederick II.

The Riso family of Messina can be cited as a good example of the Sicilian elite which sided with the Angevins against the rebels.[42] Here again we are looking at long-standing allies of the crown, at a family which had played a role under Frederick II, and which transferred its loyalty to Charles I. This is all the less surprising in view of the intimate ties between Messina and the toe of Italy; Calabria and Messina were economically interdependent, and Messina looked away from the rest of Sicily in significant respects. Still, this did not serve the Riso family well in the long run: Messina too rose against its Angevin master; the rebellious Commune imprisoned the Risos in the castle of Matagriffon, and the city fell into the grasp of Alaimo da Lentini, who proposed to the pope – naturally without success – that he himself should be appointed boss of Messina under papal suzerainty.[43] Yet it is important also to bear in mind the character of this Sicilian nobility: the island, unlike the mainland, possessed no 'world class' nobles comparable to the great nobility of northern France or indeed of northern Italy; the social

41. Bresc, '1282', p. 256.
42. See now Catalioto, *Terre*, pp. 233–49.
43. Runciman, *Sicilian Vespers*, pp. 239–41.

structure at this level is more reminiscent of Catalonia or the Latin East, a world in which really great nobles were a rarity, but in which there existed an extensive nobility of more than moderate means. If the prosperity of the leading families depended heavily on their ties to the royal court, it is not difficult to envisage the problems engendered when the royal court itself was based far away in Naples, and when the king seemed more preoccupied with business in Provence and even Anjou than with Sicily. There was, then, a disjuncture: the mainland, which had posed difficulties for earlier kings because of the extent of baronial power there, was the ideal base from which to conduct an active policy in northern Italy and further afield; but it was on the island of Sicily that royal power had traditionally been expressed most forcefully through the effective exclusion of noble grandees who could rival royal authority. Put differently, the crown was based in the wrong place to achieve the necessary degree of political coexistence with its island subjects, whose relationship to the crown existed on a different basis to that found in southern Italy. It could be said that Norman government was predicated on the assumption that the island would be the base and focus of royal government; Hohenstaufen and Angevin government thus appeared from Sicily to be exclusively dedicated to maximising income from Sicily's resources, notably the massive grain trade which the Angevins always took care to police with thoroughness. Government no longer seemed to be geared to the prime interests of the island's more powerful inhabitants.

Another complication in 1282 that is often cited is the Byzantine issue. The opposition of the Greek population of eastern Sicily to Charles's Byzantine crusade has also been seen as a factor in the rebellion, notably in studies by Deno Geanakoplos.[44] The argument that the Greeks were hostile to Charles because of his enmity towards the Byzantine emperor Michael VIII seems implausible, however, at a time

44. D.J. Geanakoplos, 'The Greek population of South Italy and Sicily and its attitude to Charles of Anjou and Michael Palaeologus before and during the early phase of the Sicilian Vespers', *XI Congresso di Storia della Corona d'Aragona: La Società mediterranea all'epoca del Vespro. VII Centenario del Vespro Siciliano*, 4 vols (Palermo, 1983–84), vol. 3, pp. 177–82; repr. in D.J. Geanakoplos, *Constantinople and the West* (Madison, Wis., 1989), pp. 189–95.

when the Byzantine world was very fragmented and when the Greeks in southern Italy and Sicily had long experience of communion with Rome. They were a shrinking group, barely represented among the trading community of what had once been their greatest centre in Sicily, Messina. The future lay, rather, with the 'Lombards' who had been swamping eastern Sicily for up to two centuries.

What is clear is that the term 'popular rebellion' should be applied to the Sicilian Vespers with caution. If there was a conspiracy, it is not at all certain that the occurrence at Vespers on 30 March was part of it. Nor is it certain that the Sicilian nobles, with their dream of a papal 'republic', were at one with Giovanni da Procida and his contacts. Legend relates that Palmieri Abbate, Alaimo of Lentini and Gualtiero da Caltagirone were the prime contacts of Giovanni da Procida as he wandered the Mediterranean disguised as a Franciscan brother.

It would not be surprising if the failure of the 1268 uprising left discontented Sicilian barons conspiring fruitlessly among themselves. But Procida did have someone 'waiting in the wings'; and the uprising in Sicily only acted as a spur to definite activity on the part of one who was already contemplating an attack on Sicily, perhaps while Charles's fleet was at sea: the husband of Manfred's daughter Constance, King Peter of Aragon, had behind him the navy of Catalonia. The Sicilian parliament met at Palermo and agreed to his envoys' suggestion that the King of Aragon be summoned to Sicily to take the crown in right of his Hohenstaufen wife; and in September he came fully armed to Palermo to receive the crown and defend his new kingdom.[15] Evidently, Peter III was not the first choice of the rebels, since they first sought papal protection; equally, his help became an absolute necessity once the pope had refused to support the rebels against Charles of Anjou. The crucial aspect of the Vespers that has not been sufficiently stressed is, therefore, the division of opinion concerning the future of Sicily and indeed of southern Italy: whether there should be a collection of republics under papal overlordship (an approach which must at the time have raised almost insoluble questions about

45. Runciman, *Sicilian Vespers*, pp. 248–52.

who should rule the rural expanses between the towns), or whether it was preferable to maintain a monarchy in the teeth of papal opposition, a monarchy which was nothing less than a Hohenstaufen restoration legitimised by the return of Queen Constance to her ancestors' kingdom. Events during the War of the Vespers suggest that the difference of opinion over such a fundamental question was capable of shattering the unity of the Sicilian resistance to the Angevins: Gualtiero da Caltagirone, an early leader of the rebellion, was executed for apparent contact with the Angevin enemy; and who had him executed? Alaimo da Lentini, who was himself soon proved to be in contact with the king of France, and whose fate was life imprisonment in Catalonia after he had mistakenly accepted an invitation to the court of King Peter in Barcelona during 1284. This was after a promising start as Captain of Messina and Grand Justiciar of the Sicilian kingdom. Runciman, delighting as ever in the gossip of the thirteenth century, relates by way of the chronicle of Bartolomeo da Neocastro how Alaimo's wife had made amorous advances to King Peter, which the king rejected, and which then led her into a blind fury against Queen Constance. She is said on one occasion to have competed with the queen by having herself borne a great distance through Palermo and out into the country-side in a magnificent litter which was deliberately intended to outshine that of the queen herself. More to the point, Alaimo seems to represent that group of leaders who had serious doubts about King Peter's party. Giovanni da Procida was, after all, a south Italian and not a Sicilian, a perfect example of that group of civil servants from the area of Naples and Amalfi who were the focus of so much opposition at the time of the revolt. Alaimo may also have reacted with disappointment to the destruction unleashed within Sicily by the shock troops of the king of Aragon, the *almogàvers*, who twenty years later were to win a particularly frightful reputation in Greece. A third leader, Palmieri Abbate, did not maintain his influence and drops out of sight after the Catalan-Aragonese takeover.[46] In fact, in the two years after the rebellion there were many defections to the Angevins, for it was not at once clear how Peter of Aragon could lighten

46. Runciman, *Sicilian Vespers*, p. 276.

the tax load on his Sicilian subjects, needing as he did sub-ventions to pay for the war against the house of Anjou. On balance, the Aragonese proved sensitive to the dangers of over-taxation, and yet the fact was that they had only limited resources on which to call, since their Catalan-Aragonese subjects were not keen on the foreign adventure they had undertaken, and were able, through the Catalan *Corts* and the Aragonese *Cortes*, to place limits on the king's freedom of action back home in Spain.

Not that Peter was unaware of these problems: as early as 6 October 1282 he recognised the right of the towns to choose their own judges and officials, though very rapidly he clawed back these rights. The evolution of town govern-ment in Sicily, as in mainland southern Italy, was to follow a very different path to that visible in northern Italy and even in the Papal States, taking the form of communities or *universitates* decidedly limited in their freedom of action and in their control of the countryside. Peter seems to have realised that the best way to handle the urban elites was to flatter those he considered reasonably loyal with the priv-ileges of nobility and land grants which had been denied them when central government had packed up and trans-ferred to Foggia and Naples on the mainland.

Peter's conquest of the island of Sicily did not redeem all the claims of the Hohenstaufen. Aragonese armies pushed northwards into Calabria, after defeating Charles's fleet in the narrows between Sicily and the continent. Peter hoped for major successes in the Bay of Naples, and aimed to recover every inch of Frederick II's kingdom. He had the enthusiastic help of the Ghibellines in northern Italy, who provided con-venient distraction by the eviction of papal and Angevin governors from the towns. Perugia renounced Martin IV. Where Peter could not be so confident of success was nearer his homeland of Aragon. The king of France, Philip III, was distressed at his uncle's losses; he had already warned Peter that he would support Charles, if the Catalan fleet were diverted against Sicily. Peter meanwhile proposed an ingeni-ous way to avoid further bloodshed and end rivalry: he would fight a duel with Charles in single combat; a meeting was arranged at Bordeaux in 1283, but both sides managed deftly to avoid one another, each accusing the other of bad faith. Not even a French crusade, with papal blessing, against the

Kingdom of Aragon managed to dislodge Peter III.[47] His kingdom in Spain was, like Sicily, technically a papal fief, and so like Sicily the pope assumed he could assign it to another prince. Aragon was formally conferred on Philip III's son Charles of Valois (1284) but the French crusade met with disaster; this will be discussed further in the following chapter. In Italy, too, Peter managed by a combination of luck and determination to hold and strengthen his position. Charles of Anjou's son Charles, Prince of Salerno, was captured at sea; the delighted Neapolitans took the news as an invitation to riot against the French. Although Charles I arrived soon in person to restore order, the exuberance of the Neapolitans at his son's defeat revealed how limited was Angevin support even in the areas which he himself controlled.[48]

. . .

THE AFTERMATH OF THE REVOLT OF THE VESPERS

On 7 January 1285, his work incomplete, Charles I died at Foggia. He is said to have spoken these words:

> Lord God, as I truly believe that You are my Saviour, I beg You to have mercy on my soul. Just as You know that I took the Kingdom of Sicily more to serve the Holy Church than for my own profit or covetousness, so therefore You will pardon my sins.[49]

The Sicilian Vespers should not, in fact, be seen as a revolt against Charles of Anjou so much as one against decades of tight-fisted government, accentuated by the loss of capital status of Palermo, and by the political aspirations of the island's lawyers, petty nobles and great merchants, many of whom were not deeply rooted in the island. They certainly were not simply seeking to recover a romantic past in which the island had been the home of varied communities and a glorious royal court. The republican ambitions of the rebels are so constantly emphasised that it comes as little surprise

47. J.R. Strayer, 'The crusade against Aragon, 1285', in J.R. Strayer, *Medieval statecraft and History* (Princeton, 1971).
48. For the captivity of Charles of Salerno, see M.R. Toynbee, *St Louis of Toulouse* (Manchester, 1929), pp. 49–54.
49. *Villani's Chronicle*, transl. Rose E. Selfe and ed. P.H. Wicksteed (London, 1906), p. 275, given in modernised French.

that Peter of Aragon found it hard to hold on to his supposed allies in the struggle agianst the Angevins. On the other hand, Peter was well attuned to the need to supply Sicily with its own king and dynasty, rather than to bring it, like Valencia, under his direct rule; the logistical problems of ruling Sicily from Spain apart, it was a Hohenstaufen whom the pro-Aragonese rebels wanted, not a member of the house of Barcelona. Hence it made sense to leave his wife in control in Sicily when he returned post-haste to Catalonia in 1283, in order to fend off a French invasion, and then, with the approval of a Sicilian parliament, to bequeath Sicily to his second son James, while the Spanish lands went to his eldest son Alfonso. As King Peter well understood, 1282 saw not an Aragonese conquest of Sicily, but a Hohenstaufen restoration.

· · ·

CONCLUSION

By the year 1266 the papacy had apparently achieved its great objective of securing a friendly ruler on the throne of Sicily; but it was precisely the security of Charles's tenure of the Sicilian throne that was soon placed in doubt, as rebellion broke out in 1267–68, and much more seriously in 1282. Charles was certainly dedicated to what he saw as God's purpose, and yet he found himself drawn into the same quicksands which had buried the house of Hohenstaufen: the attraction of alliances with the Guelfs in northern Italy put an end to the official notion that his sphere of operations was confined to the south; his insistence on solving the problem of the Greek Church by the sword created a host of enemies across the Mediterranean; he constantly clashed with the Aragonese over issues such as control of Tunis, Sardinia and Provence. On the one hand, the pope knew that only a well-heeled prince would be able to carry through the expensive war of conquest that destroyed Manfred; on the other hand, Charles's other lands drew him into wider affairs, and as count of Provence from 1246 he was already a significant actor on the north Italian political stage, with major interests in neighbouring Piedmont. Moreover, the papacy soon discovered that Charles's own resources were insufficient to pay for his war of conquest. Thus the invasion of Sicily drained papal reserves as well.

Charles's Mediterranean empire, extending as far as the Latin kingdom of Jerusalem, was shown to be fragile when Sicily revolted, and his power not merely on the island but in northern Italy as well disintegrated; Constantinople was saved and, as will be seen, the Holy Land was lost, for there was no opportunity now to launch a great crusade to hammer the obstinate Greeks and to succour the importuning Latins in the East. The tendency to rush into new schemes before he had fully mastered his last project was a fatal flaw in Charles. He never came to know the island of Sicily, and he misjudged the mood among a population which was dominated by a newly emergent local elite of Italian origin. Rather, he was bewitched by the sense that he had conquered an island of fabulous resources, rich in wheat and gold, which would provide a jumping-off point for victories in Italy and the Mediterranean recalling those attributed by the romance writers to his eighth-century namesake Charlemagne. Later writers were to attach not to him, but to his Aragonese rival Peter, Charlemagne's epithet 'the Great'; and Charles I of Anjou retains a reputation for hard-hearted ruthlessness, expressed most poignantly in the execution of his enemy the young Conradin of Hohenstaufen in 1268.

Chapter 4

POLITICS AND RELIGION IN THE ERA OF RAMON LLULL

. . .

THE TRIUMPH OF PETER THE GREAT

It has been seen how, during James I's reign, Catalonia-Aragon underwent an extraordinary transformation: a congeries of counties, divided by local rivalries, loosely subject to the authority of the count-king (who was himself, in Catalonia, nominally the vassal of the French king), was given a greater degree of unity as royal administration pushed into the localities, as the men of those localities were tied to the crown through frequent *Corts*, as the monarchy earned itself a Europe-wide reputation in the war against the Moors of Majorca, Valencia and Murcia. Old animosities with France were subdued, if not extinguished; but Castile remained generally a cooperative neighbour. Alongside these developments, the rise of Barcelona was no less striking: the Catalans created their own *mare nostrum* in the teeth of Italian opposition, exercising considerable influence in Tunis, Bougie and other prime trade centres of the Maghrib. James could frankly boast that his was now the most eminent of all the Spanish monarchies. It may thus appear surprising that James did not intend to pass on a single legacy, but insisted on creating a second Catalan realm, that of Majorca, in the Balearics and in Roussillon. This second kingdom was to act as an irritant in the side of Aragon-Catalonia until the mid-fourteenth century.[1]

1. On this, see David Abulafia, *A Mediterranean Emporium. The Catalan Kingdom of Majorca* (Cambridge, 1994); and for an older view A. Lecoy de la Marche, *Les relations politiques de la France avec le royaume de Majorque*, 2 vols (Paris, 1892); J.E. Martínez Ferrando, *La tràgica història dels reis de Mallorca* (Barcelona, 1960; Italian translation: Cagliari, 1993).

The chivalric playboy James I was succeeded in Aragon-Catalonia by a canny ruler whose programme of action can be reduced to a simple formula: the defence of the rights of the house of Barcelona, which now included also the rights of his wife Constance as legitimate heiress (so it was maintained) to Sicily and southern Italy. He was 'that rarity in history: the greater son of a great father', in Bisson's words.[2] Aware that it was necessary to keep relations with Castile on an even keel, he took into custody the Infantes de la Cerda, disinherited members of the Castilian royal house. Peter was not prepared to tolerate his younger brother's claim to independence, forcing James II of Majorca, in 1279, to acknowledge Peter as his overlord; he had the added motive of wishing to punish James of Majorca for supporting his enemies in a renewed struggle for mastery of Urgell. Arguably this was a serious miscalculation; Peter hoped to draw James away from the French court, which was the obvious source of support for a Majorcan kingdom that ruled over Roussillon and Montpellier, on the edges of France, and was afraid of being swamped by Aragon-Catalonia. But the resentment that James of Majorca felt for his brother only pushed him the more rapidly into the French camp when conflict between France and Aragon finally broke out. James found himself obliged, technically at least, to attend the *Corts* of Catalonia as Peter's vassal, an odd humiliation seeing that Catalonia was not even a kingdom; he was denied the right to mint his own coins in Roussillon, which Peter treated not as counties within the Majorcan state but as Catalan counties that happened to be held from him by the lord of Majorca. Under Peter's jurisdiction, James became to all intents a powerful baron distinguished by an especially grand title; and not surprisingly he and his successors worked hard to re-establish the parity with Aragon that James I had envisaged in his will: all to no avail.[3]

2. T.N. Bisson, *The Medieval Crown of Aragon. A short history* (Oxford, 1986), p. 86.
3. Could one king be subject to another? Edward I of England certainly thought so in regard to Scotland at about this time: M. Prestwich, *Edward I* (London, 1988), pp. 356–75; W. Ferguson, *Scotland's relations with England. A survey to 1707* (Edinburgh, 1977), pp. 22–8; G.W.S. Barrow, *Robert Bruce* (3rd edn, Edinburgh, 1988), pp. 1–53.

Peter's less romantic approach to politics, by comparison with that of James I, is also apparent in his handling of his north African crusade in 1282, on the eve of his invasion of Sicily. His attempts to convince the pope that he deserved a crusading indulgence fell on deaf ears (Pope Martin IV was an intimate ally of Charles of Anjou); the papacy, and the Angevins of Naples, rightly suspected Peter's motives in campaigning so close to his wife's claimed inheritance of Sicily. And, despite Peter's insistence that he had useful allies in the Maghrib who would – as the story always went – soon turn Christian, there is little doubt that Peter journeyed to Collo (Alcol) in the hope of influencing events in Sicily. In any case, his presence close to Tunis constituted a challenge to Charles of Anjou, who had been actively competing with the Catalans for influence in the Hafsid state of Tunis.[1]

A fuller account of the Sicilian uprising against Charles of Anjou can be found in chapter 3, which is devoted to his rise and fall; what will be offered here are some Aragonese perspectives on these events. Peter was not the architect of the revolt of the Sicilian Vespers, which broke out apparently spontaneously in Palermo in March 1282. But his court was an obvious place of refuge for those south Italians such as Giovanni da Procida who had found the temperature too hot under Charles of Anjou's rule. Once invited to Sicily to take the crown in right of his wife, Peter came not as an Aragonese conqueror but as the vindicator of the rights of the house of Hohenstaufen. He was sufficiently conscious of this to decree, with some local prompting, that Sicily should not be passed on to his eldest son, but be separated from the other lands of the *Corona d'Aragó* after his death, and ruled by a half-Catalan, half-Sicilian cadet dynasty (not that events quite fulfilled these expectations). What was intolerable in the case of Majorca, the separation of a conquered island territory from Catalonia-Aragon, was desirable – logistically and politically – in the case of Sicily, so much further away from his seat of power.[5]

---

4. On Aragon and Tunis, see C.-E. Dufourcq, *L'Espagne catalane et le Maghrib aux XIIIe et XIVe siècles* (Paris, 1966), *passim*.
5. F. Giunta, *Aragoneses y Catalanes en le Mediterraneo* (Barcelona, 1989), pp. 124–5.

Yet the real battle was one for survival in the face of the combined hostility of the Capetians in France and the Angevins in Naples. By early 1283 Sicily was his, and his armies were beginning to make headway in Calabria; the aim was to acquire control of the entire Sicilian kingdom, almost up to the gates of Rome. As has been seen, an attempt (brokered by Edward I of England) to resolve the feud between Anjou and Aragon by single combat at Bordeaux in 1283 turned into farce when Peter and Charles managed to avoid one another, the former perhaps rightly fearing capture at French hands. Events in the west thus lured Peter back to Spain; he left his wife in effective charge in Sicily. Peter was well aware of the precariousness of his position, for on his Pyrenean front he had to face French-dominated Navarre and French-allied Majorca, while he could never be sure of the loyalty of his own barons and cities. The Aragonese *Cortes* exploited the king's discomfiture to secure confirmation of its ancient privileges. The Catalan *Corts* demanded major concessions: not merely the usual promises not to levy a regular *bovatge*, but the dismissal of the king's Jewish officials, such as the financiers Muça de Portella, Aaron Abinafia and Mossé Alconstantini. The denial to Jews of the right to hold authority over Christians was a well established feature of the Church's policy towards the Jews; and both Aragon and Castile were rare among European kingdoms in the degree to which their rulers flouted the demands of the papacy, their bishops and Christian laymen for the dismissal of Jews. But in the present emergency, the Jews were seen as dispensable. The same *Corts* also enacted legislation *en les terres o llocs*, 'in the lands and places', insisting that unfree peasants must pay a fee for their redemption, thereby setting on a firmer basis long-term trends towards peasant servitude in Catalonia.[6] The *Corts* were clearly anxious to squeeze the monarchy while the chance was there.

Peter was obliged to march into Roussillon in search of his treacherous brother James, in an attempt to close James's territories to French armies; holed up in the Palace of the Kings of Majorca at Perpignan, James of Majorca managed first to feign illness and then to escape dramatically down

---

6. P. Freedman, *The origins of peasant servitude in medieval Catalonia* (Cambridge, 1991).

a drain while Peter's men hammered on the door of his bedroom, though he must have known that the price of escape would be the seizure of a large part of his territories by Peter's armies.[7] The pope, meanwhile, declared the king of Aragon deposed from his throne, on the grounds that Aragon was a vassal kingdom of the Holy See (a relationship that had been largely ignored since Peter II was crowned by Innocent III in 1204); the new king was to be Philip III of France's younger son Charles of Valois, a second-rate imitation of his own great-uncle Charles of Anjou. A second, massive French invasion of Catalonia, in 1285, launched as a full-scale crusade, was accompanied by civil unrest in Barcelona; this Peter ruthlessly suppressed by hanging the ringleader despite assuring him of a safe-conduct.[8] James of Majorca proved his unreliability by opening the French campaign with an attack on Elne, the sometime capital of Roussillon, in the hope of wresting it from Peter's men. The passes across the Pyrenees seemed sufficiently well guarded to hold back the French, until a route across the mountains was apparently betrayed by one of James of Majorca's men. What saved Peter was not his military skill, for he largely avoided confronting the massive French host, but the outbreak of disease in the French ranks; even King Philip III was a victim, so that the army turned back when it was already in charge of Girona, and the dying Philip was borne to Perpignan, where he died, and with him the crusade.[9]

Other factors ensured the survival of the house of Barcelona, too. The death early in 1285 of Charles I of Anjou occurred when his own heir Charles, Prince of Salerno, was – as has been seen – a captive in Aragonese hands, having been captured at sea by Admiral Roger de Lauria.[10] Peter saw the need to gain control of the western Mediterranean,

---

7. Martínez, *Tràgica història*, pp. 67–80, utilising the dramatic account of Bernat Desclot, the close adviser of Peter the Great who left an important chronicle of the reign (printed by Soldevila, *Les quatre grans cròniques*; English version: *Chronicle of the reign of King Pedro III*, transl. F.L. Critchlow, 2 vols, Princeton, NJ, 1928–34).
8. C. Batlle y Gallart, *La crisis social y económica de Barcelona a mediados del siglo XV*, 2 vols (Barcelona, 1973), vol. 2, doc. 1.
9. *Villani's Chronicle*, transl. Rose E. Selfe and ed. P.H. Wicksteed (London, 1906), pp. 277–9.
10. J. Pryor, 'The naval battles of Roger of Lauria', *Journal of Medieval History*, 9 (1983), pp. 179–216.

leaving his brilliant admiral in charge of a small but deadly fleet which challenged his foes from Malta to the shores of southern France and Catalonia, and had a starring role in the otherwise ineffective resistance to the French invasion of Catalonia. Peter's heir Alfonso was despatched to Majorca with an army that rapidly overwhelmed an island that had not yet had time to grow accustomed to the idea of independence from Catalonia-Aragon, and whose merchants, if anything, suffered during the war from lack of free access to Catalan markets. The same year, 1285, saw the death of Peter the Great; he had held on to his crown, and, whatever might still happen in Sicily, it was abundantly clear that the house of Barcelona could not easily be dislodged from Aragon-Catalonia.

. . .

PETER'S LEGACY

The new king, Alfonso the 'Liberal' (1285–91) began his reign on a high note, with the suppression of James of Majorca's rights in Majorca itself, followed soon after by the invasion of the Muslim vassal statelet of Minorca (1287), whose surrender treaty of 1231 was deemed to have been breached when the Minorcan Muslims had sent messages to north Africa advising their co-religionists of Peter the Great's Collo campaign. There were also strategic advantages in directly controlling the largest natural harbour in the Mediterranean at Maó (Mahón).[11] The mass enslavement of the Minorcan Muslims was not simply a chance to make money: Alfonso's actions were part of a wider trend towards the assertion of the Christian identity of the western Mediterranean kingdoms, and it was the same ruler who initiated the enclosure of the Jews of Majorca City in a *Call* or ghetto.[12] Such actions were perhaps all the more important for a ruler

11. Abulafia, *Mediterranean Emporium*, pp. 68–72; E. Lourie, *Crusade and Colonisation. Muslims, Christians and Jews in medieval Aragon* (Aldershot, 1990), chapter 5; David Abulafia, 'Monarchs and minorities in the medieval Mediterranean c.1300: Lucera and its analogues', in P. Diehl and S. Waugh, eds, *Christendom and its discontents. Exclusion, persecution and rebellion, 1000–1500* (Cambridge, 1966), pp. 246–9.
12. Abulafia, *Mediterranean Emporium*, pp. 81–6.

who faced the implacable hostility of the pope even after Charles of Salerno was released from captivity in 1289. Under pressure from the *Unión* formed by the nobles and towns of Aragon, and distracted by rebellious Aragonese barons in Valencia, Alfonso not surprisingly began to bend, and indicated that he would abandon his support for his younger brother James of Sicily. His unexpected death in June 1291 put a temporary end to such initatives; he was childless, and his heir was therefore none other than James of Sicily (James II of Aragon), who was not at first prepared to abandon the island for which he had fought so hard. How this could be achieved when overseas adventures evidently were unpopular with the Aragonese and Catalan political community was the first problem he would have to resolve. The price proved to be the abandonment of claims to Sicily, but by no means the abandonment of claims elsewhere in the western Mediterranean.

. . .

THE THREE RELIGIONS IN SPAIN

Excommunication and interdict did not make Peter and his family turn violently against the Church; Queen Constance in fact endowed an important convent of Poor Clares (the female wing of the Franciscan movement) at Huesca in northern Aragon; Peter continued to rely heavily on ecclesiastical advisers, such as Jaspert de Botonac, bishop of Valencia. At the king's deathbed Bishop Jaspert was suitably coy:

> Since there is no man in all the world, and above all men like you, who are an earthly prince and a king, that may not sometimes fall into sin, I pray and beseech you to confess your faults . . . and to seek forgiveness for wrongs committed, if you have committed any, and to pardon all those who have done you harm and to be at peace with those against whom you have at any time shown hatred or anger.[13]

Certainly, the good bishop was not going to blame this excommunicate king for the hideous faults attributed to him by the Church of which he was a prelate.

13. Bernat Desclot, *Chronicle*, in Soldevila, *Les quatre grans cròniques*, cap. 168.

Precisely because of the strength of their Christian faith, the Aragonese kings did not forget that they were rulers over a substantial Jewish and Muslim population whose spiritual salvation, by conversion, was an urgent aspiration of the Church. Methods of dealing with the non-Christian population varied from reign to reign. It has been seen that Alfonso III was responsible for a novel approach to the problem of the existence within his kingdoms of a Muslim population, cruelly expelled from Minorca, and of substantial Jewish communities; he enclosed the Jews of Majorca City within what was arguably the first real ghetto in Europe (in the sense that it was a place where they had to live, was walled in, and was not fully accessible to non-Jews). In order to understand the changing relationship between the Mediterranean monarchs and their non-Christian subjects, it is necessary to start with an analysis of the approach they adopted to the Jews, which then did much to mould their attitude to the Muslims. It is also essential to recall that, as they acquired more territory in southern Spain during the course of the thirteenth century, they became more aware than ever that they were no longer Christian rulers over primarily Christian subjects; in Valencia or Murcia they were Christian sultans trying to hold in check a restive 'infidel' mass.[14]

The idea of a 'Jewish problem' is one which has, after the horrors of the mid-twentieth century, at last been laid to rest, amid denunciations of anti-Semitism by the Catholic and other Churches, as well as by all responsible governments. However, in the thirteenth and early fourteenth centuries the survival of large numbers of non-Christians in Christian society was seen as an anomaly; society was by definition Christian; those who lived under Christian rule but were not Christian, whether Jews, Muslims or pagans, could only occupy a marginal role. Yet the status of Jews was especially complex. The Church permitted the practice of the Jewish religion by existing Jews, but strictly forbade conversion to Judaism, which had been quite frequent in the days of the Roman Empire. A minority of Jews was seen, as St Augustine had argued, as a demonstration of Christian truth; these were the guardians of the sacred texts which in

14. L.P. Harvey, *Islamic Spain, 1250–1500* (Chicago, 1991), pp. 55–73, for evolving attitudes to subject Muslims.

Jesus's time had constituted the divine law, and at the End of Time the remnant of the Jewish people would be converted to Christianity. Jews were not to exercise dominion over Christians; the loss of political control over the ancient land of Israel was seen as a further indication that God had abandoned the Jews because they had supposedly abandoned Him.[15] Meanwhile it was the Christians who had become the 'New Israel', living under a new law (the New Testament). In practice the application of legislation against the Jews was patchy: in the sixth century, the Visigothic kings of Spain had issued draconian legislation attempting to enslave all Jews who refused to convert to Christianity, but by 1300 Spain was notable for its disregard of such precepts. It has been seen that rulers such as James I and Peter III made full use of Jewish administrators. Mediterranean rulers often favoured the Jews, regarding them as an industrious element in the population, predominantly merchants and artisans. Some were moneylenders, but the image of the Jew as primarily a moneylender does not fit the known circumstances in either Catalonia or southern Italy at this period.[16] Further north, in northern France, Germany and England, Jews were excluded from many crafts and turned increasingly to the provision of credit. It was in northern Europe that the Jews began first to suffer from a combination of royal rapaciousness and popular hostility: in France the Jews were expelled from the royal domain by King Philip Augustus at the start of the thirteenth century, while horrific and totally unfounded misrepresentations of the Jewish religion, accusing the Jews of the human sacrifice of Christian children, began to spread out of England from 1144 onwards.[17] Their effect in southern Italy will be mentioned shortly.

Most of the Catalan-Aragonese rulers had no wish to persecute their Jewish subjects, whom James III of Majorca (for instance) praised for their usefulness in trade. But the kings came under increasingly heavy influence from those royal

---

15. For a discussion of views in the twelfth century, see Anna Sapir Abulafia, *Christians and Jews in the Twelfth-Century Renaissance* (London, 1995).
16. L. Berner, 'On the western shores: the Jews of Barcelona during the reign of Jaume I, "el Conqueridor", 1213–1276', Ph.D. dissertation, University of California, Los Angeles, 1986.
17. W.C. Jordan, *The French monarchy and the Jews* (Philadelphia, 1989).

courts where hostility to the Jews had become a significant priority. The king of France, Louis IX (d. 1270), initiated the burning of Jewish books, among them the great law code known as the Talmud which was deemed anti-Christian, though the Jews protested that the Talmud did not even mention Christianity. In 1240 a public disputation was held in Paris in which a certain Nicholas Donin, a converted Jew, attempted to show up the fundamental faults in Judaism.[18] Increasingly, Christian attention focused on the works the Jews themselves trusted, especially the Talmud, whose contents were made known to Christians by such converts as Donin. Judaism was seen as a rabbinic distortion of the faith practised in the days of the Temple, during, indeed, the life of Jesus. The Talmud was argued to contain a whole body of rules that reformed biblical Judaism into something quite different. Judaism as practised in the thirteenth century was thus nothing less than a Jewish heresy that had long ago departed from the religion of ancient Israel. Such a critique of Judaism was moulded in part by the awareness of vigorous factional debates within Judaism, particularly in Spain, which had spilled over into southern France in the early thirteenth century. The question that then arose was whether it was still appropriate to guarantee the right of Jews to practise what was no longer the religion of Jesus's day.[19]

Leaders of the campaign against the Jews were the Dominican friars, and to a lesser extent their Franciscan rivals. The Dominicans had been founded in Languedoc at the very start of the thirteenth century, to combat the menace of the Cathar and Waldensian heresies. When the order found itself under the leadership of a Catalan, Ramon de Penyafort, who was a close associate of both James the Conqueror and of Pope Gregory IX, the Dominicans hardly surprisingly became interested not just in Christian heresy, but in the question of the relationship between a Christian society and its Jewish or Muslim subjects. Penyafort was an energetic moral reformer: usury, not least the charging of unfair interest by Christian merchants, was another of his acute concerns, and here too can be seen reflected the

---

18. H. Maccoby, *Judaism on Trial. Jewish-Christian disputations in the Middle Ages* (London/Toronto, 1982), prints the key texts in translation.
19. J. Cohen, *The friars and the Jews* (Ithaca, NY, 1982), pp. 78–9, 242.

preoccupations of someone who had observed with his own eyes the extraordinary transformation of Catalonia from a county on the edge of Europe into a thriving hub of business and into the focal point of a federation of states inhabited by people of all three monotheistic religions.

The extent to which the friars were genuinely innovative in their attacks on Jews and Muslims has been the subject of vigorous debate. Jeremy Cohen has argued that the friars became involved as inquisitors with the Jews when the Church became aware of Jews trying to 'convert' Christians. (These would probably be former Jews whom the rabbis were hoping to win back to Judaism.) Only in such special cases as these would the Inquisition have authority over Jews. An 'Inquisitor of the Heretics and Apostate Jews of France', known in 1285, would have been given the brief of checking that Jews converted to Christianity were sincere and that they had abandoned such Jewish practices as refusal to eat pork or even the use of special kosher butchers. Other scholars, such as Robert Chazan, lay stress on the continuing debates within the Church about the relationship between Judaism and Christianity, debates which were of considerable importance in defining the limits of Christian belief. Chazan points out that Peter the Venerable, abbot of the great monastery of Cluny in the middle of the twelfth century, had also attacked the Talmud, and it was he who commissioned the first translation of the sacred text of Islam, the Koran, not because he wanted to compare Christian and Muslim belief in an impartial way, but because it was felt necessary to attack the rival religions on their own ground, armed with knowledge of their texts; to go and do no more than preach the Christian word was not likely to impress the enemy. Indeed, there was a growing desire to engage directly with the leaders, rabbis or imams, of the rival faiths.[20]

Chazan would certainly agree that the attack on the Jews and Muslims was intensified in the thirteenth century; and it was in Catalonia that the debate developed most vigorously. And this reflects the possibilities that were open to preachers now that the kings of Aragon could grant them privileged access to the mosques and synagogues of their

20. R. Chazan, *Daggers of Faith. Thirteenth-century Christian missionizing and Jewish response* (Berkeley/Los Angeles, 1989), pp. 7–24.

non-Christian subjects. A crucial element in the struggle was the insistence that Jews and Muslims must listen to conversionist sermons delivered by friars on their home ground. The papacy was already urging the bishops and friars of the Aragonese lands to go and preach to the Jews and Saracens as early as 1245: 'if they do not wish to come of their own will, our officials shall compel them to do so, putting aside all excuses'. James I was occasionally prepared to license such preaching, though he was also happy to withdraw the licence if the Jews offered him sums of money to get the friars off their backs. And the friars, frustrated at the sullen refusal of the non-Christians to pay much heed, for conversions were still quite few, began to develop further methods for convincing the infidel of the error of his ways.

One method that applied to both Muslims and Jews was the foundation of language academies where Arabic, Hebrew and other oriental languages could be taught to friars, so they could study the holy books of Islam, Judaism and the eastern Christian sects in schism with Rome. Cities in formerly Muslim-held territory, such as Valencia, were obvious choices for such academies; perhaps the most remarkable was one apparently established in Tunis around 1250, during a period of warm diplomatic relations between its ruler and the Aragonese, though how much it achieved and how long it lasted cannot be stated for certain.

Another approach was to tackle the 'enemy' head on, by public disputations and the publication of books aimed either at preachers or their audience, which sought to demonstrate the errors of Judaism and Islam. Best documented of the disputations is that of Barcelona (1263), briefly mentioned earlier; this was held under the auspices of King James I, and the eminent rabbi from Girona variously known as Moses ben Nahman, Nahmanides, Ramban and (perhaps) Astrug de Porta was forced to defend Judaism against the argument that the Messiah had already come. His protagonist, Paul the Christian, was – like Nicholas Donin in Paris two decades earlier – a Jewish convert to Christianity; Paul had joined the Dominican Order, and he was expected to use his knowledge (such as it was) of Hebrew literature, including the Talmud, to show that even within the Jews' own books there could be found hard evidence for the truth of Christianity. Two accounts of this disputation survive, one in Hebrew by

Nahmanides, one in Latin, and not surprisingly they give very different views of the event, with Nahmanides and the Christians each claiming victory.[21] Crucially, however, it was the Christians who set the agenda; Judaism was in the dock. Over twenty years later, in 1286, in Majorca, the Barcelona disputation was still remembered as a *cause célèbre*, a point revealed in the surviving text of a disputation held that year between a Genoese merchant and some local Jews.[22]

Vigorous attacks on Judaism and Islam increased in intensity. Ramon Martí (d. 1285/90) was a graduate of one of the early language academies, and he devoted much of his life, at the prompting of Ramon de Penyafort, to the battle against both religions. His *Dagger of Faith* was a massive study of the Jewish texts, in which he sought to distinguish what he regarded as the 'true' and the 'false' traditions of the Jews, talking of certain traditions he had found in the Talmud and other books, 'and which I most gladly raised up like pearls out of a great dungheap'. What made Martí dangerous was the extraordinary care he had taken to study his texts, so that his translations of Hebrew originals were accurate, and so that the obvious objection, that the Christians had simply misunderstood the texts they were citing, could be countered.[23]

. . .

RAMON LLULL

Of all those involved in conversionist campaigns the most extraordinary figure, even to his contemporaries, was Ramon Llull of Majorca (1232–*c.*1316).[24] The Llulls were part of the first wave of Christian conquest, settlers from Barcelona who

21. Maccoby, *Judaism on Trial*, pp. 102–50; see also R. Chazan, *Barcelona and Beyond. The disputation of 1263 and its aftermath* (Berkeley/Los Angeles, 1992).

22. O. Limor, ed., *Die Disputationen zu Ceuta (1179) und Mallorca (1286). Zwei antijüdische Schriften aus dem mittelalterlichen Genua*, Monumenta Germaniae Historica, Quellen zur Geistesgeschichte des Mittelalters, vol. 15 (Munich, 1994); Ingetus Contardus, *Disputatio contra Iudeos*, ed. and transl. G. Dahan (Paris, 1993).

23. Cohen, *Friars and the Jews*, pp. 129–69; Chazan, *Daggers of Faith*, pp. 115–58.

24. Fundamental studies are those by J. Hillgarth, *Lull and Lullism in fourteenth-century France* (Oxford, 1971); and the introduction to A. Bonner, *Select Works of Ramón Llull*, 2 vols (Princeton, NJ, 1985;

had a solid commercial background, and who in Majorca became part of a new knightly elite. As a young man, Ramon Llull lived in a society where there were still many Muslims, and where the Jewish population enjoyed handsome privileges from the crown. As a courtier of Prince James of Majorca, he had ready access to the royal court, and, according to his own perhaps exaggerated account, he led a dissolute life; he certainly married and had two children. While writing licentious poems in the troubadour tradition he began to have visions of the crucifixion, and became aware that in order to serve God he must abandon his life of luxury and devote himself to the conversion of the infidel.[25] His great ambition was to write the best book ever against the errors of unbelievers, but he could hardly hope to achieve this until he learned Arabic (which he did, with the help of a Muslim slave), and until he studied the key texts of Judaism, Islam and Greek philosophy; he had direct contact with leading Catalan rabbis, and he also paid attention to the surviving works of the Mozarabic Christians which attacked Islam with the help of a vast array of eastern Christian sources little known in western Europe.[26] This ambitious learning programme not surprisingly kept him busy throughout the late 1260s and early 1270s, for nine years. However he was what Isaiah Berlin would call a Fox: his aim was to know a great many things in no great depth (as opposed to the Hedgehog who knows only one thing, but something extremely important).[27] As well as sacred texts and philosophy, he studied law and medicine, no doubt making use of the resources of the great university at Montpellier in the lands of the Crown of Aragon.

condensed version: *Doctor illuminatus. A Ramon Llull reader*, Princeton, NJ, 1993). See also M.D. Johnston, *The spiritual logic of Ramon Llull* (Oxford, 1987), and M.D. Johnston, *The evangelical rhetoric of Ramon Llull* (New York/Oxford, 1995).

25. See Llull's autobiography in Bonner, *Select Works*, vol. 1, pp. 13–48.
26. D. Urvoy, *Penser l'Islam. Les présupposés islamiques de l' "art" de Lull* (Paris, 1980); T. Burman, *Religious polemic and the intellectual history of the Mozarabs, c.1050–1200* (Leiden, 1994), pp. 201–10; T. Burman, 'The influence of the *Apology* of al-Kindi and *Contrarietas alfolica* on Ramon Llull's late religious polemics, 1305–1313', *Mediaeval Studies*, 53 (1991), pp. 197–228.
27. I. Berlin, *The Hedgehog and the Fox. An essay on Tolstoy's view of history* (London, 1953).

Llull aimed to reach his audience directly, writing in Arabic or Catalan. He had already composed several substantial books when, in 1274, he underwent a mystical experience while contemplating God in the seclusion of Mount Randa in Majorca. He later maintained that it was at this point that God revealed to him the method he must adopt in addressing unbelievers, though there are so many indications in his earlier works that he was already beginning to formulate this method that the experience on Mount Randa must be seen as a stage in a much longer intellectual and spiritual journey. He elaborated in the several hundred long books and short pamphlets that he wrote from 1274 onwards a system for describing and explaining the entire structure of the universe (what he called his 'Art'); anyone who understood this system would be bound, he believed, to accept Christianity as the true religion. Llull's 'Art' was the medieval predecessor of the Grand Unifying Theory beloved of modern cosmologists such as Stephen Hawking:

> If we do discover a complete theory, it should in time be understandable in broad principle by everyone, not just a few scientists. Then we shall all, philosophers, scientists, and just ordinary people, be able to take part in the discussion of the question of why it is that we and the universe exist. If we find the answer to that, it would be the ultimate triumph of human reason – for then we would know the mind of God.[28]

Llull's 'Art' was also, so he believed, eminently reasonable, a means of classifying all levels of existence from inanimate objects such as stones to the attributes of God Himself in a structured and logical form, a 'spiritual logic' as Johnston has termed it, deeply rooted in early medieval interpretations of Plato's view of the cosmos. For Llull did not invent his system from scratch; the ninth-century writer John Scotus Eriugena was undoubtedly a major influence upon him.[29] To the fundamental distinctions that guide our perception of the world in which we live, such as plants, minerals, animals, correspond categories at a higher, spiritual, level; particularly important is Llull's categorisation of the Divine Attributes

28. S.W. Hawking, *A brief history of time* (London, 1988), p. 175.
29. F. Yates, *Lull and Bruno*, ed. J.B. Trapp and J.N. Hillgarth (London, 1982), pp. 9–125; Yates perhaps underestimated the changes that took place in Llull's theory over the years.

into eight, nine or more elements (the exact number varying during his writing career). Let us take nine 'absolutes': Goodness, Greatness, Duration, Power, Wisdom, Will, Virtue, Truth, Glory. To each of these may be attached a letter from B to K. Then take nine 'relatives': Difference, Concordance, Contrariety, Beginning, Middle, End, Majority, Equality, Minority. Again, these can be given a letter between B and K. Better still, we can construct a grid, setting the letters of the alphabet, the absolutes and the relatives side by side. Then we can work in other categories that can be divided nine ways, from B to K: there are the 'subjects', for instance: God, Angels, Heaven, Mankind, the Imaginative, the Sensitive, the Vegetative, the Elementative, the Instrumentative. We can thus set these categories out as follows:

	Absolutes	Relatives	Subjects
B	Goodness	Difference	God
C	Greatness	Concordance	Angels
D	Duration	Contrariety	Heaven
E	Power	Beginning	Mankind
F	Wisdom	Middle	Imaginative
G	Will	End	Sensitive
H	Virtue	Majority	Vegetative
I	Truth	Equality	Elementative
K	Glory	Minority	Instrumentative

The quasi-triangular letter A was reserved for the Trinity. All sorts of combinations are possible, and grand deductions can be made from the elaborate grids or circle patterns that then result: 'Saturn is of the complexion of Earth, which is signified by C and is masculine, diurnal and bad'. All of this was directed at the high aim of converting the infidel, for 'if the Catholic faith is unprovable by the intellect then it is impossible for it to be true'.

Llull elaborated his holy algebra not merely in complex and lengthy books aimed at potential missionaries. A little tract survives intended for Catalan and other merchants who might find themselves in Alexandria or another Muslim city, and who should then seize the chance to attempt the conversion of those they met. His argument here was that it was proper for God to be worshipped in that way that did Him the greatest honour; he thus did not deny that Muslims and Jews worshipped the same God and sought to honour Him, but he argued that their religions were inadequate because they were incomplete; but even to recognise in them partial truth was an unusual concession in late medieval Europe. Llull's novels – such as *Blanquerna*, written in Montpellier in 1283–85, or *Felix*, written while on one of his visits to Paris – are structured around a popularised version of the 'art'.[30] And the aim of such books was not simply to increase Christian devotion among his Christian readers, but to prompt them to support his campaign for the conversion of Muslims and Jews. Simply by lending their support, Christians could earn merit for themselves. It was a matter of bitter disappointment that his attempts to secure the aid of sundry popes and monarchs, including the rulers of France, Naples and Cyprus, never seemed to secure long term results. His own language school, founded for Franciscan missionaries with papal approval around 1276, was based at Miramar in the north-west of Majorca, and benefited from the patronage of Llull's old friend King James II of Majorca. But it fell victim to the chaos of the War of the Vespers. Later, the Council of Vienne took further his attempts to stimulate the teaching of oriental languages in the existing universities: there was a brief upsurge in the study of Hebrew at Oxford, for instance. But long-term results were few.

His own expeditions into north Africa, in the hope of explaining his 'art' and converting large numbers of Muslims were not successful, either. His books written in Arabic do not survive; perhaps that very fact is significant of their lack of impact, though a book-within-a-book written in Catalan, the *Book of the Lover and the Beloved*, reveals strong influence from the Sufi mystical tradition within Islam.[31] Llull's aim while he was in Tunis (in 1293) was to engage in direct discussion with the Muslim imams, tempting them into verbal combat with the suggestion that he would become a Muslim if they could convince him of the truth of Islam. But the only result was that he was expelled and forbidden to return. In Bougie, in 1307, aged seventy-five, he stood up in the main square, shouting out a denunciation of Muhammad in the

30. Ramon Llull, *Blanquerna* (London, 1923); *Felix* may be found in Bonner, *Select Works*, vol. 2, pp. 647–1105.
31. Text in *Blanquerna*, pp. 411–68; a new translation by E. Bonner is in A. Bonner, *Doctor Illuminatus*, pp. 173–237; also transl. M.D. Johnston, *The Book of the Lover and the Beloved* (Warminster/Bristol, 1995).

hope of drawing attention to himself. He was again thrown out of the city, though he came within an inch of securing the martyrdom which at times he probably craved. When hopes of persuasion failed, he occasionally laid plans for armed crusades; but the essence of Llull's message to the crowned heads of Europe was that the highest form of crusade would involve a verbal, intellectual battle with the enemy.

In Llull's *Book of the Gentile and the Three Wise Men*, which perhaps slightly antedates the vision on Mount Randa in 1274, Llull addresses Jews and Muslims not separately (as in most of his works) but together. It is an extraordinary and puzzling book.[32] A pagan philosopher or 'Gentile' is worried about the meaning of life; he has no knowledge of God or of the afterlife. Saddened by his ignorance, he travels far in search of truth. One day he sees coming towards him three wise men, in friendly discussion. They explain to him that God does indeed exist, revealing in typically Llullian fashion His 'goodness, greatness, eternity, power, wisdom, love, perfection'. The Gentile, illuminated by divine radiance, begs to be converted. But then to his astonishment he discovers that each of the Wise Men is of a different religion: one a Jew, one a Christian, one a Muslim. It becomes vital to the Gentile that he should discover which religion is correct. Each Wise Man thus speaks in order of seniority of his religion, attempting to demonstrate that his faith is best. The accounts provided by Llull of Judaism and Islam are not entirely fair (thus both Jews and Muslims are gently mocked, in very different ways, for their ideas about the nature of the afterlife); but the chapters of the book on Judaism and Islam reveal extensive knowledge of the rival faiths. It is even left to the Jew to demonstrate the Oneness of God, a point on which all three Wise Men are in accord. The Christian makes the fundamental Llullian point, of course:

> If you remember, understand and love God better through what I have said to you in proving my articles, rather than through what the Jew has said or what the Saracen will say (because by their arguments you cannot remember, understand or love God as profoundly as you can by what I have told you), therefore my religion is shown to be true.[33]

32. Bonner, *Select Works*, vol. 1, pp. 110–304.
33. Ibid., pp. 256–7.

Given that the work survives in a Catalan version intended for a Christian audience, it is only to be expected that the Gentile will become Christian. (It is likely that the book was intended to serve as a didactic aid to would-be missionaries.) And yet at the end of the story there is a surprise. The Gentile is deeply impressed by all he has heard; he makes his choice in his mind, but before he can tell the Wise Men, he sees two fellow pagans approaching. Rather than waiting to hear which religion he has chosen, the Three Wise Men insist on leaving now; the reader is never told explicitly which religion the Gentile has chosen. Indeed, one of the Wise Men bewails the divisions between the three religions in what seems almost an ecumenical spirit:

> Just as we have One God, One creator, One Lord, we should also have one faith, one religion, one sect, one manner of loving and honouring God, and we should love and help one another, and make it so that between us there be no difference or contrariety of faith or customs, which difference and contrariety cause us to be enemies with one another, and to be at war, killing one another and falling captive to one another.[34]

It would be wrong to exaggerate Llull's openness to Judaism and Islam. Elsewhere in his works his characters weep at the 'obstinacy' of the Jews. But his acceptance of Judaism and Islam as partially true was an admission few were ready to make in the era of Ramon Martí and the increasing seclusion of Jews behind ghetto walls, or indeed their total expulsion from France, England and elsewhere. It mirrored the Muslim and Jewish belief that the other monotheistic religions were roads that led some way towards the ultimate truth. It was only rarely that Llull supported tough measures against the Jews, or full-scale crusades against the Muslims. He was in many ways an old-fashioned figure, out of line with the thinking of the Dominican inquisitors, even though he seems to have enjoyed reasonable relations with them. He was a product of a society in which the three religions coexisted, though uneasily, and his works reflect that background even while trying to achieve the conversion of all the Jews and Muslims who lived under Christian rule. It was only in 1492 that the

34. Bonner, *Select Works*, vol. 1, pp. 301–2.

Jews of the Aragonese lands, and in 1525 the Muslims, were given the choice of conversion or expulsion.

. . .

ABRAHAM ABULAFIA

Llull's activities have to be understood against a background of vigorous intellectual activity among the Jews of Spain. This was the great age of Kabbalah, a Hebrew word that literally means 'that which is received', 'tradition', but which is used as a label for a variety of mystical movements current in Aragon and Castile at this time. Girona was, according to Gershom Scholem, the base for a group of mystics 'who between the years 1230 and 1260 did more than any other contemporary group to unify and consolidate what was pregnant and living in the Kabbalism of Spain'.[35] The leading figure in Girona was none other than Nahmanides, the opponent of Paul the Christian in the Barcelona debate of 1263. There are striking similarities between lists of the Divine Attributes (*sefirot*) drawn up by Jewish Kabbalists and those provided by Ramon Llull; contact between Llull and the Jews was a two-way process, in which he learned from Jews, and perhaps learned some of that respect shown in his *Book of the Gentile*.[36] Although the most influential work produced by Spanish Jewish mystics at this time, the *Zohar* or *Book of Splendour*, was written in Castile and purported to be a much more ancient text, Aragon-Catalonia was itself the birthplace of other strands of Kabbalistic thought. Abraham ben Samuel Abulafia (d. *c.*1291) hailed from Saragossa, though his first great mystical experience occurred in Barcelona, and his activity later centred on southern Italy and Sicily;[37] he developed a theory of the soul which argued that the soul is sealed up in the human body by the distractions of daily life, which turns the

---

35. G. Scholem, *Major Trends in Jewish Mysticism* (New York, 1946), p. 173.
36. See H. Hames, 'Judaism and Ramon Llull', Cambridge University PhD thesis, 1995.
37. Abraham Abulafia has been a favourite of novelists, including James Joyce in *Ulysses* and Umberto Eco in *Foucault's Pendulum*. Eco derives his knowledge of Abulafia from the works of Moshe Idel: *The mystical experience in Abraham Abulafia* (Albany, NY, 1988); *Studies in ecstatic Kabbalah* (Albany, NY, 1988); *Language, Torah and Hermeneutics in Abraham Abulafia* (Albany, NY, 1989).

mind away from the infinite and clutters it with finite objects. Only by intense meditation can the soul free itself to contemplate the Divine; Abulafia saw in the letters of the Hebrew alphabet – which were mere forms, meaningless in themselves, rather than 'objects' – a vehicle for mystical devotion. The art of combining letters was seen as a special means to launch the soul on its spiritual journey towards God. It is important, therefore, to recall the difference between what both Abulafia and Llull called the art of combining letters. (It is quite possible they knew one another, for Llull certainly had some contact with rabbis in Aragon-Catalonia, and Abulafia tells of his own discussions with a Christian scholar who could well be Llull.) Abulafia's letters were not the key to a framework for describing the material and spiritual universe; if anything, they were a key to clearing the mind of the distractions of the here and now. Contemplation focused particularly on the letters that made up the Name of God, a name so holy that it was not even pronounced by Jews; Abraham Abulafia combined the letters of the Name into elaborate versions which were the key to knowledge of God. In the highest state of contemplation, the soul leaves the body and witnesses the ineffable Glory of God.[38]

Abraham Abulafia is remarkable for other reasons. A great traveller, who had voyaged as far as the Holy Land and maybe still further east in search of the Ten Lost Tribes of Israel, in August 1280 he found himself in Italy, near Rome, where he intended to meet Pope Nicholas III and probably to reveal himself as the Messiah awaited by the Jews. (Nahmanides had referred in the Barcelona disputation of 1263, which Abulafia could well have witnessed, to the tradition that the Messiah would present himself to the pope.) Instead he found that the pope had suddenly died, and he was held captive by the Franciscans for four weeks. He is last heard of eleven years later, leading a contemplative life on Comino, between Malta and Gozo, amid the chaos of the War of the Vespers.

It is perhaps not completely nonsensical to talk of a common mystical culture in the late thirteenth century, with its centre of gravity in Aragon-Catalonia; this common culture was shared by such figures as Ramon Llull and Arnau de

---

38. See for instance Abraham Abulafia, *L'épître des sept voies* (Paris, 1985).

Vilanova (of whom more presently) among the Christians, Abraham Abulafia and the Girona kabbalists among the Jews, and there were certainly Muslim mystics, many by then long dead, whose works were known to both Llull and Abulafia. The wars of the late thirteenth century, with conflict in Sicily as well as Mongol and Mamluk campaigns in the Near East, heightened the sense that the world was falling part, and that its salvation lay in finding God again. The time that had been prophesied seemed to have come, when Gog and Magog stalked the world spreading fear and chaos. Thus the duel of the kings was not seen as the obsession of rulers distant from the concerns of their subjects, but as something that touched everyone directly, and dangerously. It is now necessary to see how the Vespers War actually drew to an end, temporarily at least.

.   .   .

CONCLUSION

Peter the Great's triumph stands in notable contrast to the collapse of Charles of Anjou's great empire. Peter too faced uprisings and disloyalty back home in Catalonia, as well as the flagrant opposition of his own brother the king of Majorca; he experienced a massive French invasion, and his nominal overlord in Aragon, the pope, Martin IV, was exceedingly hostile to him. Yet he managed, with the help of what his biographers believed was Divine Providence, to shake off most of his enemies; illness carried away the French, and the fragile Majorcan realm was easily expropriated. Yet his resources were far inferior to those of the Angevin king of Sicily. The sheer skill of his naval captains, working with a small but effective fleet, and the support at critical moments of the Sicilian population, keen to see the back of the French and to restore the descendants of Frederick II to the throne, brought him vital successes. Had bets been taken on Peter's chances in 1282 (and Charles of Anjou at least was a betting man, blamed for playing dice while on crusade to the East in 1248), he would not have seemed a good prospect. Indeed, the Sicilians were at first keener on the idea of establishing independent city republics than on the restoration of the monarchy. He came up from behind, and emerged as a convincing winner.

The sense that these were stirring times in which God was judging the crowned heads of Europe was expressed in apocalyptic literature portraying the War of the Vespers and other contemporary conflicts as the wars of Gog and Magog. Christian missionaries emphasised the need to convert the Jews and Muslims to their faith, and new methods were adopted to win over non-Christians, including the close study of the religious texts of Judaism and Islam. Catalan conquests and commerce had enlarged the day-to-day contact between Christians and Muslims, though Ramon Llull was in many respects an exceptional case of someone who made an effort to read and understand Islamic texts. Even so, the message of his work was clear: that the best way to know and love God was through his own religion. On the frontier, awareness of religious differences remained sharp, and the question how to deal with those subjects who persisted in their 'obstinacy' by denying Christianity remained an issue at the courts of the Mediterranean monarchs.

PART II

FOURTEENTH-CENTURY CRISES

Chapter 5

THE MEDITERRANEAN IN THE AGE OF JAMES II OF ARAGON

. . .

THE END OF THE WAR OF THE VESPERS

The heir to Charles I, Charles the Lame, prince of Salerno, was still a prisoner of the Aragonese at the time of his father's death.[1] And his inheritance, not merely Sicily but parts of the mainland too, was not even in the hands of Angevin officers. The recovery of the kingdom from such an inauspicious beginning to a new reign was a remarkable achievement, partly attributable to the determined efforts of Martin IV and his successors Honorius IV (1285–88) and Nicholas IV (1288–92). As suzerain of the kingdom of Sicily, Martin IV sent troops and administrators south to Naples soon after Charles I's death; and he installed a papal emissary as joint regent with the royal nominee, Robert of Artois. Martin's successor Honorius continued to emphasise the claims of the Holy See to control south Italian affairs during Charles of Salerno's captivity, but he made important efforts to remove the causes of discontent in the south and to reconcile warring factions in the north. His critical awareness of the existence of past abuses in the Kingdom of Sicily, and his willingness to seek compromise between Guelfs and Ghibellines in the northern towns earned him a reputation as a lukewarm defender of Angevin interests; but what he really saw was the impossibility of sustaining aggressive Angevin policies at a moment of near ruin for both Angevin and papal interests in Italy. In the 'Constitution concerning the government of the Kingdom of Sicily' (*Constitutio super*

1. M.R. Toynbee, *St Louis of Toulouse* (Manchester, 1929), pp. 49–54.

ordinatione regni Sicilie, 1285), Honorius IV proclaimed signi-ficant changes in south Italian administration, intended to remove the 'abuses' attributed to Frederick II and Charles I and to return to the good old days of William II the Nor-man.[2] This appeal to old law might easily be taken for a formal statement, echoing the phrases of previous rulers of the south; but Honorius IV's bull was unusually specific in detailing the abuses. As well as providing new regulations, the bull sought to forbid excessive financial demands by the crown: the general taxes known as the *collecta*, first levied by Frederick II, were to be reduced and controlled; some Hohenstaufen checks on feudatories were abolished or modi-fied, notably controls over inheritance to fiefs; the towns too would benefit from lower demands for taxes and for military or naval services, while royal control over the move-ment of goods was also reduced. These measures in one sense strengthened the Angevins in Naples and Apulia, where the support of the coastal cities and of the barons was desper-ately needed. What is less clear is whether Honorius IV was strengthening the crown in the ways it most urgently needed. A dynasty at war needs money, yet less was to be found if the strict letter of the papal constitution were observed. The Angevins needed also men and victuals for their fleet, but these too were less easy to obtain. In one way the papacy did try to ensure the Angevin monarchy could find adequate resources: alienation of the crown's own lands was forbidden. But in fact the greater part of the old royal demesne had been lost along with Sicily: the rich grain estates of the island were now in Aragonese hands, contributing to the war fin-ances of Charles II's deadliest enemies.[3]

It is here, in fact, that a crucial issue in the modern his-toriography of the Vespers comes to the fore. Bresc's notion of the Vespers as a key moment defining the future of Sicily as an 'underdeveloped' region, a 'colonial' society whose economy was dominated by outside interests – notably the Genoese and the Catalans with their involvement in the

2. L. Cadier, Italian edition prepared by F. Giunta, *L'amministrazione della Sicilia angioina* (Palermo, 1974), pp. 159–76.
3. M. De Boüard, 'Problèmes de subsistances dans un état médiéval: le marché et le prix des céréales au royaume angevin de Naples', *Annales*, 10 (1938), pp. 483–501.

island's grain trade – can be paralleled by similar arguments in favour of a gradual takeover of the trade networks of mainland southern Italy on the part of the Florentines and other north Italians.[4] In particular, the loss of Sicily forced the Angevin kings of Naples into the arms of the north Italian bankers, because a crucial source of income, grain sales from Sicily, was no longer available once the island was in Aragonese-Catalan hands. What grain southern Italy could offer was effectively mortgaged to the businessmen of Florence. More recent research by Stephan Epstein has modified the force of Bresc's argument, but the link between war finance, foreign loans, privileges to alien merchants and grain sales remains a prominent feature of government policy both in Angevin Naples and in Aragonese Sicily after 1282.[5]

The division of Sicily from Aragon in 1285 in fact helped the papacy negotiate a truce between Alfonso of Aragon, James of Sicily and their Angevin captive. Charles II was in sufficient despair at his captivity in Spain to agree to surrender all rights over Sicily, but Honorius rejected these drastic terms. An arbiter, Edward I of England, suggested instead that Charles II be released and that three of his sons be sent to Aragon in his place as hostages. Charles would promise to negotiate a proper peace within the next three years. Edward's adjudication was published during a papal vacancy and the College of Cardinals, lacking leadership, reluctantly agreed to it. Immediately on his election as pope, Nicholas IV promised the French king that he would not permit such an ignominious truce, but it was essentially these terms which Alfonso of Aragon accepted in 1288.[6] Charles II himself seems to have been keen to find a way to peace, but even after he was released the king of France bullied him and insisted on renewing the war. The French king, Philip the Fair, notorious later for his vituperative attacks on the

---

4. H. Bresc, *Un monde méditerranéen. Économie et société en Sicile, 1300–1450*, 2 vols (Rome/Palermo, 1986); G. Yver, *Le commerce et les marchands dans l'Italie méridionale* (Paris, 1903); David Abulafia, 'Southern Italy and the Florentine economy, 1265–1370', *Economic History Review*, ser. 2, vol. 33 (1981), pp. 377–88.

5. S.R. Epstein, *An island for itself. Economic development and social change in late medieval Sicily* (Cambridge, 1992).

6. S. Runciman, *The Sicilian Vespers. A history of the Mediterranean world in the thirteenth century* (Cambridge, 1958), pp. 264–6.

papacy which he now enthusiastically supported, seems to have assumed that he could use Charles II as his own agent in a grandiose Mediterranean policy. He looked forward to firm Guelf ascendancy, the recovery of Sicily, and the conquest of Aragon, to which his younger brother Charles of Valois maintained his questionable claim.

After his release Charles II travelled via Anjou and the French court on his way to Italy and his coronation at Rieti, just outside his kingdom, in May, 1289. A theme of moral reform entered at once into his government: he expelled the Jews, Lombards and Cahorsins (the bankers from southern France), all accused of moneylending, from Anjou and Maine shortly before renouncing the counties in favour of Charles of Valois, who was thought to deserve a consolation prize after failing so dismally to win power in Aragon. Tough measures were also introduced against the Jews in southern Italy, this time accused of putting children to death in mockery of the crucifixion, an old *canard* already denounced by Frederick II and by Pope Innocent IV. Mass conversions took place, notably at Trani, and Dominican inquisitors were introduced into southern Italy. Drawing on French concepts, Charles and his leading advisers, such as Bartolomeo da Capua, appear to have reasoned that it was their duty to establish a Christian kingdom in southern Italy; as well as the political battle for control, a moral battle, which might even determine that political one, needed to be fought. A further reflection of this can be seen in the sudden arrest of the Muslim inhabitants of Frederick II's colony at Lucera, whose goods and persons were confiscated in 1300; as well as bringing much-needed funds to the king, the sale of the Lucerans into slavery was the fulfilment of old Angevin promises to purify the kingdom of its heathen inhabitants.[7]

Bolstered by papal insistence that the war must be continued, and by a Florentine Guelf victory (Campaldino, June 1289), Charles worked hard to recover territories and loyalties in southern Italy. The Angevins found themselves surprisingly well placed in dealings with their enemies; they

---

7. David Abulafia, 'Monarchs and minorities in the medieval Mediterranean *c.*1300: Lucera and its analogues', in P. Diehl and S. Waugh, eds, *Christendom and its discontents. Exclusion, persecution and rebellion, 1000–1500* (Cambridge, 1966), pp. 250–1.

benefited from the death of Alfonso of Aragon and the transfer of James of Sicily to the throne of his brother in Spain. James defied his father Peter's will and did not maintain the separation of the kingdoms of Aragon and of Sicily; his brother Frederick was appointed royal lieutenant in Sicily but was denied the royal title. Like Peter, James did, however, maintain the traditional order of priority: Aragon-Catalonia became henceforth his own base; Sicily soon proved too distant to control from Spain. By 1295 James of Aragon was willing to renounce control of Sicily in exchange for a dynastic alliance with the Angevins and the suppression of French claims to his own crown in Spain. He valued, as a successor to a line of kings who had acknowledged papal overlordship over Aragon, the chance to return to the obedience of the Church. He saw a chance of compensation, too, in an offer of rights over the island of Sardinia, like Sicily a source of wheat and raw materials.[8] James and his new allies were wrong, however, in assuming that an agreement between the kings of France, Aragon and Naples and a pope – the redoubtable Boniface VIII (1294–1303) – would bind the Sicilians themselves.

Frederick, James's younger brother, was expected under the terms of the treaty to marry into the family of the Latin emperors of Constantinople and to help restore the fallen fortunes of the Franks in Greece. But he renounced a prospective career in the east for the certainties of rule in Sicily. He activated his claim to rule Sicily as a kingdom separate from that of Aragon, under a cadet member of the Aragonese royal house. The meetings of the Sicilian parliament of barons and townsmen confirmed these wishes enthusiastically; indeed, Frederick was more disposed to obey the papacy than were those who offered him his crown. Frederick's court rapidly became the focus for anti-Angevin agitation in Italy, attracting also the Ghibelline exiles of northern Italy.[9] By March 1296 Frederick was king of the island of Sicily. All

8. F.C. Casula, *La Sardegna aragonese*, 2 vols (Cagliari, 1990), vol. 1, pp. 70–6.
9. Indeed, Frederick became the focus for apocalyptic movements which saw in him the 'Last Emperor' who would redeem the world, his Hohenstaufen namesakes having failed to do so. See C. Backman, *The decline and fall of medieval Sicily. Politics, religion and economy in the reign of Frederick III, 1296–1337* (Cambridge, 1995).

that had been achieved by James, Boniface and partners was a separate peace for Aragon itself.

The Aragonese in Spain began to give solid support to the Angevins against the inhabitants of the island James himself had so recently defended. The able naval commander Roger de Lauria pressed the Sicilians hard at sea; there was strong resistance to them on the Italian mainland; by 1298 Angevin armies were disembarking in Sicily itself, though they did not progress far. Boniface also sought to acquire his own special champion in papal causes, bestowing attractive honours upon Charles of Valois, who attempted to build a power base in Tuscany and to reconquer Sicily, to no avail. By the treaty of Caltabellotta (1302) Frederick agreed to withdraw his own armies from the Italian mainland. He was to remain as king of Sicily, or rather, of 'Trinacria', an antiquarian name for the island unearthed to avoid conflict between Frederick's title and that of Charles II. Charles was to hold the south Italian mainland as 'King of Sicily' and he or his heir would inherit the island of Sicily on Frederick's death. In other words, Frederick was king of Sicily for a single creation; his own heirs would receive lands elsewhere in the Mediterranean: Sardinia, Cyprus, Albania were all at times mooted. Charles of Valois, Charles II, Frederick of Sicily, James of Aragon were all keen to sign; Boniface VIII, in difficulty on several fronts, was far from pleased to learn that terms had been agreed, the more so since he was nearing the climax of a bitter ideological struggle with the King of France and he was thus both preoccupied and isolated. A twenty-year war had ended.[10]

. . .

CHARLES II AND THE EASTERN QUESTION

The Sicilian war took place at a time when Christian navies were urgently needed in another of Charles II's kingdoms: that of Jerusalem. In the brief period between Charles II's coronation at Rieti and the loss of Acre (1289–91), the Neapolitan king continued to take an interest in the affairs of the kingdom of Jerusalem. After the fall of Acre he helped formulate a plan for a massive assault on the Mamluks,

10. T.S.R. Boase, *Boniface VIII* (London, 1933), pp. 290–2.

including the forces of all the great Military Orders.[11] He could hardly launch a crusade while the rebels were still installed on the mainland of southern Italy. Indeed, his struggle with Frederick seemed only to possess greater justice since the Sicilians were preventing him from going east to save Acre or recover the Holy Land. The only blows he could strike were those of his officials who rounded up and sold the Muslims of Lucera. After the treaty of Caltabellotta in 1302 appeals continued to arrive from the east, but Charles II was by now engaged in active expansion in north-western Italy. The Levant had become a distraction, however great the shock of the fall of Acre; Charles's elaborate crusade plans came to nothing. Meanwhile Serbs and Greeks whittled away Angevin power in the Balkans, where the Angevins lost much of their past influence in Albania, gaining however rights in the Peloponnese (Achaia) when Charles's son Philip married into the family of the deposed Latin emperors of Constantinople.

Shadowy territorial rights in Achaia were matched by extension in other areas too. Charles II took willing advantage of appeals by the towns of Piedmont, where Charles I's authority had earlier fallen apart; he intruded Angevin administrators into Piedmont, and they worked hard to win the submission of the great local lords such as the marquis of Saluzzo. Between 1303 and 1309 the 'county of Piedmont' became a political and administrative reality as it had never been before. As Émile Léonard said, 'Charles I was content to let himself be recognised as seigneur of this town or that; Charles II, on the contrary, was going to bring together into organic unity the lands he aspired to reconquer, and to make of them a real principality'.[12] His aim was as much to protect the frontiers of Provence as to strengthen his position in northern Italy. But there too the Angevins managed to consolidate their alliances in the years after the peace of Caltabellotta. Robert, Charles II's third son, was busy in Tuscany against such Ghibelline strongholds as Pistoia. He

---

11. S. Schein, *Fideles Crucis. The Papacy, the West and the recovery of the Holy Land, 1274–1314* (Oxford, 1991), pp. 107–11, who is, however, more doubtful about the sincerity of the king's commitment than I am, but there were clearly ups and downs in his devotion to the crusade.
12. É. Léonard, *Les Angevins de Naples* (Paris, 1954); Italian edn, *Gli Angioini di Napoli* (Milan, 1967), p. 247.

began to build the close relationship with Guelf Florence which was to characterise his reign.

Another area of success was newer to the house of Anjou. Existing marriage alliances between the house of Anjou and the Hungarian royal family resulted in an Angevin claim to the throne of a powerful eastern kingdom whose dominions stretched to the shores of the Adriatic, though it took from 1296 to 1310 for that claim to be made real, under Charles Robert (Carobert), grandson of Charles II of Naples. There is no need here to examine in detail the successes of the Angevins in Hungary. Efficient financial management, a vigorous policy of territorial aggrandisement, and the taming of the great native families resulted in the creation of a strong state with considerable influence in the politics of central Europe, not to mention the Adriatic. The stability of this structure must be partly attributed to Carobert's awareness of Italian Angevin precedents. He did not surround himself with an imported nobility, but relied on the native peoples of the Hungarian kingdom. His chamberlain (*comes tavernicarum*) in charge of royal finances was a native, Nekcsei Démétrius. He did, however, consolidate the royal demesne and extend feudal ties where practicable. It will be seen that marriage ties were maintained with Angevin Naples, not always to desired effect; the Neapolitan-Hungarian link became a constant in European diplomatic relations, and was still visible under the new dynasties that ruled both Naples and Hungary at the end of the fifteenth century. The proximity of Hungary to the Mediterranean, by way of the Adriatic, as well as a yearning for access to cultural fashions being developed in Italy, explain why the Angevin branch in Hungary helped to draw that land into the European mainstream, politically and culturally.[13]

Charles II died in 1309; he was clearly less ambitious than his father and lacked the dangerous pretensions of his cousin Charles of Valois. Possibly the disappointment of his crusading hopes, possibly his keen interest in the more radical

---

13. Balint Homan, *Gli Angioini di Napoli in Ungheria, 1390–1403* (Rome, 1935) remains the only major work not written in Magyar, the work of an author who was finally arrested in 1945 for serious war crimes; see also O. Halecki, *Jadwiga of Anjou and the rise of east central Europe* (New York, 1991), pp. 19–32, but this is not the best work of a distinguished historian.

branch of the Franciscans, the Spiritual movement, provide a key to his outlook. This attitude certainly had an impact in his family, where one son, the future St Louis of Toulouse, renounced the throne to become a Franciscan, so that Naples and Provence passed to his third son Robert.[14]

. . .

JAMES THE HONEST, 1291–1327

James II of Aragon was perhaps the wiliest of the thirteenth-century Aragonese rulers. Like most kings of Aragon he earned a sobriquet which was held to encapsulate his qualities.[15] Known as James the Honest, he could well have earned the name James the Hypochondriac, or equally James the Wily. He was able to beguile the Angevins and the papacy into plans for an exchange of Sicily for some other Mediterranean territory; Cyprus was one option for an exchange, but Corsica and Sardinia were closer and larger, and there was no single existing ruler who would need to be displaced. In any case, the Sicilian nobility insisted that only a descendant of Frederick II could sit on their throne; and the prospect of an Angevin return was firmly rebutted with the connivance of James's own younger brother Frederick, royal lieutenant in Sicily, who had his own royal ambitions. And so Frederick was elected king by his Sicilian friends, finding himself subsequently at war with James, who sent troops and ships in rather half-hearted aid of the Angevins, while maintaining a loving private correspondence with his brother. In 1297 Boniface VIII granted the title to the *Regnum Sardinie et Corsice*, kingdom of Sardinia and Corsica, to James II, but the pope was deceiving himself if he imagined that James was now firmly in his camp.[16] In 1298, resisting unsuccessfully, James of Aragon had to concede the restoration of his uncle

14. Toynbee, *St Louis of Toulouse*, pp. 100–9.
15. Most of the sobriquets were apparently posthumous, though James I seems to have been known as *El Conqueridor* in his own lifetime. The titles provide a valuable means of distinguishing hordes of Peters, Alfonsos and so on, when the numbering of the kings according to the Catalan, Aragonese, Valencian, Sicilian and Neapolitan sequence differs. On James II, see J.N. Hillgarth, *The problem of a Catalan Mediterranean Empire, 1229–1324* (English Historical Review Supplement no. 8, 1975), pp. 30–4.
16. Casula, *La Sardegna aragonese*, vol. 1, pp. 61–77.

James II of Majorca to power in the Balearics and Roussillon, though the Majorcan kings were obliged to acknowledge again the overlordship of the ruler of Aragon-Catalonia. This did not prevent James of Majorca from initiating ambitious schemes to establish tariff barriers around his kingdom: a new customs station at the port of Collioure claimed the right to tax Barcelonan merchants, similar measures were enforced in Majorca, and the king of Majorca began from 1302 to create his own consulates along the coast of north Africa, in open rivalry with James II of Aragon; the merchants of Barcelona responded with trade boycotts aimed at Majorca.[17] So too the treaty of Caltabellotta in 1302 did not end the rivalry of Sicilian Aragonese and Neapolitan Angevins for control of Sicily; but it drew the houses of Barcelona, Naples and indeed Majorca closer together by means of marriage alliances and, later, trade treaties. But the unity of the Catalan-Aragonese commonwealth should not be exaggerated. Three dynasties of Aragonese origin held sway in mainland Spain, Majorca and Sicily, sometimes at odds with one another.

James II's character is one of the best known of late medieval kings; beginning a great Catalan royal tradition, he was a prolific letter writer, corresponding with Frederick of Trinacria throughout the War of the Vespers, and with the best medical practitioners in Europe (whom he hoped to attract to his court). It has been remarked that 'he obviously perceived illness as always imminent and always potentially serious'; fortunately he did have trust in his physicians, who included the eminent and prolific medical and religious writer Arnau de Vilanova. James's constant bouts of severe hypochondria do not seem to have incapacitated him politically, even though he spent the last years of his life as an invalid incapable of going two paces without knowing that a doctor of medicine was at hand.[18] He was constantly worried

17. This uneasy relationship, after a more open period under King Sanç of Majorca (1311–24), who accepted his obligations to his Aragonese overlord, culminated in the defiance of the king of Aragon by James III of Majorca and the invasion and incorporation of his kingdom in 1343–44. Thus long-term problems were shelved rather than resolved. See David Abulafia, *A Mediterranean Emporium. The Catalan Kingdom of Majorca* (Cambridge, 1994), and A. Riera Melis, *La Corona de Aragón y el reino de Mallorca en el primer cuarto del siglo XIV* (Barcelona, 1986).

18. M. McVaugh, *Medicine before the plague. Practitioners and their patients in the Crown of Aragon 1285–1345* (Cambridge, 1993), pp. 4–28.

about not just his own health, but also that of his family; as a matter of fact, the succession to the throne was less smooth than he hoped, because his eldest son James decided to abandon both his bride and the world, becoming before long head of the semi-monastic Military Order of Montesa. There was currently a vogue for such renunciations; royal heirs in Naples and Majorca took a similar course about this time, opting for spiritual rather than earthly glory.

A good demonstration of James II's true abilities is provided by his diplomatic skills, which brought him in 1312 the long contested Val d'Aran to the north-west of Andorra, in the face of French claims to the territory, which was said by France to lie on the French side of the Pyrenean watershed.[19] Such successes were rendered much easier by the increasing efficiency of a royal administration that moved towards a common standard in presentation of fiscal accounts, under a single *Mestre Racional* for all his realms, though in virtually all other respects the three states had separate bailiff generals responsible for the king's lands, and separate procurators representing the itinerant crown in judicial matters.[20] Attempts to integrate the territories into a single whole were thus no more noticeable than they ever had been. This was, then, a personal federation, and the Privilege of Union of 1319, which declared that whoever was king of Aragon was also king of Valencia and count of Barcelona, must be seen as an attempt to prevent the fragmentation of the house of Barcelona into potentially rival statelets in addition to Majorca and Sicily-Trinacria, rather than part of a strategy for drawing Catalonia, Aragon and Valencia under a single government. The Privilege stipulated that neither in the will of the king nor by any royal donation could the lands be divided or fragmented, though small donations that did not detract from the authority of the count-king were, of course, acceptable. The Privilege was to constitute part of each king's coronation oath. As important, perhaps, as the Privilege of Union was the consolidation of the count of Barcelona's control in independently minded areas such as Urgell, and on

19. J. Reglà i Campistol, *La lucha por el Valle de Aràn*, 2 vols (Madrid, 1951); J. Lladonosa, *Invasions i intents d'integració de la Vall d'Aran a França* (Barcelona, 1967), pp. 14–24.

20. T.N. Bisson, *The Medieval Crown of Aragon. A short history* (Oxford, 1986), p. 98.

the lands of the Knights of the Temple, which were expropriated by the crown-dominated Order of Montesa. Internal consolidation was a major theme of the reign; Aragon-Catalonia recovered in significant measure from the effects of the War of the Vespers, and the king wisely bided his time before attempting renewed conquests in the Mediterranean towards the end of the reign.

James well understood that the interests of the house of Barcelona in the western Mediterranean could be fatally compromised by internal conflict within his Spanish lands. He began his reign as a conciliator, travelling widely to make his presence felt at a time when political dissent within Catalonia and his other realms was still simmering; he then permitted regular sessions of the *Corts* in Catalonia and the *Cortes* in Aragon, so that the internal opposition that had been focused in the 'Unions' of Catalan and Aragonese barons and towns against Peter III and Alfonso III was effectively defused. Another sign of James's political abilities can be found in his relationship with the other Spanish powers. Casting envious eyes on Murcia, the Catalan-populated territory ruled by Castile to the immediate south of the kingdom of Valencia, James conspired with a disaffected claimant to Castile, and invaded Murcian territory, eventually winning recognition of control over Alacant. He made up to the Castilians by helping them in a campaign against the remaining Muslim kingdom in Spain, Granada, in the vain hope of acquiring control of the celebrated port of Almería. Such ambitious projects were not entirely successful, but they reveal a constant urge to play a part in the management of Iberian affairs equal to that of the kings of Castile.[21]

. . .

THE CATALAN COMPANY IN GREECE

Elsewhere in the Muslim world James II of Aragon found a chance to establish far more cordial relationships. The king of Aragon pursued an intermittently vigorous Levant policy which brought him recognition as the effective protector of

21. L.P. Harvey, *Islamic Spain, 1250–1500* (Chicago, 1991), pp. 167–9, 171–80.

118

the Christian communities in the Holy Land and in Egypt. Papal boycotts did not damage the lucrative trade with Egypt, from which the Aragonese king benefited directly: in 1306 James II of Aragon was sent embroidered and plain cloths in a variety of colours, produced in the state factories in Egypt, and made of silk, linen and cotton; some of the cloths were hand-painted, one possibly with pictures of peaches; the sultan also sent balsam and incense, and some crossbows.[22] Revenue from the 'fines' levied on Catalan merchants trading to Egypt became one of the major sources of income of the king of Aragon. The formal prohibition of trade rapidly became a means to its informal promotion.

James did not neglect other potentially profitable corners of the Levant. James II's bid to become heir to the crown of Cyprus by marrying Maria de Lusignan brought him an elderly bride whom – he was later to complain after her death in 1322 – he had not found sufficiently companionable, and who failed to bear any children; nor in the event did she bring him Cyprus, but as Edbury remarks, this was 'arguably the best match ever made by a member of the Cypriot royal house'.[23] Had the plan succeeded, Cyprus, like Sicily and Majorca, would have been ruled in due time by an Aragonese cadet dynasty, while James's senior male heir took charge of the Spanish lands. Besides, the crown of Cyprus carried with it the title to Jerusalem as well; and James was anxious to confirm his Mamluk-approved sponsorship of the holy places. If he could acquire grand titles and influence in the Levant, he would once again have scored a point off his family's old rivals, the Angevin 'kings of Jerusalem and Sicily' based in Naples.

22. A.S. Atiyah, *Egypt and Aragon. Embassies and diplomatic correspondence between 1300 and 1330 AD* (Abhandlungen für die Kunde des Morgenlandes, 23:7, Leipzig, 1938), pp. 26–34.

23. P.W. Edbury, *The kingdom of Cyprus and the crusades, 1191–1374* (Cambridge, 1991), p. 138. The throne of Jerusalem and Cyprus held a dangerous fascination for the Aragonese. On other occasions Frederick of Trinacria had been offered Albania, Cyprus or Sardinia if he were prepared to abandon Sicily; in 1309–10 the King of Naples, Robert the Wise, was approached by the Aragonese in the hope that he would cede his claim to the crown of Jerusalem to Frederick: Edbury, *Kingdom of Cyprus*, pp. 107–8; David Abulafia, 'The Aragonese kingdom of Albania. An Angevin project of 1311–16', *Mediterranean Historical Review*, vol. 10 (1995), pp. 1–13.

A venerable Catalan historical tradition looks elsewhere, however, for signs that the Catalans were beginning to create an empire stretching from southern Spain to the Near East. The success of the mercenaries of the Catalan Company in establishing a Catalan Duchy based in Athens and Thebes has been celebrated as yet another great conquest since the time of Ramon Muntaner, the Catalan chronicler who had himself been a military commander in the Greek wars. For Muntaner, looking back on the Greek campaigns from the 1320s, the successes scored in the former lands of the Byzantine Empire were further proof of God's favour to the Catalan race, and were a clear demonstration that Catalan soldiers were the bravest in the world, each worth ten Sicilians in battle. Muntaner's story, which he told within the framework of a vast, optimistic chronicle of the achievements of the kings of Aragon, Majorca and Sicily-Trinacria (all of whom he knew personally and well), had a massive influence on later historians such as the sixteenth-century Aragonese annalist Jerónimo Zurita or the seventeenth-century narrator of the Greek wars, Moncada. Major twentieth-century studies of the Catalan 'Empire', such as that of the Catalan politician Nicolau D'Olwer, assumed that the history of the Catalan Company was an integral part of the process of Catalan imperial expansion. The result was that the events leading up to the Duchy's creation acquired a significance in historians' eyes that is now much more keenly doubted.[21]

That the Catalan Company was a by-product of the War of the Vespers is, however, clear. The Catalan mercenary was a well-established feature of Mediterranean military life, present in large numbers at the courts of the north African emirs such as the ruler of Tlemcen; many mercenaries had also fought with distinction in the War of the Vespers. As the demand for paid recruits fell away after the Peace of Caltabellotta in 1302, Catalan and other mercenaries who had been fighting in Sicily on behalf of Frederick of Trinacria

24. *The Chronicle of Muntaner*, transl. Lady Goodenough, 2 vols (Hakluyt Society, London, 1921), vol. 2, pp. 480–587; Zurita, *Anales de Aragón* (Saragossa, 1610, and later editions); F. de Moncada, *Expedición de los catalanes y aragoneses contra turcos y griegos* (Madrid, 1987); N. D'Olwer, *L'expansió de Catalunya en la Mediterrània oriental*, 3rd ed. (Barcelona, 1974); K. Setton, *The Catalan Duchy of Athens* (Cambridge, MA, 1958); cf. J.N. Hillgarth, *The problem of a Catalan Mediterranean Empire, 1229–1324* (English Historical Review Supplement no. 8, 1975), pp. 43–4.

began to look for other employers, which meant looking for other wars. Byzantium, already an actor in the events surrounding the Sicilian Vespers, was no longer directly threatened by Angevin armies, though the Angevins retained their patronage of their close kin the exiled Latin emperors, and continued to exercise overlordship in important areas of the western Peloponnese held by Frankish barons descended from the commanders of the Fourth Crusade. On the eastern front, however, the Byzantine emperor, Michael IX, faced an ever more intense threat from the Turks. The Catalan, Aragonese, Sicilian and other motley mercenaries who offered to help clear the Turks out of the border lands in Asia Minor – whence they threatened Constantinople – were under the command of a former Templar whose family, of German origin, had come south in the service of Frederick II: Roger de Flor, whose real name is assumed to have been Roger Blum, was a charismatic commander who proved able to bring discipline to one of the most feared fighting forces in the Mediterranean, the *almogàvers*. These were men who fought on foot, armed to deadly effect with javelins, a traditional element in the army of the Catalan-Aragonese rulers. Accompanied by about four thousand *almogavers* and perhaps two and a half thousand other men, Roger de Flor led his men into Asia in 1304, so successfully that Michael IX felt obliged to hail him as a hero, offering him in 1305 the title Caesar, which conferred great ceremonial status, though less real power. Yet Michael became so fearful of Roger de Flor's ambition that he had him and many of his companions murdered, whereupon, in revenge, what survived of the Catalan Company (1,462 men) went on the rampage in Thrace, to the west of Constantinople, destroying all that fell into their hands, before moving west and south through Thessaly into peninsular Greece.[25]

It has been suggested that the line of march of the Catalans can be traced in a line of impoverished, depopulated villages that appear in the early fourteenth-century Byzantine tax records, surrounded by better-off areas which the Catalan Company evidently did not reach.[26] Once in southern Greece,

25. A popular account is in A. Lowe, *The Catalan Vengeance* (London, 1972); also Moncada, *Expedición*.
26. A. Laiou-Thomadakis, *Peasant society in the late Byzantine Empire* (Cambridge, MA, 1977), pp. 240–1.

the Catalans became inextricably involved in the complex political rivalries between the Frankish warlords, some of whom were favourable to the house of Anjou; the Catalans themselves switched their loyalty back and forth, as well as suffering bitter internal rivalries in which Muntaner was a major actor. The confusion was settled, after a fashion, when the Company slaughtered the Frankish duke of Athens in battle in 1311. James II observed what was going on in Greece without ever seeking to take responsibility. The Genoese were worried at Catalan successes and asked him to intervene; the king, somewhat ingenuously, replied that 'the Aragonese and Catalans who are in Romania [the Byzantine Empire] did not go there at his own wish, command or counsel, and so he cannot very well recall them'.[27] The Catalan Duchy of Athens was able to survive in Attica and Thebes until the 1380s, administered by a regent or vicar-general who represented the higher authority not of the king of Aragon but (perhaps unsurprisingly) of the Aragonese king of Sicily, from 1312 to 1379; several governors, including an illegitimate son of King Frederick III, were members of the Sicilian royal house, though the actual title of duke tended to be held by legitimate princes of Sicily. Within the duchy, order was maintained by a policy of excluding the native population from government (although Greeks became increasingly valuable in the civil service); it was assemblies of Catalans, anxious always to maintain their distinct identity, who managed local affairs, and met together occasionally in parliaments. The devolution of power was modelled on Catalan ideals, and the elitist democracy of the Catalan *Corts* had to all intents been imported on to Athenian soil. Catalanisation of the church proceeded slowly. There was a large, virtually unbridgeable, gulf between Catalans and Greeks.[28]

The result of the Catalan conquest of Athens was that proxy wars between supporters of the Angevins of Naples and the Aragonese of Sicily continued to break out in southern Greece throughout much of the fourteenth century. In 1312 there was concern in Naples and Paris at the future of Frankish fiefs in areas such as Argos, dangerously close to the Catalan conquests. Aragonese princes such as Ferran

---

27. Cited by Hillgarth, *Problem*, p. 44.
28. Setton, *Catalan Duchy*, for social relationships.

of Majorca intervened, in this case unsuccessfully, in the Greek conflicts; but in reality the political ties even to Sicily were slight, and Catalan Greece was a world unto itself. It should be remembered, too, that Athens was not a place of great significance in the Middle Ages; Catalan traders did not make extensive use of the Duchy as a commercial base, though they received privileges occasionally for trade in the heartlands of the Byzantine Empire (or what little remained of it): Constantinople and its surrounds. The Catalan Duchy had strategic significance only insofar as it might act as a check on further Angevin expansion in the Balkans, and insofar as it tied up Angevin energies which might otherwise have been directed at Sicily itself.

James II articulated his view of the need to create a line of communication to the east, a 'route of the islands' (*ruta de las illas*), in a letter to the pope in 1311, written when the Holy See was trying to stimulate new enthusiasm for a crusade against Mamluk Egypt. Often interpreted as a description of the trading network of the Catalans, James's statement is increasingly recognised for what it explicitly is: an assertion that the Aragonese-Catalan commonwealth could serve a future crusade extremely effectively:

> The Christian army, proceeding eastwards by the sea route, should always stay close to the Christian islands, namely Majorca, Minorca, Sardinia and Sicily, from which it may receive food and refreshments and people to reinforce the said army and to populate the new territories, and then by acquiring this series of bases it can, with God's help, reach the Holy Land.[29]

Interestingly, there is no reference to the activities of the Catalans in Greece, in the very year when they seized the duchy of Athens, for James's real interest lay still further east than Athens.

. . .

THE INVASION OF SARDINIA

Of the lands mentioned in James II's letter to the pope, only Sardinia did not yet lie under the rule of a member

---

29. Abulafia, *Mediterranean Emporium*, p. 236, for a discussion of various interpretations of this passage.

of the house of Barcelona; but even there, as the pope well knew, the king of Aragon was waiting to activate his claim. Sardinia was important, in fact, not simply as a base for armies heading eastwards. The island was rich in medium quality wheat, harvested by a thinly spread and hard-driven population of peasants who suffered what was perhaps the lowest standard of living of any sizeable area of western Europe. Unhealthy conditions made it impossible for population to grow as rapidly as it was increasing elsewhere in Europe; but large open spaces made the island another important Mediterranean granary, like Sicily and the heel of Italy, exporting its wheat to Florence, Pisa, Genoa and Barcelona. It was also a significant source of salt, while the substantial pastoral sector produced meats, cheese, hides and other basic animal products. The silver mines of Iglesias, in the southwest, had come to be dominated by the Pisans, and were an obvious attraction. Virtually no luxuries were produced, and few sold, on the island, though coral was fished in the waters off Alghero, a business that was heavily dominated by Provençal merchants.[30]

Sardinia may thus have presented the illusion that it was a half empty island waiting for effective government. Pisan and Genoese lordship, established in coastal areas and over the main towns since the eleventh and twelfth centuries, generated discord rather than reduced it, since Genoa and Pisa were constantly at one another's throats in the hope of winning the valuable resources of the island all to themselves. In the middle of the twelfth century, at the court of the Holy Roman Emperor Frederick Barbarossa, both sides had engaged in unprepossessing arguments about who had the right to control Sardinia, though as well as the emperor the pope was certain that he had ultimate jurisdiction over the island. External claims to the right to dispose of Sardinia were largely irrelevant; discord among the native Sards, divided into four petty states or 'judgeships', and the Pisans and Genoese who sought to control the island's exports, meant that even

---

30. On the economy, see J. Day, *La Sardegna sotto la dominazione pisano-genovese* (Turin, 1986), originally published as part of the UTET *Storia d'Italia*, ed. G. Galasso; M. Tangheroni, *La città dell'argento* (Naples, 1985), on Iglesias; C. Manca, *Aspetti dell'espansione economica catalano-aragonese nel Mediterraneo occidentale. Il commercio internazionale del sale* (Milan, 1966), on Sardinian salt.

Sardinia could not escape the intense factionalism that characterised thirteenth- and early fourteenth-century Italy. Attempts by the emperor to provide the island with a king – such as Enzo, son of Frederick II – led to nothing; in 1267–69, as has been seen, the house of Anjou and the house of Barcelona were engaged in yet another battle for influence when both James prince of Majorca and Philip of Anjou were nominated before the pope as candidates for the putative crown of Sardinia, which Clement IV then wisely declined to grant to anyone.[31]

At the start of the fourteenth century, Sardinia was still dominated by the Genoese and the Pisans, exercising power both directly and through great feudal lords of Genoese or Pisan origin, such as the Genoese Doria family in the north-west or the Pisan Donoratico family in the south. Meanwhile, James II's claim to the island was left in abeyance all the way from 1297, when the pope had granted him the island together with Corsica, to 1322, when he made arrangements for an invasion that commenced the following year, drawing gratefully on financial help from his Jewish subjects. Corsica, still at this point largely in Pisan hands, was left off the agenda of the kings of Aragon until the fifteenth century; but from 1297 to 1323 James II of Aragon made optimistic use of the title 'king of Sardinia and Corsica' on his charters, and he meddled occasionally in Sardinian affairs.

The massive campaign of 1323–24 should be called 'invasion' rather than 'conquest' for two reasons. One was, quite simply, that James was invited into Sardinia by the ruler of Arborea, the central judgeship among the four that made up the island. Their aim was quite simply to play off the Catalans against the Pisans, who were a declining force since their defeat at the hands of the Genoese in the battle of Meloria (1284). But the Arboreans, as will be seen, soon had reason to turn against the overweening attitude of the Aragonese. The second reason for calling this an invasion is, quite simply, that the conquest of Sardinia did not really prove possible. The invasion intensified the existing commercial rivalry between the Genoese and the Catalans, both

---

31. F. Artizzu, *La Sardegna pisana e genovese* (Cagliari, 1985); Casula, *Sardegna aragonese*, vol. 1; Abulafia, *Mediterranean Emporium*, pp. 235–45.

seeking mastery of the western Mediterranean trade routes. The Pisans, a much weaker force than the other two commercial powers, proved a lesser problem to the Aragonese, and were even granted extensive rights in southern Sardinia once they had accepted the new order.

The price the native Sards paid for their own resistance was as high as that paid in earlier conquests by the Muslims. Indeed, the Sards were treated as if they were no better than subdued infidels, partly because they had resisted their true lord the king of Aragon; and partly, perhaps, because the low standard of living on the island brought out in the Catalans contempt for a primitive society that still seemed a fossil of Carolingian Europe. The judges of Arborea were, naturally, speedily disenchanted with their supposed allies. In 1330–33, 166 substantial fiefs were distributed, as well as many hundreds of smaller grants, generally in favour of Catalans, Valencians and Majorcans. Although many of those who came to settle were discouraged by the difficult conditions on the island generated by continuing warfare and a low standard of living, there was still a powerful trend towards catalanisation, expressed in the repopulation of Sassari in 1329; not for the first time, native Sards were turned out of what had been one of the few significant cities on the island, to be replaced by Catalan Christians and indeed Jews. Other beneficiaries included the Majorcans; in return for the supply of several much needed galleys, King Sanç of Majorca (1311–24) secured for his subjects a handsome trading privilege in Sardinia.[32] The 'Kingdom of Sardinia and Corsica' was never offered to a cadet dynasty. It was subsumed into the Privilege of Union; Sardinia was simply too valuable to hand to a younger son, and it was thus the first overseas conquest to be permanently incorporated from the start in the core territories of Aragon-Catalonia.

The brief reign of Alfonso IV of Aragon, from 1327 to 1336, saw some old wounds reopen as the king's second wife laid plans for her sons by an earlier marriage to acquire lands and power in Spain. It was Alfonso who had actually led the Catalan-Aragonese army into Sardinia, and it was in his reign that the difficulties in governing the island became

---

32. Abulafia, *Mediterranean Emporium*, pp. 245–52 [with the text of the Aragonese privilege].

ever more obvious, with the rebellion of Sassari and the outbreak of wider conflict with the Genoese, which brought
bloodthirsty Catalan raiding parties to the coasts near Genoa,
and which resulted in constant atrocities by Catalan privateers
against Genoese shipping in the western Mediterranean, and
vice versa. The Sardinian and Genoese conflicts distracted
Alfonso from plans for a Europe-wide crusade against the
Muslim kingdom of Granada; Spanish Muslim raiding parties
penetrated without much difficulty into the southern lands
of the kingdom of Valencia (1331). Thus Alfonso began to
learn the lesson that overseas adventures and the internal
affairs of the Iberian peninsula were difficult to manage at
the same time. Like his father, James, he was obsessive about
the monitoring of his health, though perhaps with good
reason: the king died at the age of twenty-seven, conceivably
laid low by disease picked up in his Sardinian campaign.

· · ·

THE GOLDEN AGE OF CATALAN TRADE

The fortunes of Catalan trade in the early fourteenth century can be measured by looking at the extensive evidence
that survives from Majorca. Majorca City (Ciutat de Mallorca),
a boom town of the late thirteenth century, was dangerously
isolated during the War of the Vespers, for the quarrel between the king of Aragon and the king of Majorca denied
the Majorcans free access to the Catalan coast. In 1284, a
year from which there survives a collection of licences issued
to sailors wishing to leave Majorca, the Majorcans were trading intensively along the coast of what is now Algeria, mainly
in small or medium size vessels; larger boats linked Majorca
to Tunis, Genoa and Seville; all the evidence indicates that it
was in north Africa that the Catalan merchants of Majorca,
including a sizeable Jewish population, made their profits.
Majorca City contained up to one half of the population of
the island of Majorca, so that dependence on outside supplies
of grain and other necessities was always heavy: attempts by
James II of Majorca to stimulate local agricultural production
by the foundation or extension of small rural 'agro-towns'
were reasonably successful, but Majorca became known as a
centre for the production of rather specialised foodstuffs such

as figs; the island lived from its trade. Indeed, the papacy had conferred special privileges following the conquest of Majorca by James I, permitting intensive trade with the Muslims since it was otherwise unclear how the inhabitants could survive.

Majorca City thus became a great emporium or entre-pôt through which there passed a startling variety of goods: cowrie-shells and cinnamon from the Indian Ocean, gold, wax and leather from north Africa, dried fruits from Moorish Spain and Majorca itself, wine from Valencia, woollen cloth from Catalonia, Languedoc and Flanders, raw wool from England, grain from Sicily and Sardinia, butter from Minorca, salt from Ibiza, and, last but not least, large numbers of Muslim slaves, whether the captive population of Minorca in 1287 or the inhabitants of the mountainous interior of Libya. Attempts were also made to imitate Barcelona (by 1300 a major textile centre) by creating a vibrant woollen cloth industry on the island, but this only took off in the late fourteenth century. By 1300 the king of Majorca was minting his own coinage on the island, too, emancipating Majorca from dependence on the currency systems of Valencia and Barcelona. Close links to the mainland possessions of the king of Majorca, Perpignan and Montpellier, brought further advantages; both cities were active centres of manufacture, trade and banking, heavily involved in the trans-European textile traffic, and Collioure, the outport of Perpignan, became a flourishing secondary centre of trade by 1300.[33]

Treaties with other Mediterranean rulers fostered the interests of merchants from the lands of the Majorcan king: there were treaties with Castile in 1284, 1310 and 1334; with Aragonese Sicily in 1305 and 1313; and with Angevin Naples in 1325; the invasion of Sardinia in 1323–24 brought a further trading privilege to the men of Majorca and Roussillon; relations with the Muslim world were fostered by treaties with Tunis in 1271, 1278 and 1313; with Tlemcen in 1313, with Bougie in 1302, and with the Nasrid kings of Granada in

33. Abulafia, *Mediterranean Emporium, passim*; F. Fernández-Armesto, *Before Columbus. Exploration and colonisation from the Mediterranean to the Atlantic, 1229–1492* (London, 1987), pp. 13–31; Riera Melis, *La Corona de Aragón y el reino de Mallorca*; F. Sevillano Colom, J. Pou Muntaner, *História del puerto de Palma de Mallorca* (Palma de Mallorca, 1974).

the same period. Peaceful trade became the prime objective of the Majorcan monarchy, which drew a handsome income from the taxes levied on ships calling in at Majorca City. In the early fourteenth century the crown could expect to receive at least £20,000 per annum in taxes on the economic activities being conducted in the Balearic islands. The foundation of Majorcan consulates in north Africa, in the teeth of strong Catalan opposition, further enhanced the revenues of the crown, with profits from the Majorcan warehouses at Bougie, Tlemcen, Bône, Algiers and several other key towns in the Maghrib.[34]

Particularly important in the long term was the development of trading links between Majorca and the Atlantic Ocean, which offered facilities to Italians and others trying to reach either the Atlantic coast of Morocco, where Anfa (now Casablanca) was a favourite base, or, much further afield, the ports of England and Flanders. The first hard evidence for Majorcan shipping in England dates from 1281; the presence of Majorcans alongside Genoese, exporting raw wool out of England, is impressive testimony to the navigational skills of the Catalans, but also to their diplomatic skill, since sailing out of the Straits of Gibraltar was impossible unless reasonably good relations were cultivated with the Muslim and Christian powers in the neighbourhood.

Catalan navigators learned by the late thirteenth century how to keep the sea lanes to Majorca open in all weathers; by the early fourteenth century hardly a day passed, even in mid-winter, on which a vessel failed to come into port in Majorca City. Some were from no further away than the lesser Balearic islands, others from Venice (great galleys bound for Flanders), the Basque country or the Cantabrian ports in northern Spain; and most were from Catalonia and Valencia. Majorca became famous in the early fourteenth century, and for long thereafter, as a centre for cartography; some of its leading mapmakers were Jews, who may have drawn on the technical knowledge available in the Islamic world. Portrayed on their maps were newly discovered Atlantic islands, in the

34. Abulafia, *Mediterranean Emporium*, pp. 160–1; Riera Melis, *La Corona de Aragón y el reino de Mallorca*, pp. 301–2 [for the key documents]; C.-E. Dufourcq, *L'espagne catalane et le Maghrib aux XIIIe et XIVe siècles* (Paris, 1966), pp. 419–22.

first place the Canaries, which were the target of a flotilla sent out from Majorca in 1342, in the hope of claiming these remote islands for King James III.[35]

There were, of course, some distinctive features that marked out the trade of Majorca from that of the rest of the Catalan world, notably Barcelona with its flourishing textile industry. Majorca was much more open to Italian traders than was Barcelona, and had to be so if it was to function as an entrepôt between Italy, southern France, Spain and north Africa. The lesson of attempts to tax Barcelonan merchants coming into Majorcan ports, between about 1299 and 1311, was that Majorca's success really depended on the maintenance of open supply lines; when the Catalans threatened to boycott Majorca if the charges were not lifted, the king of Majorca had before long to give way. But in many respects Majorca can be taken as a prime example of the rapid and effective intrusion of Catalan sea-power and trading capital into the western Mediterranean, a sea that had since the end of the eleventh century been dominated by older naval powers: by Genoa, still a menace to Catalans and Majorcans when it chose to pick a quarrel (as it did over the invasion of Sardinia in 1323), and by Pisa, already past its peak by the early fourteenth century. In part the answer was that along the trade routes many animosities were shoved to one side, and Genoese, Pisans, Florentines, Catalans and others invested side by side in the massively profitable trade linking Mediterranean Europe to the Muslim world and to the Atlantic Ocean.

The ending of the War of the Vespers liberated trade across the western Mediterranean, restoring links between Sicily and Barcelona, and reducing greatly the danger from the privateers who prowled the seas under licence from the warring Mediterranean kings. The open question remained how long the Angevins of Naples would tolerate the survival of an independent island kingdom of Sicily.[36]

35. Fernández-Armesto, *Before Columbus*, pp. 156–9.
36. For the break in trade between Sicily and Barcelona, see D. Abulafia, 'Catalan merchants and the western Mediterranean, 1236–1300: studies in the notarial acts of Barcelona and Sicily', *Viator: medieval and Renaissance Studies*, 16 (1985), pp. 232–3.

. . .

CONCLUSION

The disentanglement of the Angevins and the Aragonese was a slow and difficult process; when King James of Sicily inherited the throne of Aragon, and indicated his willingness to renounce Sicily, he did not appear to take into account the wishes of the Sicilians themselves, who elected his younger brother and lieutenant, Frederick, as their king in right of his mother Constance of Hohenstaufen. That James suspected this would happen is not unlikely; his support for papal and Guelf interests after 1296 was spasmodic, and yet by clever diplomacy he was able to win from Pope Boniface VIII, a man difficult to please, the promise of the crown of Sardinia and Corsica in return for the abandonment of Sicily. James's claim to Sardinia was only turned into reality in 1323–24, when a Catalan-Aragonese army invaded the island, with a keen eye of its food and silver resources. Meanwhile, Sicily was not surrendered: Frederick's ability to hold out against his enemies finally brought him wider recognition in the face of continuing papal mistrust; but even after peace was agreed at Caltabellotta in 1302, the Neapolitans continued to harbour plans for the recovery of the island of Sicily, concentrating for the moment on diplomacy and on the hope that the island would revert to Naples on the death of King Frederick III of Sicily. Meanwhile there was plenty of reconstruction work to be done, in Sicily (of which more in a later chapter) and on the mainland, where Charles II expressed his gratitude to God for his release from prison by unleashing persecution first of the Jews and then, in 1300, of the last remaining Muslims based at Lucera. Charles II was not merely leader of the Guelfs in Italy, but he was also a Christian king who sought to rule in accordance with Christian principles, relying in addition on the teaching of the Roman lawyers at his court. Men such as Bartolomeo da Capua and Andrea da Isernia boosted the standing of the crown by emphasising that the king was a Roman-style *princeps* or ruler, and it will be seen shortly how important such concepts became when once again a German emperor came to Italy and challenged the overweening power of the house of Anjou, which by 1309 had succeeded in welding together the county of Piedmont, and other north Italian possessions, into a reasonably coherent domain.

As a Christian king, Charles II was also dedicated to the cause of the crusade, including the difficult question of the Frankish lands in Greece, over which he sought to establish his authority. The loss of Acre in 1291 proved the impotence of the Angevins in the East; and in Greece it was not the Angevins but a group of mainly Catalan freebooters who were most successful in asserting their authority at the start of the fourteenth century. Though the Catalan Company was not an agent of the house of Barcelona, the Duchy of Athens which it established eventually accepted the overlordship of the Aragonese king of Sicily, and southern Greece became the theatre of proxy wars between the supporters of the Sicilian Aragonese and the Neapolitan Angevins. On the other hand, the Duchy of Athens did not provide the Catalans with important trading opportunities, and north Africa remained the prime target of the merchants of Barcelona and Majorca who, particularly in the years after the peace of Caltabellotta, were able to resume peaceful trading in the western Mediterranean. Thus continuing political tensions did not cancel out the commercial dividends of peace.

Chapter 6

ROBERT THE WISE OF NAPLES, 1309–43

.   .   .

HENRY VII AND THE ITALIAN CRISIS

In the fourteenth century two Kingdoms of Sicily vied for influence in Italian affairs, and one, that based on the mainland, also sought again and again to reabsorb its island rival. Such conflicts were a severe drain on the resources of the combatants; they also necessitated increasing reliance on powerful regional nobles and on foreign banking houses. The dissolution of political power was accompanied, as a result, by economic dislocation, particularly in the countryside. The fourteenth century saw, therefore, a significant change in the character of the southern realms; the open question is how permanent the damage was, the more so since the calamity of war was compounded by the mortality of plague. In Sicily, recovery was stimulated by the arrival at the end of the fourteenth century of the royal house of Aragon-Catalonia, which took advantage of the extinction of the cadet Aragonese dynasty of Sicily to reimpose its authority, with growing success and with beneficial effects on the island's economy. On the mainland, recovery was hindered by the persistence of weak government, characterised by serious internal strife within the ruling Angevin dynasty itself.

The accession of Robert of Anjou, 'the Wise', in 1309 coincided with developments which were greatly to influence the Angevin kingdom of Naples. At the end of 1308 Henry, count of Luxembourg was elected King of the Romans by the German princes. During the same decade the residence of the popes became fixed not in Italy but at Avignon in the Angevin county of Provence. The proximity of the popes to

133

the Angevin court in Provence and the popes' absence from Italy elevated Robert to the status of prime defender of Guelf interests in Rome, Tuscany and Lombardy. Robert could confer with the pope on his frequent visits to Provence.[1] Equally, the papacy had to take care not to allow the Angevins to consolidate their hold over the whole of Italy. Thus there were tensions pulling several ways: towards the policies of the French or Angevin courts; towards a possible mediator who could create a non-Angevin peace in Italy. The papacy never ceased to hope that the Angevins would lead a crusade, and the priority given to the recovery of Jerusalem naturally attracted them still more to the self-styled 'Kings of Jerusalem and Sicily'.[2] But at the time of the accession of Robert the Wise the temptation to place trust in a new peacemaker briefly triumphed. Pope Clement V welcomed the election of Henry VII in Germany and agreed to instruct his cardinals to confer the imperial crown upon him in Rome, the traditional place of coronation as Holy Roman Emperor. This was an especially brave political act since Clement had not felt able to take up residence in turbulent Italy, and was residing in Provence in the shadow of the French king's influence: Philip IV's defeat of Pope Boniface VIII resulted in the seventy-year long transfer of the papacy away from Rome to Avignon in the Angevin county of Provence, on the very edge of France proper.[3]

The reason for the pope's decision to go ahead with the coronation of the first full emperor (rather than mere King of the Romans, i.e. king of Germany) since Frederick II was that Clement rapidly came to conceive of Henry as a balance to Robert of Anjou. Maybe a new era in papal-imperial relations was about to dawn, now that well over half a century had elapsed since the papal deposition of Frederick; maybe Henry would counterbalance also the influence of the French monarchy over the papacy. But the pope also had important reservations, aroused by Henry's insistence on entering

1. David Abulafia, 'Venice and the Kingdom of Naples in the last years of King Robert the Wise', *Papers of the British School at Rome*, 48 (1980), pp. 187–8.
2. N. Housley, *The Avignon papacy and the Crusades, 1305–1378* (Oxford, 1986), pp. 20, 26, 28, etc.
3. G. Mollat, *Les Papes d'Avignon, 1305–1378*, 10th ed. (Paris, 1965); English translation of earlier edition as *The Popes at Avignon* (London, 1963).

Italy as soon as possible with an imperial army, rather than negotiating a tentative date in the future. Henry, elated by his new status, saw himself as a peacemaker who would end the rivalry of Guelf and Ghibelline towns and bring back the exiled factions into their home cities. Certainly he was inadequately informed about the depth of division that existed. He did not try to resolve practical problems, such as what would be done with the property of Ghibellines confiscated and sold long ago. He was a pious, well-meaning man who saw the solution to Italy's problems in the spiritual act of reconciliation. This attitude scared Pope Clement. Peace was to him the consolidation of the present order, the Guelf ascendancy, by the careful extinction of existing rivalries and trouble-spots. Moreover, Henry naturally enough attracted to his court, by his very existence, groups of Ghibelline or White Guelf exiles, whose constant support swung Henry in their favour, and whose constant presence irritated the Black Guelfs and aroused their suspicions.[4]

Even so, Clement V tried to encourage Robert to show grace to Henry. Henry aroused Robert's suspicions when his ambassador instructed the citizens of Asti, in Angevin Piedmont, not to pay homage to King Robert (1310). Robert was, of course, technically an imperial vassal, since the county of Piedmont was held from the emperor; it was a delicate situation. Looking for allies who were strongly Guelf, Robert visited Florence in 1310 and was lavishly entertained by his bankers, the Peruzzi, with whom he stayed for some weeks in their magnificent palace.[5] In addition, Clement appointed Robert his 'Rector' in Romagna despite his reluctance, in common with earlier popes, to let the Angevin king hold office in papal lands in northern Italy. The front line of the papal states had to be held in the event of a German invasion.[6]

Henry VII did begin to heal some of the wounds of faction-fighting in the Lombard towns during 1310–11, notably in Milan. But Florence was determined to resist Henry. Henry

4. W. Bowsky, *Henry VII in Italy* (Lincoln, Nebraska, 1960); see also K. Pennington, *The Prince and the Law, 1200–1600. Sovereignty and rights in the western legal tradition* (Berkeley/Los Angeles, 1993), pp. 165–201.
5. E.H. Hunt, *The Medieval Super-Companies. A study of the Peruzzi Company of Florence* (Cambridge, 1994), p. 30.
6. Bowsky, *Henry VII*, pp. 123–4.

avoided Florence. He went to Rome, but the city was partly occupied by Angevin troops. He was crowned amid street-battles in June, 1311. The presence of an Angevin army, hostile to his own forces, only helped Henry swing more towards the Ghibelline groups who had his ear. It would be interesting to know how he reacted to Dante's thundering letters, urging him to tame Florence and bring imperial peace to Italy.[7] But it is clear that he reacted decisively against Robert. His daughter would now be sent in marriage to the Aragonese court in Sicily, that established focus of Ghibelline interests. Frederick of Sicily became 'admiral of the empire'. Pennington remarks: 'if Henry misjudged the Italian political situation badly, he committed an even graver error by binding himself with the Aragonese king Frederick III, who would prove a completely ineffective ally.'[8] Papal attempts at mediation were rapidly set aside. Henry had no difficulty in choosing the ideal targets for a war in defence of imperial interests: Florence, which he besieged (1312–13) and the kingdom of Naples. He demanded that Robert of Anjou appear before him before three months were out on the charge that he did treasonably support rebels fighting the emperor in Tuscany and Lombardy, not to mention the city of Rome itself, and that he did enter into treaties with the emperor's enemies. Since by 26 April 1313 Robert had still not appeared before the emperor, the Neapolitan king was stripped of all imperial honours (such as the county of Piedmont) and even of his throne. A savage touch was the decision to condemn Robert to death by beheading, exactly the punishment that his grandfather had imposed on the last Hohenstaufen, Conradin.

The problem was how to justify such grandiose claims to suzerainty over the pope's vassal, the king of Naples. There were several pamphleteers who insisted that Sicily (i.e. Naples) was as much part of the emperor's jurisdiction as anywhere else in the whole world: 'all the world is the emperor's . . . and I say that Sicily is especially part of the empire'; for them, the view that the kingdom of Sicily is part

---

7. Dante Alighieri, *Monarchy and Three Political Letters*, ed. and transl. D. Nicholl (London, 1954), pp. 97–115, for letters v, vi, vii.
8. Pennington, *Prince and the Law, 1200–1600*, p. 169.

of the Patrimony of St Peter is simply wrong. In the same way that a beekeeper keeps his bees in a hive, and lets them go when he chooses, the emperor has charge of all people and places. The emperor even has authority over the Church. These arguments chime well with the anachronistic and often unsubtle protests of Dante in his vigorous tract *De Monarchia*, arguing that the restoration of a universal empire was necessary for perfect world order.[9] Such pamphleteers were not writing good law, but they were writing what the emperor wanted and needed to hear. Against these arguments the famous jurist Oldradus da Ponte was soon to argue: 'one bee who is king is not king of all bees'. He concluded that the emperor was not in fact 'lord of the world', an explicit recognition, grounded in law, of a reality that theorists of imperial authority had long sought to avoid. Pope Clement V in the decree *Pastoralis cura*, issued in Provence in March 1314 after Henry VII had in fact died, attempted to clear up some of these issues, arguing that Robert could not be summoned from beyond the imperial frontiers, that he was not an imperial but a papal vassal, and that due regard had not been paid to his fundamental right to defend himself against the charges. Importantly, the pope insisted that as papal authority in any case exceeded imperial, it was within his rights to review the case.[10]

Henry planned an invasion of Naples; and Clement, now fully roused, riposted with a threat to excommunicate anyone who attacked his vassal Robert. Italy was saved from a papal crusade against Henry and from new havoc in southern Italy only by Henry's death from fever in August 1313. He was buried at Pisa, the city which had served as his base in Tuscany. During his four-year reign, Henry's optimism and idealism had given way quickly to a righteous sense of determination; he had learned how difficult it was to practise pacification without drawing blood. The will to compromise he had expected had not been there. And this was partly the result of the successes of the Guelfs in the decade before his election; indeed, his visit to Italy had done more to revive old rivalries than to settle them.

9. Dante, *Monarchy*, p. 26.
10. Pennington, *Prince and the Law*, pp. 171, 187–201.

. . .

GUELFS, GHIBELLINES AND KING ROBERT

Robert of Anjou's initiation into Italian politics was marked also by another conflict: the crusade launched against Venice in 1309, and the struggle between Pope Clement V and the Venetians for suzerainty over Ferrara. Ferrara had been bequeathed by its ruler Azzo VII d'Este (who was also Robert's brother-in-law) to an illegitimate son, Fresco, rather than to his legitimate heirs. Fresco invited the Venetians to accept suzerainty over Ferrara, a city they had long coveted, if they would maintain him as its lord. The pope maintained Ferrara was an unredeemed part of the papal state. He preached a crusade against the Venetians, and aroused the wrath of King Robert against the Venetians. Their goods were confiscated in the trading cities of Apulia, where previously they had benefited from royal favours. Robert was keen to establish harmony with the papacy over common objectives in northern Italy. He was ready to do Clement considerable favours in return for support in vigorous new 'crusades' against Sicily and other objectives. He was confident that, with the support of other allies, Venetian political support was superfluous.[11]

The first experiences of Robert as king seemed to urge him into more decisive action against the Ghibellines and their allies in Sicily. He realised that southern Italy was in danger of being trapped between two anti-Angevin forces: the resurgent Ghibellines who had drawn encouragement from Henry VII's brief career, and Frederick III of Sicily (as he now called himself in disregard of the treaty of 1302). Robert's first assault on Sicily, in 1314, achieved nothing, but promised more trouble in the future. In the north of Italy he did acquire titles: the death of the Emperor Henry left Pope Clement free to dispose of imperial offices in northern Italy, according to the debatable position that, *vacante imperio*, during an imperial vacancy, the pope assumed temporary authority over the empire. Robert became imperial vicar in Italy at papal behest (1314), and was encouraged to turn against the

11. Abulafia, 'Venice and the Kingdom of Naples', pp. 187–8; cf. N.J. Housley, 'Pope Clement V and the crusades of 1309–10', *Journal of Medieval History*, 8 (1982), pp. 29–43.

most powerful Ghibelline family in Italy, the Visconti of Milan and against the anti-papal champion, Castruccio Castracani, who gained power at Lucca in 1314.[12] Disaster struck at Montecatini (August, 1315), when the Tuscan Ghibellines aided by Matteo Visconti of Milan left members of the house of Anjou dead on the battlefield. But Robert proved able just to hold his position, exercising influence as leader of the Guelf factions from Piedmont to Tuscany.

The creation of an Angevin seigneury in Genoa was perhaps the most ambitious attempt at resistance to Matteo Visconti and the Ghibelline revival. It signalled, also, the inception of a close but uneasy relationship between Robert and Pope John XXII (1316–34), an ambitious pontiff whose fulminations against his foes placed him in the same class as Innocent IV or Boniface VIII. Like them, he was keen to use the crusade as a weapon for the defence of papal interests in Italy, preaching holy war against Milan and Sicily. This determination to use the full force of papal armaments made him a useful ally for Robert; but John's insistence on rigorous respect for papal rights could also lead to tension between the allies; John's remark that, *vacante imperio*, he could dispose of the imperial county of Piedmont and could not see by what right Robert assumed the right to control it was perhaps good law, but it was also bad statesmanship. They did not even agree on the fine points of theology: King Robert's learned treatise on the Beatific Vision of the saints clashed with John's eccentric views.[13] Essentially, though, it was Robert who made the important military decisions in Italy; and that was what mattered while the papacy was confined to Avignon.

In Genoa the conflicts between noble factions were expressed with an extreme bitterness and an extraordinary persistence which threatened to undermine the city's trading position and laid it open to attempts by outsiders to seize sovereignty over the town. The Genoese had submitted voluntarily to Henry VII (1311). But there were also Genoese who saw salvation in the rise of the house of Anjou: members

---

12. L. Green, *Castruccio Castracani. A study on the origins and character of a fourteenth-century Italian despotism* (Oxford, 1986).

13. Robert d'Anjou, *La vision bienheureuse. Traité envoyé au pape Jean XXII*, ed. M. Dykmans (Miscellanea Historiae Pontificiae, Rome, 1970).

of the Grimaldi family, Guelfs, earlier took control of the fortress of Monaco which was situated indeterminately between Genoese territory and the lands of the Count of Provence (1297).[14] From there the Genoese Guelf exiles terrorised the seas in the name of King Charles II and King Robert; the doge of Venice was forced on several occasions to send strongly-worded complaints to Robert of Anjou about Guelf pirates from Monaco who assailed Venetian shipping in Provençal or south Italian waters.

At the end of 1317 the Guelf families seized power in Genoa, and their rivals appealed to Matteo Visconti for armed help. The Guelfs in reply appealed to Robert to send men, money and ships to defend their besieged city. They recognised him as lord of Genoa, jointly with Pope John; Robert even transferred a small crusading flotilla, waiting at Marseilles, from campaigns in the east to the relief of Genoa. Robert's lordship was renewed until 1335, when a government of reconciliation ejected the Angevins; before then the king spent some months in Genoa, seeing the city as a lever for the extension of Angevin authority eastwards from Provence along the coasts of north-western Italy.[15] For much of the period of the Angevin seigneury Genoa was actively besieged by the *extrinseci*, or pro-Visconti exiles, who camped in the suburbs and assaulted Genoese shipping. Genoa had in effect become two hostile cities. The cost of this war to Genoa was enormous; overseas trade was in disarray and the major overseas colony, at Pera outside Constantinople, raised the Ghibelline flag.

Robert spent several years in Provence, from 1319 to 1324, in the hope that he could influence John XXII's plans. In 1322, Matteo Visconti, already excommunicated, became the object of a large and widely-preached papal crusade. The lord of Milan was accused of rank heresy. This accusation opens an important and difficult problem. John XXII's use of the 'political Crusade' as a weapon is often described as

14. The Grimaldi still hold Monaco, though the line all but died out in the nineteenth century.
15. David Abulafia, 'Genova Angioina, 1318–35: gli inizi della Signoria di Roberto re di Napoli', *La storia dei Genovesi*, vol. 12. *Atti del Convegno internazionale di studi sui Ceti Dirigenti nelle Istituzioni della Repubblica di Genova, 12a Tornata, Genova, 11–14 giugno, 1991*, part 1 (Genoa, 1994), pp. 15–24.

a perversion of crusading ideals, a deviation from the prime objectives: crusades for the recovery of Jerusalem and for defence against the Turks. The appeal of a war in Italy, in defence of the papacy, was naturally less than that of a war in the Holy Land; yet it was also easier to reach Italy, and the same spiritual privileges, remission of sins, in particular, could be achieved at lighter cost. Some of those who fought Venice in the Ferrara crusade were saved from a journey of thousands of miles by a journey of perhaps only a few, if they lived in north-eastern Italy: an easy way to expiate one's sins. Yet the very fact that the papacy followed these ancient models in formulating its bulls calling for crusades reveals some of the tensions between the holy war in the east and the 'political crusades'. The bulls insisted that the same crusading privileges would be conferred on those fighting the papal wars in the west as on those who fought in the Holy Land. From the papal point of view this was not necessarily a cynical use of the crusade, whatever contemporary critics may have thought.[16] The theory of the holy war, developed at the papal court, was argued on an abstract plane and did not normally isolate the 'just cause' of fighting the Muslims from the 'just cause' of fighting groups within Europe, such as heretics, political foes and pagans on the Baltic frontier.

This problem of 'political crusades' deeply involved the house of Anjou. For the 'political crusade' was seen, sincerely enough by the papacy, as part of the process of launching crusades to the east. The Visconti and their allies were accused of distracting the house of Anjou from the more urgent task of the redemption of that 'Kingdom of Jerusalem' whose title Robert bore. The papal-Angevin crusade against the Visconti almost but never quite broke their power. By 1324 Robert of Anjou's diplomatic intervention secured from Matteo's son a promise to resist any future imperial adventures in Italy. This success in diplomacy was all the greater because by 1324 the claimant to the throne of the Holy Roman Empire, Ludwig of Bavaria, had begun to interfere

16. David Abulafia, 'The Kingdom of Sicily and the origins of the political crusades', *Società, istituzioni, spiritualità. Studi in onore di Cinzio Violante*, 2 vols (Spoleto, 1994), vol. 1, pp. 65–77; N. Housley, *The Italian Crusades against Christian lay powers, 1254–1343* (Oxford, 1982), pp. 15–24.

directly in north Italian politics. Ludwig of Bavaria posed a greater danger to the pope than to King Robert. He surrounded himself with scholars critical of papal pretensions, such as the political theorist Marsiglio of Padua and the philosopher William of Ockham. He scorned papal excommunication (1324); he appointed his own pope, the Spiritual Franciscan Nicholas V, who was as a matter of fact a native of Robert's kingdom (1328): a puppet pope, but a shrewd choice, since John XXII had condemned the doctrine of the 'absolute poverty' of Christ and had persecuted the Spiritual Franciscans who were its main proponents. Nicholas V then crowned Ludwig as emperor, a title few of course recognised. Robert of Anjou showed little sign of being greatly scared by Ludwig, even when the emperor was crowned in Rome in 1328. He seems to have reasoned that wars in Tuscany would distract Ludwig from interference in Neapolitan affairs. Another dimension to Robert's attitude was probably his irritation at John XXII. Whether its source lay in the excessively vigorous attempts of this aggressive pope to guide Angevin policy, or whether it lay in Robert's affection for the Spiritual Franciscans whom John persecuted, the late 1320s saw the paths of Robert and John diverge.[17]

This is not to say that the Angevins failed to recognise the danger of a Ghibelline revival in Tuscany. The brilliant soldier Castruccio Castracani frequently, though not constantly, gained the upper hand in battles with the Guelfs. A whole series of victories brought Robert's enemies power and influence in the Romagna by 1315, and in Tuscany by 1325; notable were the Ghibelline victories at Altopascio (May, 1325), and further north at Zappolino (November, 1325). The Guelfs were increasingly on the defensive; even the Florentines thought they could only guarantee their liberties by accepting an Angevin governor. Robert had tried to foist one on them as long before as 1317, but the Florentines insisted that a royal vicar would be incompatible with their traditions of freedom. But in 1325 they offered the seigneury of the city to Robert's heir, Charles duke of Calabria. He was to bring with him several hundred knights, and he was to receive 100,000 florins per annum from the

---

17. É. Léonard, *Les Angevins de Naples* (Paris, 1954); Italian edn, *Gli Angioini di Napoli* (Milan, 1967), pp. 302–35.

city to cover his expenses. Other Guelf communes nearby also accepted him; after three years he died, after achieving moderate successes for the Tuscan Guelfs, but leaving too a sour taste in Florentine mouths.[18] The Florentines were not to accept another Angevin governor till 1342. However, it was in the last years of John XXII's pontificate, until 1334, that irrefutable signs of a breach between the Avignon papacy and the Angevin king emerged.

The arrival in Italy in 1330 of John, king of Bohemia, opened the way to unexpected co-operation between Guelfs and Ghibellines, and the Angevins too, against eccentric papal policies. John was the son of Henry VII, but he did not seek to become emperor, nor to displace Ludwig of Bavaria whose Italian links were by now very attenuated; it was rather that the Italian towns began to see in him a herald of peace reminiscent of his father Henry. Brescia stood in the front line; and its former protector, Robert of Anjou, seems to have made no effort to help defend the city against the Scaliger lords who were trying to overwhelm it. Brescia, and then Milan, saw in John of Bohemia the saviour they needed. The papal legate in Italy was impressed, and made an alliance with the king of Bohemia, but when the legate was defeated in battle soon afterwards, the adventure came to a premature end.[19]

Robert of Anjou decided that his place also lay with the opponents of Bohemian intervention, which he apparently identified with earlier imperial intervention. Giovanni Villani, the Florentine chronicler, observed that the motive of King Robert in supporting Ghibellines, of all people, lay in his resentment at the papal-Bohemian alliance and his fear of Ludwig of Bavaria and John of Bohemia. It was with French armies behind him that King John re-entered Italy in 1333, only to be defeated three months later at Ferrara, by the Lombard League of Guelfs, Ghibellines and Angevins. By 1334 Robert of Anjou and Ludwig of Bavaria were showing signs of rapprochement. The Guelf alliance had disintegrated,

18. F. Schevill, *Medieval and Renaissance Florence*, vol. 1, *Medieval Florence* (New York, 1961), [earlier published as *History of Florence*, New York, 1936], pp. 203–4, 207–8.
19. G. Tabacco, *La casa di Francia nell'azione politica di Giovanni XXII* (Rome, 1953); Léonard, *Angioini*, pp. 328–35.

and yet Robert had managed to remain master of himself, an influential, agile and able politician who deserves his sobriquet 'The Wise'.

. . .

THE CRUSADE AGAINST SICILY

To understand Robert's lack of enthusiasm for some of John XXII's north Italian schemes it is necessary to consider the king's other preoccupations. Sicily, above all, demanded attention, for King Frederick had allied himself to Ludwig and the Ghibellines; moreover, Frederick broke the terms of the treaty of Caltabellotta in 1320 by naming his son Peter as his heir, since the island was supposed to go after his death to the Angevin king. In addition, the successors of James II of Aragon gave open support to Frederick of Sicily from the 1330s onwards. Thus the years of the Bohemian entry into Italy saw an intensification of Robert's struggle for dominion over Sicily; between 1330 and 1343 six Angevin expeditions were launched against Frederick and his heirs. There were striking successes in the short term, such as the capture of a castle at Palermo and of Milazzo, near the straits of Messina; in 1346, three years after Robert's death, Milazzo was in fact permanently occupied, but during his lifetime none of the conquests lasted long and they could not even be used to force the Aragonese into negotiation.[20] The failure of the expeditions is all the more surprising since the Sicilian nobility was deeply divided between two factions, the 'Catalans' and the 'Latins'; there were even defections to the court of Naples, such as that of Giovanni Chiaramonte, a very illustrious nobleman who acquired from Robert what proved to be an empty title: vicar-general for Sicily. However, the accession of a child king in Sicily, Louis or Lodovico, in 1342 and the rebellion of the 'Latins' against the new regent brought no permanent Angevin success.

The Sicilian crusade was presented as the essential preliminary to a crusade to the East; and the Angevins continued to take seriously their duties in the east. There were a few Neapolitan ships in the expedition to Smyrna, on the coast of what is now Turkey, in 1337; this region had become

20. Léonard, *Angioini*, pp. 409–13.

an important theatre of war since the Knights of St John of Jerusalem occupied Rhodes in 1310.[21] In the former Byzantine lands claimed by the Angevins there was more progress. The 'Kingdom of Albania' seemed to acquire again some reality, with the co-operation of the native Thopia family.[22] The Albanian nobility was loyal to the house of Anjou in the 1320s and 1330s; probably it saw the Angevins as generous defenders of their own domains against the Serbs. In 1336–37 an Angevin prince, Louis of Durazzo, gained successes against the Serbs, fighting in central Albania. It was his family that received Durazzo and the hinterland as a fief from Robert of Anjou, founding a cadet branch of the dynasty which was to have a major role in the politics of Naples and of Hungary later in the century. So too in Achaia the Angevins enforced their authority (1338–42), or rather the authority of Charles of Valois' daughter Catherine de Courtenay, who had married into the Angevin dynasty and had brought the imperial title of Constantinople with her. More importantly, she brought to high office and royal attention a remarkable man who was greatly to help shape the kingdom of Naples in future years: the Florentine Nicola Acciaiuoli, the son of a prominent banker. For his help in holding Achaia he was awarded his first fiefs, in the western Peloponnese; and on his return to Naples he won office as justiciar of the Terra di Lavoro, the province around Naples. Thus events in the Balkans help mould the shape of those in Naples.[23]

The links between the court of Naples and the Hungarian court were intensified. A series of projects for a marriage alliance between the two Angevin dynasties reached fruition in the betrothal of Joanna, granddaughter of Robert, and Andrew, younger son of the Hungarian ruler Carobert. Joanna had become heiress after her father Charles of

21. Housley, *Avignon papacy and the Crusades*, p. 39, for Neapolitan involvement in various plans.
22. As has been seen, Frederick III declined the offer to exchange Albania and Achaia against Sicily: David Abulafia, 'The Aragonese kingdom of Albania. An Angevin project of 1311–16', *Mediterranean Historical Review*, vol. 10 (1995), pp. 1–13. On the Thopias, see D.M. Nicol, *The Despotate of Epiros, 1267–1479* (Cambridge, 1984).
23. The principal account of Acciaiuoli remains that of É. Léonard, *Histoire de Jeanne Ière reine de Naples, comtesse de Provence*, vol. 3, *Le règne de Louis de Tarente* (Monaco/Paris, 1936); also Léonard, *Angioini*, pp. 461–505.

Calabria died in 1328, and a responsible prince was needed to help her rule her future kingdom. The boorish Andrew was in fact a questionable choice as royal consort, and he aroused sufficiently intense hatred to be murdered in 1345, to no great regret. of Queen Joanna. But the murder of Andrew meant also that Robert's good intention in bonding Naples and Hungary led rather to conflict. Andrew's elder brother Lajos, or Louis, the Great led two devastating expeditions into southern Italy to avenge his death. These unforeseen results of Robert's Hungarian alliance, after that king's death, should not be allowed to detract from his real achievement: after careful negotiation the king of Naples secured an arrangement which was intended to lead neither to the union of the two Angevin kingdoms nor to the automatic acquisition of a crown by Andrew. In addition, Robert took care to set aside papal claims to assume authority in the vassal kingdom of Naples should he die before his granddaughter came of age.

· · ·

THE KING AND THE BANKERS

The lengthy, bitter wars of the Angevins had somehow to be funded. The resources of the house of Anjou shrank at once with the loss of Sicily, whose grain had produced tax revenue, military supplies and valuable political leverage over centres of consumption in northern Italy. A sophisticated redistribution system under Charles I had ensured that mainland provinces, especially the area of Naples, that were habitually short of grain could be fed from the generally abundant spare resources of the island. Expenditure on the recovery of Sicily was thus seen as investment in the restoration of state finances. It is not, then, surprising that the monarchy took large loans from foreign bankers to finance its wars and its other needs; moreover, the existence of good wheat lands in Apulia and other corners of southern Italy meant that the crown could still to some degree capitalise on the great tradition of grain production. The relationship with foreign merchants can be seen in its most extreme form in the instance of Angevin favours to the great Florentine banks. In 1284 members of the Bardi, Acciaiuoli and Mozzi houses made Charles II a loan of a thousand ounces of gold, and in return were permitted to export two and a quarter thousand tons of wheat from Apulia. Charles de la Roncière has counted over forty grants of export rights to these and lesser Florentine banks in the thirty years from 1290 to 1329, all of them secured by handsome loans to the crown. In 1311 alone the quantity of recorded grain exports was about 45,000 tons; and the steady rise in the volume of these exports was aptly matched by massive amounts of gold advanced to Charles II and Robert the Wise, such as a sum of over 18,000 ounces in 1305.[24] Repayment took many forms, such as permitting the banks control over the collection of revenue from royal assets, including the fishing port of Castellamare near Naples, the royal mint or harbour taxes in various provinces.[25] Meanwhile, access to south Italian markets gave the bankers the chance to sell considerable quantities of Florentine cloth in Naples. It was a profitable relationship, not so much for the government of Florence as for the bankers and textile producers of the city; the relationship also took pressure off the food supply of Florence, which depended heavily on imported wheat.

Such activities planted in the minds of the rulers of Naples schemes to develop internationally successful textile industries of their own. Native assets appeared to make such plans viable: the existence of a local wool supply, in which Charles I had expressed interest as early as 1279; the existence of a dyeing industry in such centres as Salerno, where the Jews had a special role; this industry was given further impetus by Charles II in 1299 when he tried to set up new dyeing workshops in southern Italy. Later in his reign Charles II paid two brothers from Florence the sum of 48 ounces of gold to encourage them to set up a textile factory in Naples. These efforts, which have ample contemporary parallels in neighbouring lands such as Majorca, were repeated under Robert the Wise; but success was limited, and even the monarchy's attitude cooled when it became apparent that there were heretics among the north Italian textile workers who came to Naples.[26]

24. C. de la Roncière, *Florence, centre économique régional*, 4 vols (Aix-en-Provence, 1976), vol. 2, pp. 565, 571–3, 625.
25. D. Abulafia, 'Southern Italy and the Florentine economy 1265–1370', *Economic History Review*, ser. 2, vol. 33 (1981), pp. 380–1.
26. R. Caggese, *Roberto d'Angiò*, 2 vols (Florence, 1922–30), vol. 1, pp. 530–6.

The great banks, the Bardi, Peruzzi and Acciaiuoli, whose size was not even rivalled by the Medici and Strozzi in the fifteenth and sixteenth centuries, were deeply involved with the Angevins not merely in their rise to prosperity, but also in their cataclysmic fall in the 1340s. The peak of Florentine involvement in Naples was reached before 1330. Thereafter a number of cracks appear in this neat façade. Internal squabbles reduced the effectiveness of the Florentine government in influencing papal and Angevin affairs. External quarrels brought Florence into expensive wars, such as the Lombard League of 1332 in which such improbable allies as the Visconti joined Florence and King Robert in an attempt to rebuff King John of Bohemia. The result was that by 1341 Florence had to ask its allies for help with its war expenses; the commune turned, improbably enough, to King Robert of Naples: 'We are spending an uncountable amount of money nowadays on Lombard affairs, so that all our existing and future revenues have already been taken up.' The Florentine banks were either reluctant to help or incapable of helping. The economic historian Armando Sapori suggested that the Peruzzi at least were being drained of funds: in 1331 the firm reorganised, with £60,000 capital, but by 1335 virtually every penny had already gone.[27]

The collapse of the Bardi and Peruzzi in 1343–45 marks the end of an era of great commercial adventurousness, and the beginning of a dramatic decline in the fortunes of the Neapolitan crown. The bankers' support for Edward III's invasion of Flanders was a financial disaster, while Florentine attempts to extricate the republic from its traditional Guelf alliance against Ludwig of Bavaria excited serious alarm in Naples, on political and financial grounds. It was not clear where the Angevin rulers could henceforth turn in their search for funds; for the Florentine banks which survived the 1340s were smaller and more cautious than those which had financed Robert of Anjou. Yet there were still wars to be fought, in Sicily and against the Hungarians, and there was still a magnificent court demanding its upkeep.

This negative picture of Angevin finance must not be exaggerated. John H. Pryor has discussed Angevin attempts to

---

27. A. Sapori, *La crisi delle compagnie mercantili dei Bardi e dei Peruzzi* (Florence, 1926); but cf. Hunt, *Super-Companies*, pp. 156–229.

stimulate the economy: the careful protection of merchants travelling within the kingdom; improvements in port facilities at such centres as Manfredonia (under Charles I); the establishment of more than a dozen new fairs; the provision of ships from the royal fleet to merchants, when not needed in war; the opening of new silver mines in Calabria, whose exploitation was farmed out at a charge of one-third of the proceeds. Few of these measures were entirely new. The crown stockpiled salt, as it had done under Frederick; profits could reach 1300 per cent once the mineral was released to buyers. Export taxes were maintained and, when reformed, were sometimes increased: Charles II introduced a light tax which was actually to be levied on goods exempt from all tax (the *jus tari*); under Robert it developed into a tax on all goods irrespective of whether they were otherwise exempt.

As Pryor shows, the Angevin kings were not impoverished by comparison with their contemporaries:[28]

Ruler	Territory and date	Annual revenue in florins
Charles I of Anjou	Naples and Sicily, 1266–82	1,100,000
Robert the Wise	Naples, 1309–43	600,000
Louis IX	France, 1226–70	500,000
Philip VI	France, 1329	786,000
Visconti lords	Milan, 1338	700,000
Edward III	England and Gascony, 1327–77	550–700,000
Boniface VIII	Papacy, 1294–1303	250,000
John XXII	Papacy, 1316–34	240,000

The key difference is that the Angevin figures declined over time; the French increased, up to the Hundred Years' War. Partly this is simply attributable to the loss of Sicily, which was a source of great wealth; but in the later years of Robert's reign and during that of Joanna I there was increasingly dramatic erosion. Moreover, Charles I maintained his court and armies by failing on occasion to pay the tribute due to the pope; over 90,000 ounces of gold were due at the time of

28. J. Pryor, 'Foreign policy and economic policy: the Angevins of Sicily and the economic decline of southern Italy', in L.O. Frappell, *Principalities, Powers and Estates. Studies in medieval and early modern government and society* (Adelaide, 1980), pp. 43–55.

his death in 1285, though after the loss of Sicily the tribute was reduced to only 5,000 ounces per annum.[29] Later on, Robert diligently paid the pope what was due, despite heavy war costs: 'When military success began to wane and the Angevin domains contracted, and when revenue itself contracted, the crown became able to hold its deficit, to reduce it gradually, and finally to extinguish it.' On the other hand, Robert's abilities were not matched by those of his successors, under whom the *Regno* became the battle ground of mercenary companies.

The effects of these difficulties on the population at large are hard to estimate; the picture is distorted by the ravages of plague, which first reached Sicily in 1347. The loss of millions of records during the Second World War – in the German destruction of the Naples archive in 1943 – means that the social history of the *Regno* in the fourteenth century cannot now be written. Romolo Caggese alone made use of the Angevin registers to illustrate the violent tenor of rural life: royal protection of merchants and pilgrims often worked better in theory than in practice. Tough landlords, such as the Teutonic Knights, found their pastures invaded by the peasantry of the Barletta region (1313). The lord of Castroprignano complained not merely that his peasants refused to pay their rents and perform their services, but that he and his family had been attacked, and his bailiff killed. But the peasant case was precisely that many of the labour services were a novelty; he imposed on his peasants the duty to help repair his castle and his mills; the lord was himself guilty of grabbing royal land. It is difficult to know how typical these cases were of Robert's *Regno*, or of Europe as a whole.[30] Certainly, it was the baronage that exploited weaknesses in royal power to enhance its regional authority; the monarchy's own liberality to favoured subjects, such as Nicola Acciaiuoli, further eroded royal control of the provinces. The tendency persisted to dream of the reconquest of Sicily as the solution to all the kingdom's ills.

29. W. Percy, *The revenues of the Kingdom of Sicily under Charles I of Anjou, 1266–1285, and their relationship to the Vespers* (repr. from Princeton doctoral dissertation, 1964, by University Microfilms).

30. R.H. Hilton, *Bond men made free. Medieval peasant movements and the English rising of 1381* (London, 1973), pp. 110–12, certainly assumes that he can generalise to the rest of Europe from these cases; Caggese, *Roberto d'Angiò*, vol. 1, pp. 233–73.

. . .

A WISE KING: ROBERT AND THE ARTS

King Robert's 'wisdom' was most evident to his contemporaries in his patronage of letters and the fine arts. These activities were turned to the political advantage of the Angevin royal house and, quite apart from Robert's genuine devotion to the arts, his willingness to use his artists also as propagandists sheds light on his policies. Robert's grandfather had actively maintained the cultural patronage of the court of Sicily, inherited from the Hohenstaufen and Normans. It was the scale and fame of Robert's court excited special admiration. The Angevins were known for their interest in rich silks and damasks, expressive of their special royal dignity and wealth. Robert sought to display the legitimacy of his dynasty amid the counter-claims of his Aragonese rivals. The most eloquent document of their political interest in the fine arts is a painting by the eminent Sienese, Simone Martini, dating to about 1317. Robert's eldest brother, the saintly Louis of Toulouse, is shown conferring his crown on Robert after his renunciation of the throne in favour of life in the Franciscan order.[31] Not merely Robert's own claim to the throne of Sicily but that of the Angevin dynasty to rule in southern Italy was enhanced by the presence of a saint in the royal family. Can the Angevins be mere usurpers if the body of St Louis of Toulouse works miracles? Giotto, the unrivalled Florentine painter of the time, came to the Angevin court too, and received a pension from King Robert.[32] Around 1330 he was at work on a series of paintings, sadly now lost, showing the great classical and biblical heroes with their wives or lovers: Paris and Helen of Troy, Aeneas and Dido, Samson and Delilah.

Here were classical themes, with romantic overtones: the subject of Giotto's work reflects the combination of French 'Gothic' cultural traditions, brought by Charles of Anjou to Naples, with innovatory Italian styles and motifs. Many of the great buildings of the Angevins in Naples are heavily influenced by French Gothic architecture: the church of

31. J. Gardner, 'Simone Martini's St Louis of Toulouse', *Reading Medieval Studies*, vol. 1 (1975), pp. 16–29.
32. B. Cole, *Giotto and Florentine painting, 1280–1375* (New York, 1976), pp. 12–13.

Santa Chiara, for instance, where Robert and other Angevins are buried in lavish marble tombs which recall French and Provençal styles. Nor is this surprising in a dynasty which took a keen interest in the county of Provence, and proudly displayed in decorations the fleur-de-lys of Charles I's royal French ancestors. Provençal poets, blending with south Italian lyricists whose work had been fostered by the Hohenstaufen, remained active around the Angevin court, and Charles I fancied himself as a composer of verses. The Norman and Hohenstaufen courts were no more eclectic in taste than that of the Angevins; the close attention of the Angevins to French and Provençal courtly models simply added to the diversity at court. Like many fourteenth-century courts that of Naples patronised chivalric orders, imitated from the Order of the Star in France and of the Garter in England; ten years after Robert's death Nicola Acciaiuoli organised the 'Order of the Holy Spirit' (also known as the Order of the Knot) for the flower of the Neapolitan nobility.[33] Attention to the ideals of chivalry, at a time of growing misconduct in war, shows further responsiveness to the influence of north European courts.

More disinterested was the Angevin patronage of letters, though even there King Robert acquired glory in his own day by his friendship for Petrarch, who came to Naples in 1341 so that King Robert could examine whether he was worthy to receive the Laurel Crown, not awarded since antiquity, for his knowledge of poetry. Giovanni Boccaccio, active also in the study of classical literature, was present at Petrarch's examination in Naples. Although less lucky in his attempts to gain lavish patronage from the Angevins, Boccaccio had spent his youth in Naples, apprenticed to the Bardi bank. He was then a close friend of Nicola Acciaiuoli, though later they quarrelled. The young Boccaccio spent more time at the picnics and revels of the Neapolitan nobility, less at the royal court itself; but his admiration for Robert the Wise and the influence of his Neapolitan education upon his writing were both substantial.[34] (A reading of the *Decameron*

---

33. D'A.J.D. Boulton, *The Knights of the Crown. The monarchical orders of Knighthood in later medieval Europe, 1325–1520* (Woodbridge, 1987), pp. 211–40; Léonard, *Angioini*, pp. 463–7.
34. V. Branca, *Boccaccio. The man and his works* (Hassocks, Sussex, 1976), pp. 16–76.

provides a lively image of fourteenth-century Naples: nobles, bandits, merchants, and the destitute). Among lesser figures more permanently at court must be mentioned Barlaam, a Greek-speaking Calabrian, from whom Boccaccio learned some Greek; the Angevin court was the only European court where steadily sustained study of Greek texts could be found.[35] Scientific and medical study was also active, with the help of Jewish translators whom the Angevins protected, more it seems for their knowledge than out of tolerance. In 1308 loans from Florentine bankers were used to pay a fee for the translation of Arabic books into Latin and a stipend for the distinguished Roman painter Cavallini.

There was a further area of intellectual activity which helped the Angevin dynasty politically. It has been seen that the king's lawyers willingly demonstrated the independence of the kings of Naples from all superior control, in the wake of the conflict with Henry VII. The jurists Marino da Caramanico and Andrea of Isernia, under Charles II and Robert, used the historic legatine status of the rulers of southern Italy, the *monarchia sicula*, as evidence for the freedom of kings from day-to-day interference in royal affairs. They stressed that the king was not subject to imperial or other authority: he was emperor in his own kingdom. In his commentary on Frederick II's lawbook of 1231, Andrea of Isernia insisted that the king's decrees must be accepted as law and that his power consisted in determining the law; he was not bound by the law. This gloss on a law-book which itself stressed that the ruler's word was law helped the Angevin dynasty to claim the exalted authority of their Hohenstaufen predecessors. Though Robert was more scrupulous than Charles I and II in paying the tribute due to the pope, in other respects he was a prolific legislator, insistent on the supreme authority which his legal advisers instructed him to employ. Émile Léonard has provided a list of the vivid and varied preambles to royal decrees, rich in the insistence on the need for careful exercise of justice and in warnings against human tendencies to pervert the course of justice.[36] Robert was fond

35. R. Weiss, *Medieval and Humanist Greek* (Padua, 1977), pp. 13–43.
36. A. Trifone, *La legislazione angioina* (Naples, 1921); Pennington, *Prince and the law*, pp. 165–201; W. Ullmann, *The medieval idea of law as represented by Lucas de Penna* (London, 1946); Léonard, *Angioini*, pp. 339–66.

of delivering sermons to the captive audience of his courtiers; he drew his texts for the sermons from biblical passages which could not but arrest the attention of a warrior king: 'My soul hath long dwelt with him that hateth peace. I am for peace: but when I speak, they are for war' (*Psalms*, 120.6–7). He was a passionate amateur theologian, as befitted the brother of a saint.[37]

King Robert's attempts to present himself as a sincere advocate of peace and justice impressed many north Italian citizens. The Venetians, it is true, received from him little but rough justice; but the veneration of the citizens of Prato for their seigneur the Neapolitan king was expressed with more devotion than literary skill in a lengthy verse celebration of Robert's justice and wisdom. Of the three surviving manuscripts of the Prato eulogy one, now in the British Library, shows King Robert in a majestic profile, against a back-cloth of fleur-de-lys: perhaps a reliable portrait, with its long Angevin nose and face.[38] The message is clear: Robert did in his own lifetime impress and win the loyalty of those whose support he sought. Charles I had been an intruder in Italian politics, a strong man who could provide much-needed help to the Guelfs; Robert for his part showed great political adroitness and a highly developed sense of how to care for his subjects' interests. He could indeed pursue his policies obstinately, as his wars to recover Sicily indicate; but the more grandiose dreams of his ancestor were abandoned for more limited, more practical objectives within Italy itself.

. . .

CONCLUSION

The reign of Robert the Wise has been unjustly ignored by historians seeking to explain the series of political crises that wracked northern and central Italy in the early fourteenth century. Starting his reign as a close ally of the papacy, which was based at Avignon in the Angevin county of Provence, Robert soon found himself at odds with the first German

37. Robert d'Anjou, *La vision bienheureuse*.
38. British Library MS Royal 6.E.IX, f. 10v; A. Martindale, *The rise of the artist in the Middle Ages and early Renaissance* (London, 1972), p. 60, plate 38.

emperor since the days of Frederick II to be crowned in Rome, Henry VII of Luxembourg. The pope had hoped to use Henry as a counterbalance against the enormous strength of the Angevins in Italy; but Henry proved to be an idealist who dreamed of reconciling Guelfs and Ghibellines throughout northern Italy, and as a result only antagonised the Guelfs, who saw such moves as a threat to their ascendancy. The growing conflict between Henry and Robert developed into a propaganda war which addressed fundamental principles concerning the nature of kingship; it was only put to an end by the unexpected death of Henry in 1313. Robert's close alliance with Pope John XXII and with the Florentines (in particular the great Florentine business houses) brought substantial political and economic bonuses: sure outlets for the grain trade of Apulia; and lordship over north Italian cities such as Prato near Florence and Genoa, which not long before had accepted Emperor Henry as its lord. Control of Genoa was contested by the Ghibellines, but holding this city was seen as a key to the possession of the whole coastline from Provence eastwards along the Tyrrhenian seaboard.

Robert, like his Angevin predecessors, eventually scared the popes who were unnerved by his formidable power. By 1334 it was unclear whether the traditional triangular alliance of pope, Angevin king and Guelf Florence could be said still to exist. Robert of Anjou seems even to have thought of a rapprochement with such deadly enemies of the pope as Ludwig of Bavaria, the German king. Besides, Robert's agenda contained other items such as the reconquest of Sicily; this last became a more urgent priority once Frederick of Aragon died in 1337. Under the terms of the treaty of 1302, Sicily should now have reverted to the Angevins of Naples; but Frederick had already made plain his *nolle prosequi*. Between 1330 and 1343 six Angevin expeditions were unleashed against the island, while Robert argued that only after the recovery of Sicily and its precious resources could a truly effective crusade for the recovery of Greece and the Holy Land be launched. In other words, he continued to articulate the traditional arguments of the Angevin kings, going back to Charles I's conquest of southern Italy: the quelling of enemies in southern Italy, and indeed throughout the peninsula, would permit the final glorious push to the East.

Chapter 7

SICILY AND SOUTHERN ITALY. IN AN AGE OF DISORDER

. . .

THE ISLAND KINGDOM OF SICILY IN THE FOURTEENTH CENTURY

Both Robert the Wise and Frederick III of Sicily were deeply pious men, willing to show favour to the Spiritual Franciscans. It is thus a paradox that so Christian a monarch as Frederick should have spent so much of his career as king bitterly engaged in conflict with the papacy. Such was his respect for the Holy See that, when excommunicate, he dutifully avoided attending Mass, unlike his flamboyant ally Matteo Visconti of Milan, whose Christian devotions were employed to discredit papal accusations against himself. Indeed, one important element of Frederick's programme of reforms after 1302 was the restoration and rebuilding of churches and monasteries, and the establishment of schools for the teaching of religion.[1] Frederick emerges as a pious evangelist, aware of the need to generate recovery, and similar to his Angevin rivals in his insistence that moral reform would generate lasting peace and welfare. His interest in the abstruse edges of Christian belief culminated in his patronage of the missionary mystics Ramon Llull and Arnau de Vilanova.

Frederick became king of Sicily because he was to all intents a Sicilian. In 1295–96 the Sicilian barons were fearful of being betrayed into Angevin hands, as part of a global peace which would assign Sardinia and Corsica to Aragon in return for the renunciation of Sicily. Since Peter the Great's

---

1. C. Backman, *The decline and fall of medieval Sicily. Politics, religion and economy in the reign of Frederick III, 1296–1337* (Cambridge, 1995).

156

arrival in 1282 it had been clear that the Sicilian rebels saw their aim as the reconstitution of a 'national' monarchy, not the creation of a Catalan-Aragonese dependency. For his part, James II of Aragon made cynical use of his own agreement with the papacy; he provided some troops to help the Angevins fight his brother, but also maintained a cordial correspondence with Frederick. The best outcome would be the maintenance of Frederick in power, and the maintenance of peace between Aragon, France, Naples and the papacy, just as was achieved at the Treaty of Caltabellotta (1302). There followed a series of attempts to reinvigorate religious life in an island which had long been deprived of the adequate service of priests, during long years of interdict; moral reform involved not merely the planned seclusion of the Jews of Palermo so long as they refused to undergo conversion, but also legislation to ensure that slaves were given the chance to enter the Latin church, and that they were treated humanely. Measures were also taken, more successfully in the short than in the long term, to stimulate the economy, notably by the reform of weights and measures and of commercial taxation, both of which had suffered from lack of uniformity; a large number of edicts confirmed the right of the principal towns to exemption from internal tolls; the War of the Vespers had seriously damaged important sectors of the economy of an island that lived in part from its grain trade, an enterprise that depended on both internal and external peace. High intentions were, however, increasingly frustrated by the internal strife that developed between the Chiaramonte clan and its Palizzi rivals in Sicily.

Frederick's own failure to observe the conditions of Caltabellotta (as interpreted by the house of Anjou) provided the main excuse for repeated Angevin invasions, from 1312 onwards; conflict also continued, by proxy, within southern Greece, where pro-Angevin and pro-Sicilian factions emerged, notably the Catalan duchy of Athens, under nominal Sicilian obedience. As early as 1322 Frederick elevated his son Peter II to the throne as co-king, thereby trampling on the stipulation that the island would revert to Naples after his death; Angevin expeditions into Sicily followed in 1325–27. The elevation of Peter II did not prevent rebellion the moment Frederick III died; and Peter II ruled alone only for five years (during which the Palizzi were thrown out of Sicily) before the child king Ludovico came to the throne, a plaything in the hands of the rival factions. In 1355 another minor, Frederick IV, succeeded in the midst of Angevin raids on Milazzo and Messina. The Angevin invasions of Sicily might have achieved even less than they did without the support that existed within Sicily for an Angevin restoration. Rivalries between towns, notably Messina and Palermo, were one factor; Messina constantly sought to keep open supply lines to Calabria, to which its economy was in some respects traditionally more closely tied than to the island of Sicily. But still more powerful was the impact of great barons who, under Frederick III and his successors, were able to carve out great dominions in the island: the Ventimiglia in the north and west, the Palizzi in the east, the Chiaramonti in the south, where the county of Modica offered them every opportunity to extend their power over their subjects. Royal rights such as control over capital crimes and the minting of coin were granted to, or usurped by, noble princes who were becoming more important power brokers than the king himself. The fourteenth century in Sicily (as also in Naples) was the great age of the baronage, who acquired rights over the alienation of fiefs, beginning with Frederick III's law *Volentes* of 1296, a law which stood in direct contrast to the policies of Roger II and Frederick II. On the other hand, the monarchy had little choice; despite the handsome revenues to be obtained from grain sales, the Aragonese kings were desperately short of resources with which to fight their Angevin enemies, or with which to exert influence on Ghibelline factions in northern Italy. Loans from the Bardi, Peruzzi and Acciaiuoli were available to the kings of 'Trinacria' no less than to the kings of Naples, but they could not solve the monarchy's financial difficulties. Increasingly, the great barons came to dominate even the export of grain. The monarchy tolerated the expansion of noble power in the hope of creating a strong baronial buffer against the Angevins; but the price was very high: the alienation of crown demesne land. As Epstein remarks, the civil wars that raged from the 1330s to the 1360s had 'effects on institutional and economic life far more serious and long-lasting than the War of the Vespers itself'.[2]

2. S.R. Epstein, *An island for itself. Economic development and social change in late medieval Sicily* (Cambridge, 1992), p. 317.

Masters of themselves, the Chiaramonti and their rivals, known by the factional labels 'Latin' and 'Catalan', allowed private disputes to mushroom into civil wars; the former built ties to the Angevin court in the confidence that the island kingdom could not withstand the force of a large-scale invasion. In the mid-fourteenth century, at a time when Sicily was first of all places in western Europe to be afflicted by bubonic plague, conflict carried on regardless. The barons took several decades to understand that there were no winners in a conflict that undermined their own power through devastation and unlimited expenditure on war. Seventy years after the Treaty of Caltabellotta the young Frederick IV made peace with the papacy and the Angevins on terms which were barely different from those agreed by Frederick III. But it was not a peace that could be usefully enjoyed: baronial power had not been challenged; Frederick IV himself remarked bitterly in a letter of 1363 to Francesco Ventimiglia:

> What use is the barons' peace to us, if we lack our royal justice and dignity, if our great cities and towns are usurped, if our name is invoked but others enjoy the demesne's fruits, and we live in need and are ashamed of our majesty? This seems a hard life to us, all the more so now we are adult and know how things stand: yet, if everyone knew his limits, he would render to Caesar that which is Caesar's and be content with his baronies and benefices.[3]

Finally, the death of Frederick IV without a male heir, in 1377, reopened internal rivalries. Artale d'Aragona, in charge of the 'Catalan' faction, took charge in his power base of Catania of Frederick's daughter Maria, in the hope of arranging a Milanese marriage, as much to serve his interests as to solve the island's problems; he and his rivals – Manfredi Chiaramonte of Modica, Guglielmo Peralta around Sciacca, and Francesco Ventimiglia in the area of Geraci – carved Sicily into four vicariates where they exercised virtually sovereign authority, perpetuating officially the broad divisions that had been achieved unofficially by the 1360s.[4]

---

3. Cited by Epstein, *An island for itself*, p. 320.
4. There is some worthwhile literature on the Sicilian nobility and on other social groups, in addition to the key works by Corrao, Epstein and Bresc cited in this and other chapters: V. d'Alessandro, *Politica e*

The sharing of power among potential rivals also involved the exclusion of other great barons from any share; and it was Guglielmo Raimondo Moncada, a non-vicar, who spirited Maria away from Catania to Barcelona, and to marriage with Prince Martin of Aragon. The implications of this move were clear at once; towards the end of his long reign (1337–87) King Peter IV of Aragon had been contemplating the restoration of Aragonese rule in Sicily, and the Catalan duchy of Athens had already broken its formal, and weak, links to the crown of Sicily, taking the king of Aragon as its nominal overlord. It was especially obvious after 1377 that Sicily lay open to conquest, the more so once the Great Schism and internal rivalries within the house of Anjou diverted the rulers of Naples from reactivation of their own now ancient claim to the island.

The invasion of Sicily by Aragonese armies, in 1392, was less readily welcomed by the island's nobles than had been the earlier Aragonese invasion of 1282: Manfredi Chiaramonte resisted in Palermo, and paid the price of execution. His lands passed to the leader of the invading army, Bernat de Cabrera. Prince Martin became Sicilian king as Martin I; he was not himself king of Aragon, but heir to Aragon's throne, and it was only on his premature death in 1409 that the island was reunited to the Catalan–Aragonese complex of territories, when he was succeeded by his own father, confusingly, in the circumstances, known as King Martin II. The death of Martin II a year later reopened, not just for Sicily, the question of who would control the five kingdoms and one

Società nella Sicilia aragonese (Palermo, 1963); V. d'Alessandro, Terra, nobili e borghesi nella Sicilia medievale (Palermo, 1994); C. Fisber Polizzi, Amministrazione della contea di Ventimiglia nella Sicilia aragonese (Supplement to vol. 6 of Atti dell'Accademia Agrigentina di scienze lettere e arti, Padua, 1979); E. Mazzarese Fardella, I Feudi comitali di Sicilia dai Normanni agli Aragonesi (Milan/Palermo, 1974); L. Sciascia, Le donne e i cavalier, gli affanni e gli agi. Famiglia e potere in Sicilia tra XII e XIV secolo (Messina, 1993); A. Romano, ed., Istituzioni politiche e giuridiche e strutture del potere politico ed economico nelle città dell'Europa mediterranea medievale e moderna. La Sicilia (Messina, 1992); I. Peri, La Sicilia dopo il Vespro. Uomini, città e campagne, 1282–1376 (Bari, 1981; the middle volume of a series of three by Peri, on the society and economy of medieval Sicily); I. Peri, Villani e cavalieri nella Sicilia medievale (Bari, 1993); F. Benigno and C. Torrisi, eds, Élites e potere in Sicilia dal medioevo ad oggi (Catanzaro, 1995), with essays by d'Alessandro, Epstein, Corrao, et al.

principality that made up the *Corona d'Aragó*, and threatened yet again to open up Sicily to predatory invaders such as the king of Portugal; attempts to re-establish an Aragonese cadet dynasty did not succeed.

It has been seen that Bernat Cabrera was endowed with extensive lands in Sicily. Another major beneficiary was Guglielmo Raimondo Moncada, who acquired what Pietro Corrao has called 'an enormous territorial concentration under his own lordship'; the age of great lordships was thus not at an end, but what would change would be their relationship to a more effective monarchy. The personnel of the nobility underwent rapid change, as great estates, such as those of the Alagona, were torn to shreds, and a new elite emerged, in which Catalan supporters of the crown were heavily represented.[5]

Yet what did succeed, as studies by Pietro Corrao and Stephan Epstein have made clear, was a gradual revitalisation of the economy and a gradual reassertion of royal control over the baronage. In part this may reflect a degree of exhaustion which took its toll in reduced revenues for great princes whose lands were suffering from the effects of depopulation through plague and of devastation through war. Initiatives included the establishment of fairs; local industries revived, and inter-regional trade became lively. At the same time the monarchy sought to recreate an effective administration, recovering control of the coastline (and thereby asserting control over revenues from exported grain), drawing up a register of land holdings, recovering control of serious criminal cases. The monarchy tried to find a balance between the need to recover its authority over the royal demesne and its need to placate the baronage. An important bonus was the declining revenue of the baronage in the post-Black Death era, which increased noble dependence on the crown in Sicily as elsewhere in Europe; in the long term, the towns became an important alternative source of support for the monarchy, though under Martin I the relationship of crown and town remained delicate. Efforts were made to create urban militias which would reduce dependence on feudal levies, and hence on baronial interests; urban elites were

---

5. P. Corrao, *Governare un regno. Potere, società e istituzioni in Sicilia fra Trecento e Quattrocento* (Naples, 1991), pp. 203–60.

emerging which were a potential source of strength to a revived monarchy. But it would also be wrong to exaggerate the immediate success of the monarchy, which still stood a long way from 'proto-absolutism' in its ability to command its subjects; there was stiff opposition until 1398, and the concessions to Catalan and Valencian landholders risked replacing the old great families with a multiplicity of bountifully franchised settlers. Martin's own parliaments in 1397 and 1398 made exactly this point: there were too many Catalans being granted lands, and the monarchy needed to make more effort to live of its own, which would mean an end to the disbursement of royal rights and lands. Readjustment was therefore slow and painful, and compromised by conflicting interests. Often initiatives came from below; this is perhaps especially true of the foundation of new fairs.[6] Even Martin I was distracted from his own kingdom into his father's service, sailing at the end of his reign to Sardinia, a permanent trouble spot, and dying there for Aragon, not for Sicily. Yet this was also part of his achievement: the reintegration of Sicily into the lands of the *Corona d'Aragó* resulted in the reopening of its markets to Catalan businessmen scared away by internal strife; and the issue of the reincorporation of Sicily into the Angevin realm disappeared from view.

. . .

SOUTHERN ITALY UNDER JOANNA I

The disorder which characterised Sicily in the fourteenth century began also to characterise southern Italy after the death of King Robert. The premature death of Duke Charles of Calabria left Robert's grand-daughter, Joanna, as heiress to the kingdom; the existing cadet male lines, those of Anjou-Durazzo and Anjou-Taranto were passed over, and Joanna was married to the younger brother of Louis the Great, the Angevin king of Hungary. The result was that rivalries were established within the house of Anjou; and they were accentuated when the objectionable husband of Joanna, Andrew, suffered defenestration in 1345. It is still unclear whether Joanna was a conspirator in his murder. There were many

6. Epstein, *An island for itself*, pp. 113–15.

possible beneficiaries, not least Joanna, who by all accounts detested her overbearing husband. Andrew's own expectations of a royal title were the subject of controversy. On the other hand, the cadet line of Anjou-Taranto was well placed to confirm its ascendancy over a young queen uncertain of her aims.[7]

The struggle among branches of the house of Anjou began, however, with the fierce response of the Hungarian king to his brother's murder. Ruler of a vast complex of lands that very nearly stretched from the Baltic (or at least the borders of pagan Lithuania, against which he crusaded) to the Adriatic, where he ruled the kingdom of Croatia, Louis the Great demanded of the pope, as Joanna's overlord, the cession of the entire south Italian kingdom into Hungarian hands.[8] Louis did not win over the pope; but he convinced some south Italian barons, such as Lalle Camponeschi, master of L'Aquila, that he was a viable prospect, entering the city in May 1347; an even more dangerous ally was the Roman dictator Cola di Rienzo, who saw in Hungarian support the means to consolidate his own hold on Rome. Late 1347 and early 1348 saw what appeared to be a smooth takeover by Louis of Hungary of the northern provinces of the kingdom of Naples, culminating in a troublesome occupation of the capital itself just as the plague bacillus also began to occupy the Italian peninsula. What seems to have gone wrong is that Louis failed to win the confidence of the Neapolitan baronage, acting ruthlessly against those suspected of complicity in Andrew's murder.

These were not the only difficulties that piled up on Joanna I's shoulders. Continuing disputes with Genoa over the lordship of Ventimiglia were not settled until 1350; only deft

---

7. For the years up to 1362, see É. Léonard, *Histoire de Jeanne Ière de Naples*, 3 vols (Monaco/Paris, 1927–37); for the remaining years of the reign, see Léonard, *Les Angevins de Naples* (Paris, 1954); Italian edn, *Gli Angioini di Napoli* (Milan, 1967), pp. 506–56. Lighter weight biographies include V. and L. Gleijeses, *La regina Giovanna d'Angiò* (Naples, 1990); A. Perlingieri, *Giovanna I Angiò tra storia e leggenda* (Florence, 1991); F. Froio, *Giovanna I d'Angiò* (Milan, 1992), and taken together they reveal a persistent fascination in Italy with this figure.

8. As well as B. Homan, *Gli Angioini di Napoli in Ungheria, 1390–1403* (Rome, 1935) and O. Halecki, *Jadwiga of Anjou and the rise of east central Europe* (New York, 1991), see S.B. Vardy, G. Grosschmid, L.S. Domonkos, *Louis the Great, king of Hungary and Poland* (Boulder/New York, 1986).

papal diplomacy prevented a Genoese-Hungarian military alliance being created. The arrival of bubonic plague coincided with Joanna's own decision to travel to Provence and supplicate the help of Pope Clement VI at Avignon, early in 1348. The price for favour was an agreement to sell Avignon to the pope, lord already of the neighbouring Comtat Venaissin; no longer would the papacy have to be an honoured guest on the soil of Angevin Provence, but to the Provençaux this was a *venditio maledicta*, an 'accursed sell-out'.[9] Joanna sought public exculpation for the murder of her first husband, as well as papal approval for her second marriage which had recently been contracted with Louis of Taranto, leader of the powerful Angevin faction that had been restive while Andrew was alive. (She was in fact already pregnant when she arrived at the *curia*.) Her absence from the *Regno* while it was being torn apart by Hungarian invaders, as well as by predatory mercenary bands, had little effect on the outcome of Louis the Great's invasion: as well as the ravages of plague, Venetian agitation in his rear threatened to prejudice his survival, for on control of Dalmatia depended Louis' ability to create a vast Angevin domain stretching from the borders of Lithuania to the Straits of Messina. The struggle for the Adriatic, which was to culminate in the loss of Venetian Dalmatia in 1352, now preoccupied him. The pope opposed his expedition. The south Italians themselves were restive. It was time for Louis of Hungary to go home.

This did not mean that the Hungarians evacuated the *Regno*. Louis of Taranto was active in the suppression of Hungarian units. He also purged the court of Joanna's own supporters, elevating to high office the Acciaiuoli of Florence. For Louis of Taranto's marriage to Joanna had been an attempt to secure the kingdom for Louis, more than it was an attempt at compromise between the opposing factions in the house of Anjou. A second Hungarian invasion, with Genoese support, in 1350 resulted by 1352 in a narrow victory for Louis of Taranto; but Louis' real victory lay within the *Regno*, where he was crowned king in May 1352, with papal approval, subject to the proviso that he held the throne in right of Joanna (none of whose children in fact survived).

---

9. D. Wood, *Clement VI. The pontificate and ideas of an Avignon pope* (Cambridge, 1989), pp. 48–50.

There was another victor: Nicola Acciaiuoli, the cultured Florentine businessman who had acquired lands and favour in the Morea and who now rose to be Grand Seneschal of the *Regno* and count of Melfi and of Malta; he remained a devotee of traditional knightly values, expressed most explicitly in the chivalric order he helped found. Writing in 1354, Nicola Acciaiuoli spoke of the need 'to recover the kingdom of Jerusalem after having recovered Sicily', an idea which was rooted in the past policy of Angevin kings. As the Hungarian menace evaporated, Naples turned its war machine towards Sicily again. The death of Robert the Wise had been followed by Angevin successes at Milazzo and in the Lipari islands; the 1350s saw a change in approach, with appeals from the Chiaramonte faction to the court of Naples, and the formulation of elaborate plans to ensure that the island would retain a degree of autonomy within a reunited kingdom. Without such internal support, Acciaiuoli's small fleet and army could not possibly have achieved, in April 1354, the submission of much of Sicily, including Palermo but excluding the power bases of the Catalan faction in Messina and Catania. To hold down his gains, Nicola Acciaiuoli would need further resources, but Louis of Taranto failed to provide them, and his success evaporated, though fortunes later revived to the point where the king and queen of Naples could make their triumphant entry into Messina (24 December, 1356). Other concerns dominated the king's thinking in 1354–55: there was trouble in the Abruzzi, where Lalle Camponeschi, ally of the Durazzo faction, was murdered at the behest of the Taranto faction, and where the mercenary companies continued to wreak havoc. There was trouble with the new pope, Innocent VI, who taught Louis and Joanna a lesson, excommunicating them for failing to pay their annual tribute to the Holy See; a visit to Avignon by Nicola Acciaiuoli would be required (in 1360) before this issue could be laid to rest. There was constant and serious trouble in Provence, where the Durazzo faction had powerful allies; in 1361–62 Louis of Durazzo became the focus of opposition to Louis of Taranto in Apulia, while (with Durazzo encouragement) German and Hungarian mercenary companies were unleashed on the *Regno.* A final attempt to overwhelm Sicily became enmeshed in the rivalries of Ventimiglia and Chiaramonte, as well as making ever plainer the interests of a dangerous outside party, Peter IV of Aragon, who saw himself as a possible heir to Frederick IV. The Neapolitans had continually underestimated the degree to which internal rivalries within Sicily, rather than their own intervention, were the controlling factor in the island's intricate politics.[10]

In 1362 Louis of Taranto died, perhaps of plague; two years later Nicola Acciauoli was buried in the vault of the magnificent Charterhouse he had built outside his native Florence. 'The death of Louis of Taranto caused great corruption in all the kingdom', a chronicler wrote. Louis had lacked the broad vision of Robert the Wise, but he had also had little time for political initiatives of his own, caught as he was amid the scheming of Durazzeschi, Hungarians and other rivals. Yet by appointing Nicola Acciaiuoli to high office, he had provided the *Regno* with a capable administrator who was also competent on the battle field; Acciaiuoli's fault was perhaps a desperate wish to be recognised as a true grandee, count of Melfi and of Malta, an attitude which fellow Florentines such as his boyhood friend Boccaccio tended to mock. Joanna, alone again, sought the support of a new husband, rapidly choosing James IV, son of the last king of Majorca, a figure of no political weight who was also mentally unstable, aptly described by a papal legate as *argumentosus*.[11] Before long he wandered off and found himself once again in a Spanish prison, to no great regret of Joanna. Yet he injected further instability into the government of a kingdom which was already severely fractured.

．　．　．

THE RISE OF THE HOUSE OF ANJOU-DURAZZO

The history of the last years of Queen Joanna I is a constant record of court intrigues, lightened to some degree by the final end to the Sicilian war, now that all sides accepted the treaty of 1373. The papacy sought to draw Naples into an alliance which would help clear Italy of the scourge of the mercenary bands (1371), yet this soon became transformed into a crusade against Visconti Milan. Even so far north, the

10. Léonard, *Angioini*, pp. 493–5.
11. E. Oliveres de Picó, *El rei sense reialme (Jaume IV de Mallorca)* (Barcelona, 1965); A. Lecoy de la Marche, *Les relations politiques de la France avec le royaume de Majorque*, 2 vols (Paris, 1892), vol. 2, pp. 181–2.

Neapolitans still had interests on the ground, and a positive result of the war against Milan was the recovery of several territories in Piedmont occupied by the Visconti; James IV of Majorca was involved in these campaigns until 1375, when he died of fever, to be succeeded in the queen's bed by Otto of Brunswick, a soldier who knew the *Regno* from past conflicts, and who was explicitly barred from taking the crown.[12]

Changes within Italy precipitated further crises in the *Regno*. Increasing hostility on the part of Florence towards a papal restoration in Italy reached the point where Pope Gregory XI hurled an interdict at the papacy's ancient ally (1377). At the same time definitive plans for a permanent return of the Holy See to Italy culminated in the arrival of the pope in Rome, where he died a few months later (March 1378). The turbulent conclave that followed elected the disagreeable Pope Urban VI, formerly archbishop of Bari in the *Regno*, whose high-handed actions prompted the cardinals to attempt his removal and replacement by Clement VII, from Geneva. Although at first sympathetic to Urban's claims, Joanna carefully sounded out expert opinion, and concluded, like the French king, that Clement VII was worthy of her support. Her approval went so far that she remitted to him 64,000 florins due from the census imposed on the *Regno*, an obligation she could easily have avoided; she also welcomed him into her domains. Her new problem was that opinion in Naples resolutely supported Urban, if only because he was a *regnicolo* himself; under threat of an uprising, Joanna capitulated, but Urban was not satisfied with her retraction, citing her for heresy and schism (1379).[13] Of course he could see that her power was now exceedingly frail. The question was who might replace her, and the obvious candidate was Charles, duke of Durazzo, who had also benefited from the patronage of Louis of Hungary, another supporter of Pope Urban. Against him, Joanna was inclined to favour Clement VII's adherent Louis I, duke of Anjou, a very distant relation whose line harked back to Charles II of Naples's renunciation of Anjou in favour of Charles of Valois. Already active

---

12. Léonard, *Angioni*, pp. 545, 549, 567–8.
13. W. Ullmann, *The origins of the Great Schism* (London, 1948); Y. Renouard, *The Avignon papacy, 1305–1403*, transl. D. Bethell (London, 1970), pp. 68–73.

in setting Languedoc in order, Louis was, like his Valois ancestor, something of a collector of royal titles in Majorca, Sardinia and elsewhere; but his most lasting legacy as a pretender was as would-be 'king of Jerusalem and Sicily'. In 1380 Joanna agreed to name him as her heir, in view of the fact that, even after four husbands, she had no surviving heir.[14]

No doubt Louis would have shown more enthusiasm had his brother the king of France not died in September of that year; this kept him in Paris, while Charles of Durazzo conquered the south of Italy, using an army well stocked with Hungarian mercenaries. In a sense, the plans of Louis the Great were now paying off, thirty years later, and with the added benefit of papal support from Urban VI, who obligingly crowned Charles III king of Sicily in Rome in June 1381. Queen Joanna was carried off into imprisonment. By the Summer of 1382 she had been smothered; her body was displayed in the church of Santa Chiara as a token that, after a reign of nearly forty years, her kingdom had now passed to her nearest male relative, Charles of Durazzo, who now had to face an invasion by his rival from France.

Louis I of Anjou did achieve some remarkable successes in his south Italian campaign: by 1383 he had penetrated far down the eastern side of the *Regno*; on 30 August he publicly took the royal crown, and until his death in 1384 he managed to hold his position in Apulia with a certain amount of French aid. His son Louis II took the crown in his place, but failed to hold together his father's army, so that Charles III could congratulate himself that he was safe on the throne of Naples, even after the unpredictable Pope Urban turned against him and called a crusade down upon Charles. Charles ignored Urban, and prepared for an even greater conquest, that of Hungary, which was also open to claimants after the death in September 1382 of Louis the Great without a male heir. Although he briefly established himself as master of Croatia and of the Hungarian heartlands, Charles made powerful enemies, with the result that he was struck down in his palace at Buda in February 1386, dying

---

14. E.R. Labande, 'La politique méditerranéenne de Louis Ier d'Anjou et le rôle qu'y joua la Sardaigne', *Atti del VI Congresso internazionale di studi sardi* (Cagliari, 1957), pp. 3–23; repr. in E.R. Labande, *Histoire de l'Europe occidentale, XIe–XIVe s.* (London, 1973).

not long after. In Naples as in Hungary, it had been a short reign; and, though he had shown ability and ruthlessness in winning two crowns in quick succession, he had underestimated the sheer persistence of opposition among the barons of both Naples and Hungary. Other claimants still existed, and the assumption that he could rule both Hungary and southern Italy at a time of extreme disorder in Italy, of schism in the papacy, and of uncertainty in the central European monarchies indicates a lack of practical political wisdom.

Against the brief gain of dominion in Hungary, with all the vast material resources that the central European kingdoms could offer, must be set the loss of Provence, which remained in the hands of the dukes of Anjou, providing them with a power base from which to plan further invasons of the *Regno*. Urban VI died soon after trying to launch his own much vaunted invasion of the *Regno*, but in 1390 the new pope, Boniface IX, accepted the claims of Charles III's son Ladislas to the Neapolitan throne. For nine years Louis II and Ladislas effectively divided the *Regno* between themselves; and, as in fourteenth-century Sicily, the arbiters of power were the barons, notably the house of Sanseverino, which led the pro-Provençal faction finally into the Durazzo camp in July 1399.

Ladislas's major achievement was that he at last addressed the problem of baronial power in the *Regno*, turning on those such as the Sanseverino and the Ruffo (in Calabria) who had shown sympathy for the claims of Louis II of Anjou. His brutal methods, including the mass arrest of the Marzano at a wedding feast, are reminiscent of the more famous machinations of Ferrante I of Naples nearly a century later. Even so, the threat from the duke of Anjou remained constant, punctuated by startling victories that assured him briefly of ascendancy in the papal states and posed a severe threat to Florence. Ladislas's death in 1414 thus marked the end of a period of high adventurism in which the house of Anjou-Provence had again and again failed to displace the Durazzeschi, even though they frequently occupied large portions of the *Regno* and won the support of a fickle baronage, which had worked out that its best interest lay in a weakening of royal authority.[15]

15. A. Cutolo, *Re Ladislao di Angió-Durazzo*, 2 vols (Milan, 1936).

That, indeed, was the sum total of the political changes that took place in fourteenth-century Sicily and southern Italy, though the loss of power to the barons occurred earlier on the island and was accentuated by the difficulties its inhabitants experienced in restoring order and a sound economy after the War of the Vespers. The centralised, powerful, unitary Kingdom of Sicily had given way to two fractured kingdoms of Sicily where the authority of the crown was manipulated, often ruthlessly, to serve the interest of the great lords in their provincial strongholds.

.   .   .

CONCLUSION

The internal divisions which tore apart fourteenth-century Sicily were encouraged by the Angevins, whose invasions and political machinations undid much of the work of reconstruction attempted by Frederick III. The centralised monarchy of the Normans had always, perhaps, been an ideal system, and the crown had not possessed quite that degree of control over the localities which it claimed; but the fourteenth century saw some sacred principles abandoned, notably that of royal supervision over inheritance to the great fiefs. It was the baronial families that now carved out their own powerful regional domains on the island, replicating within these territories the authority the crown had sought to obtain over the entire island; and the monarchy was increasingly reduced to the role of a cipher. To these difficulties were added the devastating effects of warfare and the Black Death, which hit Sicily in 1347, just before it hit the rest of Europe.

The emergence of strong regional power and the decay of monarchic authority took longer on the mainland; but in Angevin Naples Joanna I proved unable, despite the able support of Nicola Acciaiuoli of Florence and of her second husband Louis of Taranto, to prevent a descent into factionalism. Hungarian invasions, to avenge the defenestration of her uncouth first husband Andrew of Hungary, stimulated the fragmentation of the *Regno*, as did the serious tensions unleashed by the papal schism of 1378. Joanna's murder in 1382 did little to resolve the crisis, since her successor was drawn rapidly into Hungarian affairs and met the same fate. Rival houses of Anjou, that of Anjou-Durazzo and that of Anjou-Provence (strictly speaking not direct descendants of Charles I) contested the throne; it was through Louis I of Anjou-Provence that the French crown would in due course be able to establish its own claim to the throne of Naples. Louis I's own attempts to gain Naples were not backed up by adequate resources, and yet Louis, like his successors, was to prove able to penetrate the kingdom and to hold sizeable areas for several years. Meanwhile, the papacy, which after all claimed suzerain authority in the *Regno*, was quite unable to assert its own rights, as Urban VI and his successors in Rome competed with the rival Pope Clement VII and his successors in Avignon. Thus by the late fourteenth century both Sicilian kingdoms appeared to have descended into anarchy.

Chapter 8

THE END OF THE HOUSE OF BARCELONA

. . .

PETER THE CEREMONIOUS, 1336–87

The reign of Peter IV, 'the Ceremonious', has special importance as the period (though a long one, from 1336 to 1387)
during which the king of Aragon began to articulate more
clearly a conception of the overall integrity of the lands of
the Crown of Aragon. This marks a significant step beyond
the limited intention of James II's Privilege of Union. The
young Peter had witnessed, before coming to the throne,
the struggle for Sardinia; his reign began with the assertion of his authority in Majorca; by the end of his life he
was laying down plans for the reincorporation of Sicily too
into his dominions. Writing to his heir John in 1380, Peter
insisted that:

> If we lose Sardinia, you can be sure that Majorca will be lost
> too, for the foodstuffs that Majorca receives from Sicily and
> Sardinia will stop arriving, and as a result the land will be de-
> populated and will be lost.[1]

Hillgarth comments that 'this exceptionally clear perception
of the maritime vocation of Catalonia and of the interconnec-
tion of the islands of the western and central Mediterranean
. . . is proof of a political vision acquired, painfully, over a
long reign'.[2] The attention of historians has focused so

1. V. Salavert i Roca, *Cerdeña y la expansión mediterránea de la Corona de
   Aragón 1297–1314*, 2 vols (Madrid, 1956), vol. 1, pp. 213–14, n. 37.
2. Pere III of Catalonia (IV of Aragon), *Chronicle*, ed. J. Hillgarth and
   transl. M. Hillgarth, 2 vols (Toronto, 1980), vol. 1, p. 36. Hillgarth's

heavily on the founders of the Aragonese commonwealth in the thirteenth and early fourteenth century that Peter's role as the figure who tried, with varying success, to impose an unprecedented degree of unity on his disparate lands can too easily be passed by.

It is the case, nonetheless, that Peter IV is one of the most accessible Aragonese monarchs, since he and his advisers spent many years justifying the king's policies in an autobiographical chronicle. Some sections, notably those concerned with Sardinia, were not based on eye-witness knowledge; but the greater part of the work betrays close involvement by the king in its authorship: at one point the king mentions that he was sitting in bed reading his ancestor James I's autobiography, which first survives in a manuscript of this period. The king of Aragon was thus intensely interested in studying how his predecessors had acquired lands, fame and glory, and (even more) on what legal basis their claims to lands in the Mediterranean could be justified. The inescapable conclusion, for Peter, was that God Himself had guided the house of Barcelona; he portayed himself as a new King David: 'and truly our wars and tribulations were prefigured in the wars and troubles of David . . . and, as the goodness of the Creator delivered David out of the hand of Saul, king of the Philistines, and out of the hand of Absalom and the people who had risen against him, so the mercy of the Lord has delivered us and our kingdoms out of the hand of all our enemies'.[3] It was, he said in the preface to his chronicle, the special duty of the king to render praise to God for the favours he had granted his servant the king of Aragon, protecting him from his enemies. God sustains the entire world, and it is proper that everything the good man has should be

---

edition contains an extensive introduction outlining the reign; for the Catalan text, one can use Soldevila, *Les quatre grans cròniques*. Other studies of the reign include: R. Tasis, *La vida del rei En Pere III* (Barcelona, 1954); R. d'Abadal, *Pere el Ceremoniό i els inicis de la decadència política de Catalunya* (Barcelona, 1972); see also the collection of essays published as an annexe to the Anuario de Estudios medievales, *Pere el Cerimoniό i la seva època* (Barcelona, 1989).
3. *Chronicle of Peter the Ceremonious*, Prologue, cap. 4 (Hillgarth edn, vol. 1, pp. 128–9). Quite why Peter, otherwise so sound in his biblical knowledge, thought Saul, king of Israel, was instead king of the Philistines cannot be explained.

recognised as gifts of God. 'Because of our powerlessness, fragility and littleness, thinking, working and finishing anything good means that God is working within us.'[4] As this statement seems to confess, Peter himself was not physically an imposing figure; the sixteenth-century Aragonese chronicler Zurita contrasted his bodily frailty with his boldness and ambition, and it is clear that his heavy emphasis on the royal dignity and on the grand ceremonial that earned him his sobriquet was an attempt to mask the fact that he was no conquering giant like his ancestor James I. What he possessed that James had not shown in any particular degree was an intense piety that could, on occasion, easily turn towards self-righteousness.

Another factor that influenced Peter's outlook was the difficulty he had as a young man in making his voice heard. His mother died when he was eight, just before Alfonso IV succeeded to the throne in 1327; Alfonso's second wife had children of her own whose fortune she was determined to make, even at the expense of carving out great estates for them within the lands of the Crown of Aragon. Her son was granted such important cities as Tortosa. It is not surprising that, once king, Peter acted toughly towards those barons who had not supported him, and that he vigorously asserted royal authority, even refusing to allow the archbishop of Saragossa, despite earnest entreaties, to touch the royal crown at his coronation, in case anyone suspect that the Church possessed some authority over the monarch. The pious Peter in fact ruthlessly dominated the Church, appointing his own men to ecclesiastical office in Spain and Sardinia. On one occasion, having suffered excommunication, he suspended the pope's representative by his feet from the top of a tower in order to persuade him to lift the ban. His mastery of the Church was strengthened further by his effective control of the Military Orders within Aragon-Catalonia, and further still by the Great Schism, which left him free to appropriate church revenues until the papacy sorted out its affairs. But his undoubted piety did not make him fall victim to current antagonism to the Jews, whom he treated with great solicitude. It was this sense of the unchallengeable rights of the dynasty

---

4. *Chronicle of Peter the Ceremonious*, Prologue, cap. 3 (Hillgarth edn, vol. 1, pp. 127–8).

that permeated the policies of Peter the Ceremonious, in the face of challenges from his half-brother Ferran, from his cousin the king of Majorca, from rebellious towns and nobles who sought to emphasise the limited and decentralised character of the Aragonese monarchy. Peter challenged this trend by attempting to create a more solid bureaucracy, imitating trends in other European monarchies: Bernat de Cabrera, his powerful chief minister between 1347 and 1364, issued a set of naval ordinances in 1354 and again in 1359, while Peter issued ordinances for the management of the royal household; efforts were made to increase the accountability of the senior financial official in the royal administration, the *Mestre Racional.* The king also recognised that the lack of universities in the lands of the Crown of Aragon limited the opportunity to recruit a highly trained civil service; the single 'Aragonese' university in the past had been that of Montpellier, but the city was in Majorcan and French hands. Thus in the 1350s Peter established new universities at Huesca in Aragon proper and at Perpignan in Roussillon.

Especially valuable to the crown was learning in the law, which could be used to bolster royal rights. The test case at the start of Peter's reign was that of Majorca. During the early fourteenth century, the capacity of the Majorcan rulers to resist Aragonese pretensions was constantly being weakened. The Majorcans made a substantial contribution, as vassals of Aragon-Catalonia, to the fleet that invaded Sardinia in 1323–24.[5] On the other hand, Majorca and its mainland port at Collioure had become a flourishing trade centre, and Majorcan commercial taxes would greatly strengthen Peter, if he could lay his hands upon them. Apart from material considerations, there were genuine points of law to consider. Technically, under the terms of King James I's will, the kingdom of Majorca should have reverted to the Aragonese when King Sanç or Sancho of Majorca died without an heir in 1324. But the Aragonese were still facing tough resistance in Sardinia; they grudgingly accepted that the crown could pass to Sancho's nephew James, then a minor on whose

5. See D. Abulafia, *A Mediterranean Emporium. The Catalan Kingdom of Majorca* (Cambridge, 1994), pp. 246–7; on the limited strength of the Catalan fleet, see the classic study by J.A. Robson, 'The Catalan fleet and Moorish sea-power (1337–1344)', *English Historical Review,* 74 (1959), pp. 386–408.

behalf his devout uncle, the Regent Philip, for several years governed the Majorcan state. By the 1330s, however, James III of Majorca was beginning to become an embarrassment; his independent approach to foreign policy was made plain when he continued to promote good relations with his Muslim neighbours while the Castilians were trying to organise an Iberian crusade against Morocco and Granada. Eventually, in 1340, news came that the Valencian Muslims were ready to rise in revolt; James recognised the gravity of the situation, supplying a fleet of galleys in support of the Aragonese.

James III's policies were built on an unequivocal assumption that as king of Majorca he could be subject to no other secular power. Characteristic was his decision to issue a set of 'laws', the so-called *Leges Palatinae*, which in fact laid emphasis on the ceremonial duties of the king's principal courtiers: the butler, the marshal, the constable and so on; a magnificent illuminated manuscript of the laws, now preserved in Brussels, offers a vivid picture of a court that could live well off the handsome revenues brought by Majorcan trade. Not surprisingly, James was irked by King Peter IV's insistence that he should kneel on a cushion no higher than that of ordinary barons when he came to perform homage to the king of Aragon. Arguments broke out between James III and Peter in 1339 during a visit to the pope at Avignon; the king of Majorca was upset when Peter's horse was led a pace or two in front of his own, implying his junior status. During the fracas Peter all but drew his sword to attack his cousin.[6] Peter IV's view of the Majorcan issue is recorded in his own memoirs which insist, at considerable length, that the original grant of a kingdom to James II of Majorca 'was not valid in law, for the gift was an immense one and took away the greater or a great part of the patrimony of the house of Aragon'.[7] Peter devoted exactly one third of his memoirs to the conquest of Majorca in 1343, thus giving the events of a single year a massively disproportionate amount

6. There is a detailed account of their differences in Book 3 of the *Chronicle of Peter the Ceremonious*, and the importance Peter attached to this issue can be gauged from the fact that the king of Aragon took so much care to state his claim against the king of Majorca, an event which took place early in a lengthy reign.
7. *Chronicle of Peter the Ceremonious*, Book 3, cap. 3 (Hillgarth edn, vol. 1, p. 228).

of space in his autobiography; but he needed to present himself as both a conquering hero in the best Aragonese-Catalan tradition and the stickler for correct legal form that he undoubtedly was.

As tension grew in the years around 1340, accusations and counter-accusations flew back and forth between Barcelona and Majorca. The king of Majorca was said to have tried to kidnap the king of Aragon during a visit to Barcelona; his galley was moored next to a seaside palace, and a closed wooden bridge was constructed from the ship to the palace. James would spirit Peter away without anyone noticing.[8] Moreover, James ignored the longstanding agreement that the king of Majorca should not mint his own coins in Roussillon, where Catalan money circulated. And James was known to be making polite noises to the king of England, with a view to a marriage alliance; the English possessions in Gascony lay no great distance from the Majorcan ones in the southern Pyrenees, and such an alliance could threaten Aragonese interests in the region.[9] Finally, James sent expeditions to the Canary Islands in 1342, to claim them for Majorca and to create bases there for a two-pronged assault on Muslim Africa.[10] In short, he appeared too determined on his independence from Aragon.

Peter issued a summons to James, who was to present himself in due form to be judged for his delinquent acts at the Catalan *Corts*, where he clearly intended to divest him of his lands and rights. But by failing to appear, James became a contumacious vassal, and in 1343 Peter IV riposted by attacking Majorca. As in 1285, there was no sudden upsurge of enthusiasm for the Majorcan monarchy. The mainland territories too were overwhelmed in 1344, though there Peter encountered more resistance. Only Montpellier and nearby lands were left in the hands of James III; and, desperate to raise money with which to pay an army, James sold Montpellier to the king of France in 1349. He attacked Majorca with his followers, but was almost immediately killed in battle,

---

8. *Chronicle of Peter the Ceremonious*, Book 3, caps. 16–17 (Hillgarth edn, vol. 1, pp. 246–7).

9. Abulafia, *Mediterranean Emporium*, p. 201.

10. F. Fernández-Armesto, *Before Columbus. Exploration and colonisation from the Mediterranean to the Atlantic, 1229–1492* (London, 1987), pp. 156–9.

leaving a small son (James IV) who was never able to claim his inheritance though, as has been seen, he later married Queen Joanna of Naples. Majorca became another of the constituent crowns within the Aragonese-Catalan union, governed by a lieutenant; the mainland possessions reverted to their role as counties within the principality of Catalonia (as it was increasingly termed); but in the short term the Majorcans could hope for greater prosperity as a result of their reintegration into the wider Catalan trading world, and Peter IV celebrated his coronation as king of Majorca with generous grants to the island's inhabitants, including trade privileges. What Peter had gained was a strategic advantage that was well worth having; so long as Sardinia remained recalcitrant, the existence of a naval base half way between Catalonia and Sardinia would be very valuable; and so long as the Genoese remained hostile, following their losses to the Catalans in Sardinia, control of Majorca would strengthen Catalan influence in the western Mediterranean.[11]

As desired, the conquest of Majorca brought the young king of Aragon the popularity he needed; but other problems refused to disappear completely. In Valencia and Aragon 'Uniones' were formed, as restive barons and towns sought to gain greater influence over the internal affairs of the Crown of Aragon. The Unionists expressed disquiet at the king's choice of advisers, as well as worry at plans for the succession, since Peter still had no surviving male heir; they insisted on the confirmation of ancient liberties. Peter very reluctantly met the opposition at the *Cortes* of Saragossa in 1347, and made fulsome concessions; but the conflict turned uglier, with the Catalans showing broad support for the king, and the other Spanish states turning against him. Peter was essentially saved from humiliation in Valencia by the arrival of plague in 1348; proving the maxim 'nothing succeeds like success', Peter stormed his way to victory at a new *Cortes* in Saragossa, where he publicly dissolved the Union, defacing its seal and burning its records. Valencia proved slightly harder to crack, but here too the king scored a decisive victory by late 1348. Even so, Peter had not solved the central problem: the challenge to royal authority emanated from a

11. P. Cateura Bennàsser, *Política y finanzas del reino de Mallorca bajo Pedro IV de Aragón* (Palma de Mallorca, 1982).

contractual interpretation of the relationship between the king and his greater subjects. Catalonia and Aragon were seen from this perspective as constitutional monarchies, in which the consent of the barons was conditional on good governance. The developing legend of the oath of Sobrarbe, fully articulated in the sixteenth century, presented the first kings of Aragon as lords who had promised to respect the rights of their followers, and who expected in return the loyalty of those followers, but 'if not, not'.[12] Later in Peter's reign, the most forceful exponent of this 'pactist' outlook was the prolific Franciscan Francesc Eiximenis.

The crushing of the Unionists came at the right moment; the Black Death also brought in its wake the outbreak of yet another in the sequence of wars between Genoa and Venice. As usual, the origins of the war must be sought in the competition between the Italian republics for control of the trade routes leading through the Aegean to the Black Sea. However, the war spilled over into the western Mediterranean as well, where Genoa and Aragon had plenty of scores to settle over the question of control of Sardinia; the Venetians saw a perfect opportunity to bottle up the Genoese in the west, sending their own fleets to join those of the Aragonese off Sardinia. Peter obliged by providing some Catalan naval aid off Constantinople. His difficulties increased as the situation within Sardinia became ever more unstable; Alghero was a focus for rebellion, and the treatment of its inhabitants only served to accentuate the sense on the island that the Catalans had come as an alien force of conquerors, out for their own good. In 1354 the Sards of Alghero were sent packing, and the city was repopulated with Catalans, so successfully that the Catalan language could still be heard on its streets in the late twentieth century.[13] Sard rebels were sent as slaves to the Balearic islands, where it was hoped they would help restore population levels and cultivate abandoned

---

12. R. Giesey, *If Not, Not. The oath of the Aragonese and the legendary laws of Sobrarbe* (Princeton, NJ, 1968).

13. A. Mattone, P. Sanna, eds, *Alghero, la Catalogna, il Mediterraneo. Storia di una minoranza catalana in Italia (XIV–XX secolo)* (Sassari, 1994); J. Carbonell, F. Manconi, eds, *I Catalani in Sardegna* (Milan, 1984; also in a Catalan edition, Barcelona, 1984); A. Rognoni, M.F. Arcioini, *Altre Italie* (Milan, 1991), pp. 181–97, all of which contain material on the Catalan dialect of Alghero.

or desolate land, for instance in Minorca; the experiment was not a success. The general tone of Aragonese rule was to treat the Sards as a subject people in all respects comparable to the conquered Muslims of southern Spain, even though they were in fact Christians. The harsher the rule, the stiffer the opposition; the rulers of Arborea, having invited the kings of Aragon into the island, were now in full flood of rebellion, and the Sardinians simply refused to simmer down: Mariano II of Arborea raised the standards of rebellion again in 1358, and an Aragonese invasion force was humiliated in 1367. All this cost a fortune, not least when, in 1371, Peter tried to unleash English mercenaries on the island. The ambition was to capitalise on the resources of an island which offered good amounts of grain, salt, pastoral products and silver, but it is doubtful whether the balance sheet for Sardinia was ever anywhere other than in the red. By 1400 the Aragonese had lost all but some of the fringes of the island, around Alghero in the north-west and around the major city of Cagliari, in the south-east. The kings of Arborea dominated the interior and developed a successful administrative system under a series of rulers of whom the most famous was the regent Eleonora of Arborea, who has a special reputation as a legislator. If Aragonese rule were to become a reality on the island, it would quite simply need to be reconquered.[14]

There were other wars that cost Peter more than he could really afford, and brought him no more advantage. The clearance of the seas off Gibraltar in around 1342 had been a rare example of Castilian-Aragonese cooperation. Thereafter, Peter went out of his way to pick a quarrel with his namesake Peter I (Pedro the Cruel), king of Castile, resulting in a long drawn out war from 1355 to 1366. The official excuse was interference by Basque sailors in Majorcan shipping, the unofficial motive apparently border adjustments between Aragon and Castile, notably around Murcia. In any case, Pedro was an ally, as Castilian kings in the past had tended to be, of the Genoese, who had major bases in southern Spain, notably at Seville. If it was Peter IV's intention to enlarge the Venetian-Genoese war into a Catalan-Castilian

---

14. F.C. Casula, *La Sardegna aragonese*, 2 vols (Cagliari, 1990), vol. 2, for the evolution of an independent Arborea.

one, it was an ill-advised move that very nearly cost him an exorbitant price: Pedro sent Castilian ships against the Balearic islands, and managed to grab some lands for himself from Aragon. The solution to his difficulties was to ally himself with the bastard rival of Pedro, Pedro's half-brother Henry of Trastámara; there is something ironic in the spectacle of a king of Aragon who claimed to have suffered much from his own half-brother, who was such a stickler for legal right, and yet who supported Henry's revolt against the undoubtedly merciless Castilian king. The danger went further still, since the English supported Pedro and the French Henry. The assassination of Pedro by Henry in the king's tent in 1369 put an end to this disagreeable problem.[15]

Peter IV was well aware that his difficulty in securing control over the economic resources of Sardinia made it all the more imperative that he should not lose access to the resources of Sicily, whose independent dynasty he bonded to himself by a sequence of marriages, including his own wedding in 1349 to Eleonora of Sicily. The ultimate aim was, clearly enough, to secure the complete reversion of the island to the house of Aragon, but it was difficult to engineer the extinction of the Sicilian royal line, all the more so since female succession was well established in the Sicilian royal family. Attempting to force his way into Sicily, Peter sent a fleet to the island on two occasions, in 1378 and again in 1382, and finally he carried off the Sicilian heiress Maria, who was taken to Barcelona with a view to marriage to the heir to the throne of Aragon. The Sicilian question had not been resolved when Peter died in 1387, but the outcome would be a union of Sicily and Aragon in the person of his second son Martin I of Aragon, II of Sicily.

Peter IV sought to assert the right of Aragon to play a major part in the politics of fourteenth-century Europe. He was highly conscious of the achievements of his predecessors of the house of Barcelona. He interpreted their success in spreading the Catalan-Aragonese banner over the Mediterranean islands as a sign of God's providential outlook towards

15. C. Estow, *Pedro the Cruel of Castile, 1350–1369* (Leiden, 1995), for something of a rehabilitation; excerpts of the key chronicle of López de Ayala may be found in *Las muertes del Rey Don Pedro*, ed. D. Ridruejo (Madrid, 1971).

the royal dynasty. No earlier king of Aragon had been so clear in his mind that all the territories under the rule of princes of Aragonese descent, Majorca and Sicily as well as the mainland Spanish lands, had to be united under a single sovereign. Equally, it was becoming obvious that the monarchy faced as strong a challenge as in any of the European kingdoms from the theorists and practitioners of a limited monarchy that would rule by consent of the great estates.

. . .

MARTIN THE ELDER

In view of the care that Peter the Ceremonious took to ensure that worries about the succession were settled, and that the cadet houses of Aragon were drawn back under the authority of the king of Aragon, it is ironic that the decades after Peter's death were marked by increasing uncertainty about the succession. Peter's heir John or (in Catalan spelling) Joan I died without male heir in 1396, to be succeeded by a brother, Martin, whose own son, also Martin, had married the heiress to Sicily; but this same son predeceased his father, leaving the throne of Aragon unexpecedly vacant by 1410.

John I's brief reign, from 1387 to 1396, was marked by tension: the *Corts*, critical of royal extravagance at a time of economic uncertainties, demanded the reform of the king's household and the banishment from court of those who were thought to be leading the king and his luxury-loving queen astray. There were uncomfortable parallels with events in contemporary England, where another ruler with grandiose ideas of his office, Richard II, met even tougher opposition. The difference was that Richard developed an uncompromising political programme, which finally brought him to deposition, while John I was all threats and bluster. On the other hand, John's external relations were a mixture of successes and failures. An attempted invasion in 1390 by the count of Armagnac, who believed he had a claim to the throne of Majorca, was defeated. To head off such challenges, John arranged a marriage between his daughter and the possible claimant Duke Louis II of Anjou-Provence; in the long term, however, this created a claim in the house of Anjou-Provence to the throne of Aragon, which would be revived over seventy years later. Around this time the Catalan duchy of Athens finally succumbed to pressure from the Italian mercenary leader Nerio Acciaiuoli. The Mediterranean islands proved more problematic than John apparently expected, with a major uprising in Sardinia under the aegis of Eleonora of Arborea, a figure who has acquired legendary stature in Sardinia. The result was that the zone of Aragonese influence on the island shrank still further, and no longer even included the rebellious city of Sassari. In Sicily, the hope of securing an easy succession for Martin the Younger, as husband of Princess Maria, faced growing opposition from the barons, who saw the arrival of a Catalan prince as a threat to their already extremely extensive liberties, and who erupted in rebellion in 1393.[16]

Violent uproar was not confined to the more distant lands of the Aragonese commonwealth. The economic difficulties that enveloped Barcelona and the Catalan towns included not just depopulation after repeated attacks of plague but banking crises, the emergence of a populist opposition party, known as the *Busca*, in Barcelona itself, and growing difficulty in maintaining regular supplies of precious metals for the mint, with serious effects on the health of the Catalan monetary system. Among the rural peasantry, too, there was agitation by the many unfree serfs jealous of the liberty of other peasants who had managed to escape the imposition of feudal obligations such as labour services and marriage fines (the *mals usos*, or 'bad customs'). The monarchy was generally sympathetic, now and later, to the unfree peasants, and often showed support for the *Busca* against the more patrician *Biga* faction that had dominated Barcelona in the past. It is in this context that the outbreak of violent anti-Jewish pogroms must be understood. Increasingly isolated from the rest of urban society by their enclosure within reserved areas of the city, or *Calls*, the Jews became the target of fierce preaching campaigns in 1391, first of all in southern Spain, where Ferrán Martínez, archdeacon of Ecija, led a virulent campaign which in June 1391 exploded in anti-Jewish violence on the steets of Seville, the major centre of Jewish population in the south of the kingdom of Castile.

16. The accession of Martin I and II in Sicily has been discussed already: see pp. 160–2 *supra*.

Political boundaries were no barrier to the spread of the pogroms towards Valencia and Barcelona, and even, by 1392, to Sicily. On 9 July 1391, in Valencia, a crowd of thugs began to abuse the Jews. A few managed to penetrate into the ghetto area, which was walled off. They then found themselves trapped behind closed gates which the Jews refused to reopen for fear of letting in the mob baying outside. The result was that the Christian mob assaulted the ghetto walls, found a way in, and began to massacre the defenceless Jews. Jewish property was seized. Jews were forced to convert under threat of death. Throughout Spain vast numbers of Jews underwent immediate forced conversions, either at the point of a sword or out of terror at the certain consequences of what would happen if they refused to convert.[17]

In Majorca, too, violence could not be contained. Here, social unrest was certainly a major factor. What began as a march on the governor's residence by a motley crowd of discontented peasants was deflected from Bellver Castle on the edge of the city into an attack on the Jewish *Call* in Majorca City which left very many dead, and many others forcibly baptised. As the violence exploded, townspeople joined the peasants in slaughtering Jews and despoiling their property. In Girona, an important Jewish centre, there were demands for the abolition of taxes levied at the city gates; in other words, the attack on the Jews was part of a wider set of issues. In Barcelona, massacres broke out on a Sabbath afternoon in August, and many of the Jews who escaped with their lives fled to the New Castle, only to find themselves besieged by a peasant militia. Faced with starvation, the Jews came out, to find that what faced them was once again the choice between death and baptism. Many women in particular are said to have refused to convert, and to have been massacred.

The artisans and peasants involved in these ugly events had other ambitions, too. The issue was not simply the hatred for Jewish beliefs and practices which Ferrán Martínez had spread to such deadly effect. The city of Barcelona seemed about to fall under mob rule; vigorous demands, under threat of death, were made against rich Christian citizens and even against clerics, for – though enemies of the Jews – the rioters

17. Y. Baer, *A History of the Jews in Christian Spain*, 2 vols (Philadelphia, 1961), vol. 2, pp. 95–169.

were not necessarily defenders of the established Church. Demands for tax concessions resulted in the halving of a wine tax and an official enquiry into the management of city finances. Meanwhile the monarchy, which consistently defended its Jewish subjects against such outrages, began to clear up the mess, arresting the ringleaders, hanging some of them but often issuing pardons, which had to be paid for. King John I wrote to the city officials of Perpignan, where the persons, but not the property, of the Jews was saved by bringing the Jews into the castle, that 'Neither civil nor canon law allow that a person should be made Christian by force; this can only happen in complete freedom.'[18] The authorities were well aware that attacks against the Jews led to a serious breakdown in public order, and what is striking about the events of 1391 is the way that social grievances overlapped with anti-Jewish pogroms. The whole Crown of Aragon seemed powerfully infected by a resentment of the Jews that had deep roots not merely in religious rivalries but in the need to find a scapegoat at a time of economic uncertainty and social convulsion.

John's successor, Martin I, was in Sicily at the time of his brother's death, and was not faced with a smooth succession; a number of French nobles mounted stiff challenges, gaining some support within the realm. It was only in 1399 that Martin went to Saragossa for his coronation, an indication how long it took to suppress the troublemakers. In Sicily, King Ladislas of Naples was making mischief by supporting the anti-Aragonese factions. In Sardinia, the succession to the kingdom of Arborea was being contested by the viscount of Narbonne. It was thus an achievement for Martin to pursue hard the recovery of royal rights. Alienations of crown lands under Peter IV and John I had reached a dangerous level, undermining the ruler's ability to derive significant revenue from his lands, and depriving him of jurisdictional powers even in the heartlands of Old Catalonia. Martin was well aware that his political survival depended on a delicate relationship with the *Corts* and *Cortes* in his Spanish lands, and he managed his parliaments well, securing from some meetings, in Aragon and Valencia, grudging support for the recovery

18. P. Wolff, 'The 1391 pogrom in Spain. Social crisis or not?', *Past and Present*, 50 (1971), pp. 4–18.

of crown lands, and from other meetings help against Muslim piracy and other afflictions. In 1398–99 raids into north Africa, licensed as crusades by Pope Benedict XIII, and in 1403 a treaty with the king of Tunis, helped ease the danger of Muslim piracy.[19]

Martin took events in Sardinia seriously. He was also the first Aragonese king to set foot, though briefly and without lasting results, in the other half of the kingdom James II had won: Corsica. The recovery of control in Sardinia warranted a decision to commission Martin of Sicily, here acting not as king of Sicily but as an Aragonese general, to invade Sardinia. The expedition began with Martin the Younger's arrival in late 1408, and proceeded very satisfactorily, culminating in victory in June 1409, only to be followed in three and a half weeks by the death of young Martin, who was a victim of the widespread malaria with which the island was infested. Martin the Elder had been pursuing relentlessly Peter IV's grand stategy in attempting to keep the Italian islands securely under Aragonese-Catalan rule. It seemed at the height of Martin I's rule in Aragon that the foundations had been laid for the integration of Sicily and Sardinia into the Aragonese federation. But the unexpected price of empire-building in Sardinia and Sicily was the extinction of the house of Barcelona: Martin the Younger had no heir, and Martin the Elder outlived him by less than a year.

· · ·

THE COMPROMISE OF CASPE

There were no fewer than six reasonable candidates to succeed Martin, who had not actually named an heir; among them was Duke Louis of Anjou, member of a dynasty ever hopeful of a crown and never seeming to obtain one. However, the most potent were a great-grandson of Alfonso IV and son-in-law of Peter IV, James, count of Urgell; and a grandson of Peter IV, Ferdinand of Trastámara, often called Ferdinand of Antequera after a resounding victory he had scored against the Moors. James had received a few signs

---

19. R. Brunschvig, *La Berbérie orientale sous les Hafsides*, 2 vols (Paris, 1940–47), vol. 1, pp. 220–3.

of approval from Martin, notably his nomination as royal lieutenant; but he damaged his reputation, perhaps irretrievably, when he was implicated in the murder of the archbishop of Saragossa, who was known to oppose his candidature. The danger was that the federation itself would disintegrate, though there were influential forces, such as Pope Benedict XIII, who were pulling vigorously the other way. The real victory was in creating a panel of nine electors drawn from the three major states, Catalonia, Aragon and Valencia, containing a combination of churchmen (in the majority) and eminent lawyers; and in June 1412, at Caspe, the nine declared that after long study they had determined Ferdinand of Antequera to possess the best claim, as Martin's closest relative. This was a somewhat surprising argument, because, whatever Ferdinand's virtues, there were others, including even the king of Castile, who might have better been able to press a claim based on closeness of blood ties. On the other hand, it is difficult not to be impressed by the way that the federation survived two years of interregnum, during which *Corts* met, administrators soldiered on, and even the far flung territories overseas were not after all lost, though there were strong moves in Sicily, predictably enough, to re-establish an independent monarchy. Open civil war did not break out, even though battle was joined between the parties of Ferdinand and James at Murviedro, in January 1412, with Ferdinand's men gaining the upper hand. But the battle did not decide the issue. That is crucial. It was the electors at Caspe, the well-named 'Compromise of Caspe', who determined the outcome.[20] It was a step into the unknown, certainly resented by some contemporary commentators, for Aragon-Catalonia to link itself so decisively to the Castilian royal family, and to a Castilian prince who spoke no Catalan but who retained vast tracts of land in Castile. Perhaps indeed the electors had the vision to see that this could mean not the domination of Aragon by Castile, but the domination of Castile by Aragon, so long as Aragon had effective rulers with decisive policies.

---

20. S. Sobrequés i Vidal, *El Compromís de Casp i la noblesa catalana* (Barcelona, 1973; originally published in article form in the *Anuario de Estudios medievales*, 7, 1970–71); F. Soldevila, *El Compromís de Casp* (3rd edn, Barcelona, 1994).

There was, of course, a reaction. James of Urgell invaded, hoping for English aid from Aquitaine, and penetrated to Lleida in Catalonia. But support inside the Spanish lands was not to hand. Indeed, the Aragonese and Catalan parliaments gave financial and moral support to Ferdinand I, in return for the usual guarantees that the king would respect the rights of the *Corts* and *Cortes*. This straightforward approach appealed to his subjects, and helped earn him the sobriquets conferred by later historians, Ferdinand the Just and Ferdinand the Honest.[21] Before long Count James was in Ferdinand's hands, and safely in prison.

Well aware of the dangers that stemmed from his contested succession, Ferdinand rapidly obtained papal confirmation of his title to both Sicily and Sardinia. He even appointed his second son John viceroy of Sicily, thereby hinting politely that Sicily would neither be neglected nor be allowed to resume its complete independence from the kings of Aragon; later, in 1469, the heir of John II, Ferdinand II, would even take the title 'king of Sicily' while remaining based in Spain. Winning the approval of Benedict XIII was a clever enough move at the time, but the continuing scandal of the schism in the papacy was accentuated by Pope Benedict's refusal to resign the Holy See, which was now contested by two other would-be popes. As the Council of Constance unwound the Great Schism, with the result that Martin V was eventually elected pope in 1417, Benedict became increasingly isolated, and by 1416 Ferdinand himself had realised that there was no advantage in supporting this obdurate old man. It is perhaps an exaggeration to asssign to Ferdinand a key role in ending the schism, given that Pedro de Luna paid no attention to his abandonment by the king of Aragon, holding out in deluded isolation in his palace at Peñiscola.[22] Looking westwards, Ferdinand had no difficulty in securing the approval of Castile for his acquisition of the Aragonese crown, though in the longer term the acute instability of Castile meant that few advantages were to be gained from cooperation between the kingdoms.

---

21. The short work by I. MacDonald, *Don Fernando of Antequera* (Oxford, 1948) is not entirely satisfactory.
22. A. Glasfurd, *The Antipope (Peter de Luna, 1342–1423)* (London, 1965) offers a quirky biography of Benedict XIII.

Mention must also be made of a rare change in outlook among the kings of Aragon on one issue: Ferdinand was less keen to resist attempts to coerce the Jews into conversion than his predecessors or his successor proved to be; the Disputation of Tortosa in 1413 was held in a difficult atmosphere, in which leading Churchmen unashamedly denounced Judaism in a spirit some way removed from that of Ramón Llull a century earlier. Royal support for the conversionist campaign was itself stimulated by the enthusiasm shown by the antipope Pedro de Luna for anti-Jewish measures. Such pressures, in the wake of the pogroms over twenty years before, greatly accelerated the decline of the Jewish communities of Aragon, so that by the middle of the fifteenth century Castile greatly overshadowed Aragon-Catalonia in numbers of unconverted Jews. The loss of the Jewish administrative and even intellectual elite to Christianity was a dire blow from which Aragonese Jewry failed to recover. For this reason, Ferdinand II in 1492 could contemplate the expulsion of the remaining Aragonese Jews with relative equanimity; the major Jewish centre in the fifteenth-century Crown of Aragon was probably Sicily, rather than any of the Spanish lands.

The difficulties faced by an outsider in understanding the ancient and generous privileges accorded to the Catalans became obvious when the new king refused to pay to the city of Barcelona a tax on the food supplies needed by the royal household, objecting that all clerics, as well as all the nobility, were exempt from such a tax. Ferdinand had the good sense to settle up before leaving Barcelona, but the incident left a sour taste. Soon after this incident he died at the age of about thirty-seven. His achievement lay in simply managing to have himself accepted as king without Aragon undergoing great convulsions. He did not solve Catalonia's problems; but he survived the crisis of his accession, and in doing so enabled the federation of states that he ruled to survive as well. The Compromise of Caspe must, in any case, be seen as a crucial moment in a much longer transition from the end of Peter IV's long reign to the vigorous reassertion of Aragon's Mediterranean interests under Ferdinand's successor Alfonso the Magnanimous, a period not just of political but also of economic uncertainty, in the wake of the Black Death and vicious trade wars.

· · ·

CONCLUSION

The fourteenth century, which saw such difficulties emerge in southern Italy and Sicily, was for Aragon-Catalonia a time when its rulers began to articulate a more coherent conception of their territories as an organic unity, bound together by political loyalty and by trade. The reconquest of autonomous Majorca and Roussillon by Peter IV of Aragon in 1343 was a clear statement that the authority of the crown extended over even the grandest of its supposed vassals. Peter's own idea of kingly authority, soundly based in his reading of biblical texts, has to be seen as well as a response to the challenge that existed within his lands, where the idea of a limited monarchy bound by some sort of contract with the community of the realm was more and more persistently pressed by the *Corts*, and later on by such theorists as Francesc Eiximenis. Peter expressed his sense of royal dignity through his love of courtly display, which has earned him the sobriquet 'the Ceremonious'. He needed to gain control of the resources that would emanicipate him from dependence on his parliaments, and this was not a new problem; but Sardinia proved an increasingly heavy liability, drawing Peter IV and Martin I into bitter wars with the Genoese, who also had interests on the island, and with the local kings of Arborea. Beyond Sardinia, Peter eyed Sicily, and by the end of his reign it was clear that the kings of Aragon intended to put to an end the independent Sicilian monarchy, just as they had earlier put to an end the Majorcan one.

The years either side of 1400 saw serious problems emerge. Social tensions in Aragon-Catalonia were clearly expressed in the anti-Jewish pogroms of 1391, which the Aragonese crown sought to restrain, but which resulted in the virtual collapse of the once glorious Jewries of Catalonia-Aragon. The process was hastened by a public disputation at Tortosa in 1413–14, when the Church set out, with the approval of the new king and the antipope, to humiliate the Jews. This king, Ferdinand I, had only gained the throne after the house of Barcelona died out in 1410. The transition from the ancient dynasty to the Castilian house of Trastámara was effected remarkably smoothly, and yet signs of tension were soon visible in, for instance, his disagreement over taxes owing to the city of Barcelona. As will soon be plain, these were unsettled times for the merchants of Barcelona, and the ability of the monarchy to soothe the fears of the powerful business community was to become a major issue in the fifteenth century.

PART III

FIFTEENTH-CENTURY VICTORIES

Chapter 9

ALFONSO THE MAGNANIMOUS AND THE FALL OF THE HOUSE OF ANJOU

. . .

JOANNA II, 'THE STRAW QUEEN'

The reign of Joanna II of Anjou (1414–35) expressed neatly all the difficulties that had been piling on the dynasty's head in Naples since the contest between Joanna I and her rivals, and the victory of the Durazzo branch of the house of Anjou. Joanna II was credited with more lovers than Joanna I had husbands, a sordid reputation that grew in the telling. What is more certain is that she had an ability to change her mind, or worse still not quite to make up her mind, that played further into the hands of the south Italian baronage and into those of aspirants for her throne. Pope Martin V excommunicated Joanna II in 1419, declaring that the house of Anjou-Provence was entitled to wear her crown; not surprisingly the queen looked elsewhere than the rival Angevin house for an heir, nominating Alfonso, king of Aragon and Sicily in 1421, but then backtracking in 1423, and giving Duke Louis III of Anjou the right to succeed, a claim which then passed to his heir René, of whom more shortly. This see-sawing created instability within the *Regno*, even before competing armies descended on the kingdom's shores. Other examples of her inconsistency are legion: favours to a Jew-baiting friar, Giovanno da Capestrano, led to a sudden reversal of the traditional royal policy of protecting the Jews, and soon Joanna herself was persuaded to abandon the friar and to renew the privileges of the Jews. Joanna's Grand Seneschal Gianni Caracciolo was a member of a leading south Italian noble family, and his undue influence, which appeared to extend inside the royal bedroom, led to his assassination in 1432. Equally disastrous was her decision to show favour to a family of mercenary captains from outside the *Regno*: Muzio Attendolo and his son Francesco, both called Sforza ('strongman'), were looking for land and titles like many another *condottiere* who originated among the Italian petty nobility, but even the acquisition of estates in southern Italy did not ensure the loyalty of the Sforzas.[1]

Thus under Joanna II tendencies already clearly visible under Joanna I gained further impetus: the power of the nobility was accentuated, as families such as the Carraciolo, Sanseverino and Balzo Orsini (princes of Taranto, and lords of much else besides) learned that it was possible to exercise power as effectively by paying little attention to an ineffective and mercurial monarch as it was to try to mould that monarch's policy in their favour. Ultimately, they determined what happened on their vast estates; they, and not the crown, increasingly controlled the income from the towns or from the growing pastoral sector. Most importantly, it was the barons who exercised military power, many of them offering their services for money, as did the formidable Jacopo Caldora and as did the Caracciolo.[2] Since the monarchy was the object of competition between the house of Anjou-Durazzo, that of Anjou-Provence and that of Aragon, there were plenty of opportunities to earn fame and funds as a soldier, and to increase control over alienated royal lands as well. As Alfonso of Aragon was eventually to realise, it was not possible to dismantle such formidable power at a stroke; what was needed was the formulation of a new policy towards the nobility which would bring internal peace and restore the finances of the crown.

How empty, then, were all the titles on Joanna II's tombstone: 'Here lies the body of Joanna II by the grace of God queen of Hungary, Jerusalem and Sicily, of Dalmatia, Croatia, Bavaria, Serbia, Galicia, Lodomeria, Romania, Bulgaria, countess of Provence, Forcalquier and Piedmont.' She was a 'queen of straw', *una regina di paglia*, lightly tossed back and forth between competing factions of nobles and between

1. L. Boccia, *Giovanna II. Una regina di paglia* (Naples, 1980) is a colourful biography, but the 'queen of straw' epithet in the title is apposite.
2. N.F. Faraglia, *Studii intorno al regno di Giovanna II d'Angiò* (Naples, 1895, repr. Cosenza 1990), pp. 11–18.

claimants to a crown whose grand titles were no more than an empty façade.

. . .

RENÉ OF ANJOU

René of Anjou is one of those figures whose political importance lies not so much in what he achieved as in what he failed to achieve. His significance lies too in a formidably positive reputation going back at least to the sixteenth century, and still perpetuated by those seeking to promote interest in the châteaux of the Loire or of the lower Rhône, where *le bon roi René* has become the symbol of chivalry, bonhomie, splendid display and moral rectitude.[3] His impact in the cultural sphere, both as a capable author and as a patron of the arts, has to be set against a political career which brought him the promise of the crown first of Naples and later of Aragon, as well as strategic territories delicately situated on the eastern edge of France. His political sensibilities were built on a code of honour which had little appeal to those Italians he sought to bring under his control or influence; arguably he was no match for the brilliant scheming of the Sforzas or the Aragonese kings of Naples. His fundamental political principle was the vindication of the ancient rights of the house of Anjou in the Mediterranean; but the framework within which he worked was that of an Arthurian hero. His rivals, Alfonso of Aragon and his heir Ferrante, had a keener understanding of how to create successful and lasting political relationships within the Italian peninsula.

René had no great reason to expect a throne. He was born in 1409, but an elder brother, the future Louis III of Anjou, stood to inherit the duchy of Anjou and county of Provence as well as the claim to southern Italy that Louis I and II had already, after endless labour, failed to make real. René's mother, Yolande of Aragon, was in the long term to supply him with a claim to succeed to the Spanish lands 'usurped' by the house of Trastámara after the Compromise

3. Typical examples of the romantic genre of biography are J. Levron, *Le bon roi René* (Paris, 1972), and M. Miquel, *Quand le bon roi René était en Provence (1447–1480)* (Paris, 1979). The authoritative history of the reign remains that of A. Lecoy de la Marche, *Le roi René*, 2 vols (Paris, 1875), but it is thin on his Italian campaigns.

of Caspe. His own immediate prospects seemed to lie in the borderlands between France and Germany, a sensitive area in which his second cousin Duke Philip the Good of Burgundy was also carving out wide domains. Granted the duchy of Bar by his uncle, a cardinal without descendants, by 1431 René also acquired the duchy of Lorraine by marriage. His father-in-law advised him: 'watch out for the duke of Burgundy. Never do anything against him. Live in peace with the Burgundians.' But this was easier said than done. René, already an admirer of Joan of Arc in the war against the English king, became sucked into the politics of what is now eastern France with disastrous results, supporting the French crown against the potent alliance of England and Burgundy; the result was severe defeat at the hands of the Burgundians and their allies at Bulgnéville in July, 1431, and the consignment of René to captivity at Dijon.

It was while René was a prisoner that news came of the premature death of his brother Louis III of Anjou, far away in the toe of Italy in November 1434. He had no children; René was now in line to succeed Joanna II as ruler of Naples. Indeed, he possessed a double claim: as descendant of Louis I, who had been recognised as heir by Joanna I, but never made good his claim; and as heir of Joanna II, whose own father had displaced Louis I. The prospect was renewed of a great Angevin dominion incorporating both Provence, lost to the kings of Naples since the coup d'état of Charles of Durazzo, and southern Italy.[4] The problem was, of course, that Alfonso, king of Aragon, had also been nominated heir to Naples by the feckless, confused Joanna II; and, whereas the king of Aragon was hard at work building his influence in the western Mediterranean, René was locked in a prison in the heart of continental Europe. Hopes became slimmer still as news arrived of the death of Joanna II in February 1435, and as the duke of Burgundy confined René in ever more miserable conditions, to secure a promise that he would in future keep out of Flemish politics.[5]

4. R. Duchêne, *La Provence devient française, 536–1789* (Paris, 1976), pp. 70–1; despite its title this useful book concentrates heavily on the fifteenth century.
5. A. Ryder, 'The Angevin bid for Naples, 1380–1480', in David Abulafia, ed., *The French descent into Renaissance Italy, 1494–5. Antecedents and effects* (Aldershot, 1995), pp. 55–69.

Then things began to improve: the duke's terms were accepted; an embassy to Filippo Maria Visconti was well received in Milan in June 1435; René's arch-rival Alfonso fell into the hands of the Genoese at the battle of Ponza in August 1435, after which Alfonso was passed to the Milanese duke as overlord of Genoa. In the Summer of 1435 both of Joanna II's possible heirs were actually prisoners; but, knowing his release was imminent, René despatched his wife Isabelle of Lorraine to Provence and thence to Gaeta. On her arrival in the *Regno* the Angevin queen discovered that, far from being able to rely on the full-bodied support of the Milanese, René had been completely abandoned by the duke of Milan, who was so charmed by his royal captive Alfonso that he had made peace with him.[6] The immediate consequence was that both Isabelle and Alfonso were able to establish themselves in southern Italy, the king of Aragon in Gaeta and the duchess of Anjou in Naples itself. The duchess understood that three factors would really determine who could be king of Naples. One was the outlook of the Neapolitan barons, who had acquired such extensive landed power since the mid-fourteenth century. Another was the support of the other Italian states, which was compromised by the defection of Milan and the studied neutrality of Venice and Florence. The third plank on which Angevin success would have to rest was the support of the papacy, which after all claimed suzerainty over the kingdom of Naples. Pope Eugenius IV was irritated by Alfonso the Magnanimous for supporting unfriendly factions at the Council of Basel which sought to set limits to papal authority. It is thus not surprising that, once he had firm news of a solid Angevin presence in southern Italy, he lent it support by approving René's claim to the throne in February 1436. Even so this was a papal gamble: Isabelle was short of funds, and René did not arrive in Naples to lead the campaign until May 1438; meanwhile mercenaries, under the formidable Jacopo Caldora, had to be paid, and money was so short that the duchess found herself pledging her jewels to raise funds. Moreover, the Aragonese made steady gains in the

6. G. Peyronnet, 'The distant origin of the Italian wars: political relations between France and Italy in the fourteenth and fifteenth centuries', in Abulafia, *French descent*, pp. 38–9.

hinterland. But the clearest sign that the battle was far from won by René was the seizure by the Aragonese, in early 1437, of the two seaside fortresses of Naples itself, the Castelnuovo or Maschio Angioino, built by Charles I of Anjou, and the Castel dell'Ovo in the harbour.

René's lack of firm direction is perhaps seen in his tendency to concentrate on the clearance of Aragonese supporters out of the northernmost region of the *Regno*, the Abruzzi, when the prime target should have been consolidation of Angevin power around the capital. René operated under the illusion that the Abruzzi themselves could serve as a power base from which to sweep down on the Aragonese forces which remained in command of much of the coastline between Naples and the papal states. With the death of Jacopo Caldora in November 1439, and his replacement by his son Antonio, René perhaps learned his lesson about the geography of the *Regno*; he travelled north in the depths of winter, poorly supplied, meeting his demoralised mercenary captain in the Abruzzese capital of L'Aquila; but Antonio Caldora was disenchanted. In 1440 he led his troops into what was supposed to be a decisive engagement against Alfonso at La Pelosa, only to fail to commit his men to the battle on the grounds that perhaps it was too risky after all. What might have been René's historic victory turned into an indecisive encounter that gave Alfonso the chance to regroup and return to combat another day. René's attempt to punish Caldora by imprisoning him indicated, too, the risks that a would-be Italian ruler could run in antagonising his *condottieri*. Caldora's supporters turned ugly and the duke of Anjou had to release his prisoner, who then predictably enough offered his services (gratefully accepted, for a suitable fee) to the king of Aragon.

By now it was becoming clear that René had lost his chance to hold the *Regno*. Naples was under full-scale Aragonese assault from November 1441; the siege lasted until June 1442, and only ended when, in imitation of tactics adopted by the sixth-century Byzantine general Belisarius, the Aragonese dug a tunnel into the city and sent through some soldiers who then opened the gates to Alfonso's army. The magnanimous king of Aragon allowed René to depart without interference; he sailed to Genoa, still a pro-French base in Italy, and thence retired via Provence to his lands in the Loire valley. Yet, even though his attention focused in the next few years on the struggle of Charles VII against the English, in which René served the French king loyally, the duke of Anjou was incapable of forgetting his Italian ambitions.[7] What marks out René's Italian campaign of 1438–42 from his later campaigns is the increasing involvement of the French monarchy in René's schemes, to the extent that it was sometimes the French king, rather than the titular king of Sicily, who appears to have pushed hardest. In 1453 René won the approval of Charles VII for another Italian expedition which Charles saw as an opportunity to strengthen his ties with the Sforza duke of Milan. René entrusted the management of his campaign to his son Jean, titular duke of Calabria; the fall of Genoa to the Angevins in 1458 provided René with a bridgehead for another invasion of southern Italy.[8] Yet the occupation of Genoa was a political calamity; Francesco Sforza, ever subtle in his conduct of diplomacy, realised that it was one thing to be able to call on the French for political and military aid in a crisis, but quite another to have a French presence on his doorstep, in a city over which Milan too had claims. A general Italian peace had been patched together following the Peace of Lodi in 1454–55, which guaranteed the security of the five major Italian powers, Milan, Venice, Florence, the papacy and Naples. Thus Sforza lost interest in René; Jean's own successes and final defeat in southern Italy, at the hands of King Ferrante, between 1458 and 1465, will be examined shortly; but failure in Naples resulted only in the rebellion of Genoa against the French and thus in further humiliation for the house of Anjou.

That the foundations had been laid for the French descent into Italy in 1494 is clear. René's close association with Charles VII, and Charles VII's ambitions in Genoa, where the French flag had fluttered periodically since the 1390s, certainly resulted in the view within Italy that the 'Franzesi' had become a menace and must be cleared out of the peninsula. It was not always easy to distinguish Jean de Calabre's strategy for the conquest of southern Italy from wider French hopes of hegemony in Italy.

7. Lecoy de la Marche, *Roi René*, pp. 263–88.
8. Ryder, 'Angevin bid', pp. 64–5; Lecoy de la Marche, *Roi René*, pp. 288–95.

The later career of René and Jean reveals a continuing restlessness. René married his daughter Margaret to the English king, Henry VI, amid hopes of sealing a peace between France and England; he remained loyal to King Louis XI when the new king faced internal opposition within France. Attractive, all the same, was the offer that reached René in 1466 of the title to Aragon and Catalonia. Louis XI had taken advantage of the revolt of the Catalans against John II to seize Roussillon and Cerdagne, though he expressed himself ready to accept a ransom for their return to the king of Aragon. Louis could hardly object if the Catalans also identified in René, as the son of Yolande, a princess of the defunct house of Barcelona, a possible replacement for the ruler they now rejected, who was in any case a member of the 'foreign' house of Trastámara, of Castilian descent. René accepted the Catalan offer with aplomb, adding the gold and scarlet bands of Catalonia to his already elaborate escutcheon. *Renatus dei gratia Rex Aragonie Hierusalem Sicilia citra et ultra Farum Valencie Maioricarum Sardinie et Corsice Dux Andegavie et Barre Comes Barchinone Provincie Forcalquerii ac Pedemontis etcetera*: he laid claim from 1466 to all the Aragonese territories, including the Italian islands and the Balearics (which had even earlier been summoned out of thin air to act as part of a planned, and highly fantastic, dowry for his daughter Margaret).[9] Jean de Calabre scored impressive successes on his father's behalf, and was installed in Barcelona itself when, at the end of 1470, he suddenly died; short of resources, the Angevins had been chased out of Spain by the end of 1471.

René offers an instructive contrast to the Aragonese kings of Naples in the character of his patronage. The Provençal court of Louis I and II had acted as points of contact with the culture of early Renaissance Italy, though by the time of René, contact with Italian culture was primarily expressed in the presence at his court of Italian exiles such as Roberto di Sanseverino.[10] The set of values that predominated were those of what might be termed 'late Gothic culture': an

9. A good number of René's kingdoms and duchies are portrayed heraldically on the coat of arms of the Cambridge college his daughter helped found, Queens'; on heraldic devices at René's court, see C. de Mérindol, *Les fêtes de chevalerie à la cour du roi René* (Paris, 1993).
10. A. Coville, *La vie intellectuelle dans les domaines d'Anjou-Provence de 1380 à 1435* (Paris, 1941).

emphasis on chivalric duty, on feats of arms and public display as well as on chivalric literature.[11] René himself is said
to have been a painter of passable merit, who learned his
craft while imprisoned by the duke of Burgundy at Dijon;
he was certainly a distinguished poet, and his *Livre du Cuer
d'Amours Espris* ('The Book of the Heart of Captive Love'),
of 1457, is a major fifteenth-century poetic discourse on
the nature of love, an allegorical fantasy concerning the
adventures of the knight Cuer, or Heart, who travels with
his faithful squire Desire to find Lady Mercy, trapped by
Danger in the lands of Rebellion.[12] The work was influenced
both by the celebrated *Romance of the Rose* of the thirteenth
century and by the Arthurian tale of quest for the Holy
Grail. Whether the quest in any way reflects René's political
travails, amid rebellion and danger, is a more difficult question to answer.

A vigorous patron of tournaments, René's cult of chivalry
found strong political expression in the foundation of a
chivalric order based on the duke of Burgundy's *Order of the
Golden Fleece*. René's *Order of the Croissant* or Crescent was
founded in 1448. The motto of the order was *los en croissant*,
'increasing honour' or 'honour in increasing'; it has been
suggested that here too is a political reference, to the aim of
increasing the Angevin domains. Fifty knights of impeccably
noble birth, able to show no fewer than four generations of
noble descent, were elected to the order. Vassals from Lorraine, Bar, Anjou, Maine, Provence but also Naples populated
the ranks of the Croissant; it was the only institution binding
together René's scattered subjects.[13] Though second to none
in his love for gorgeous display, René was not blind to the
practical uses to which his passion for chivalry could be put.

11. de Mérindol, *Fêtes de chevalerie*; also fundamental is F. Piponnier,
   Costume et vie sociale. La cour d'Anjou, XIVe–XVe siècle (Paris/The Hague,
   1970).
12. For the illustrations, see F. Unterkircher, *Le Livre du Cueur d'Amours
   Espris* (London, etc., 1975); for the text, S. Wharton, ed., *Le Livre du
   Cuer d'Amours Espris* (Paris, 1980). Bizarre and muddled claims have
   been made that the illuminations in the Vienna codex of this work
   reveal that René was the guardian of secret knowledge about the loca-
   tion of the Grail and of the 'tomb of God' in southern France, all of
   which proves that René has lost none of his standing as a cult figure.
13. M. Reynolds, 'René of Anjou, king of Sicily, and the Order of the
   Croissant', *Journal of Medieval History*, 19 (1993), pp. 125–61.

At the end of his life (he died in 1484, the year after Louis XI), René's political hopes met yet another dead end. He had no surviving male heir, and those he nominated to succeed him proved incapable of resisting French royal pressure, and Louis XI took advantage of his weakness to seize Lorraine, Bar and Anjou itself by 1474. In 1486 Provence too, though technically outside France, passed to the French crown. It was the young king of France, Charles VIII, who inherited from René not just his lands across France, but also the fateful claim to the crown of 'Jerusalem and Sicily'. But it is now necessary to turn back to the Aragonese conquest of Naples in order to understand Charles VIII's own plans.

· · ·

THE CONQUEST OF NAPLES

Ferdinand I was succeeded by a son, Alfonso V of Aragon, IV of Catalonia, II of Sicily, I of Naples, who was slowly to bring together under his rule all the lands which have been discussed in this book: southern Italy, Sicily, Sardinia, the Spanish territories of the Crown of Aragon.[14] During his long reign (1416–58), he thus established the framework within which later rulers, such as Ferdinand the Catholic and Charles V, would exercise dominion in the western Mediterranean. Alfonso the Magnanimous was arguably the first beneficiary of a gradual upturn in the Mediterranean economy, which became visible by the middle of the fifteenth century. Indeed, he may have done something to stimulate this upturn, by creating an Aragonese-dominated lake in the western Mediterranean across which the Catalans and their allies could sail and trade. But it is necessary to turn back to the earliest stages of his involvement in southern Italy in order to identify the main currents of his Mediterranean policy.

Very soon after becoming king of Aragon in 1416 he made it plain that he intended to complete the work of Martin the Elder, looking out from Spain towards the Mediterranean islands. His first target was a new focus of interest that

14. A. Ryder, *Alfonso the Magnanimous King of Aragon, Naples, and Sicily 1396–1458* (Oxford, 1990) is the unrivalled account of the reign.

had only attracted Martin among his predecessors: Corsica. Rockier and more impenetrable than Sardinia, Corsica was less rich in the grain and minerals that made Sardinia so desirable, and it had long been dominated first by the Pisans, latterly by the Genoese. Even then, it was the local barons who held effective power in the interior. There were strategic advantages in holding Corsica, however, for it lay between Sardinia and the Italian mainland, so that its possession could bolster the weak position of the Aragonese in Sardinia, and act as a lever against Genoese pretensions. Alfonso did secure some notable results: the strong fortress town of Calvi on the north-west coast came under his control, and a staircase cut into the steep rock of the impregnable citadel at Bonifacio on the southern tip of Corsica is still identified, perhaps wrongly, as 'King Alfonso's staircase'. Bonifacio proved too well defended for Alfonso, and he left the island in the charge of an ambitious local noble, Vincitello d'Istria, who was already far more powerful in Corsica than Alfonso. Aragonese influence in the island rapidly slipped away; but consideration of the Corsican scheme offers a valuable clue to Alfonso's wider intentions.[15]

Alfonso did not leave Corsica with great regret. New opportunities beckoned, now that Joanna II of Naples needed help against the combined forces of Louis III of Anjou and the mercenary captain Muzio Attendolo Sforza, father of the future Milanese duke Francesco Sforza.[16] Against such formidable enemies, Alfonso could count on the support of powerful south Italian barons such as the semi-independent prince of Taranto, a member of a branch of the eminent Orsini family. But the outcome of Alfonso's attempts to conquer Naples did not at first sight seem very encouraging; his final conquest of Naples in 1442 was the result of over twenty years of campaigning, first of all in 1420 in a war that culminated in the sack of Naples by the Catalan navy (1423).[17] In 1432 he was planning a further major offensive; the death of both Louis III and Joanna II in 1435 gave him an extra motive for pouncing on Naples, though, as has been seen,

15. Ryder, *Alfonso*, pp. 65, 82–9.
16. C.M. Ady, *A history of Milan under the Sforzas* (London, 1907), pp. 8–12.
17. Ryder, *Alfonso*, pp. 106–7.

Louis had an ambitious successor in René, duke of Anjou, Provence and Lorraine, who gained strong support among the powerful Neapolitan baronage. Alfonso sailed out with a large fleet, to find his way blocked off the Ponza islands by the Genoese navy. The battle of Ponza in August 1435 was a resounding military defeat; but it was turned by Alfonso into a brilliant diplomatic victory. The king of Aragon fell captive into Genoese hands, but Genoa was unable to keep hold of him, since the city was subject to the higher authority of Filippo Maria Visconti, duke of Milan, to whom Alfonso was despatched. Filippo Maria found himself enchanted by Alfonso, a man of considerable taste but also a capable negotiator. Between them, captor and captive worked out a master plan for the partition of the entire Italian peninsula, an old Visconti dream. The price Filippo Maria paid was uproar in Genoa, which became instead a focal point of opposition to Alfonso and of support for René.[18] Alfonso was soon back on the battlefield, operating out of Gaeta on the northern edge of the kingdom of Naples and the southern edge of the papal state, where Pope Eugenius IV showed distinct preference for René's claim.

On 2 June 1442 the long process of whittling away at the Angevin possessions in southern Italy culminated in the breakthrough into Naples, followed soon after by the defeat in battle of the mercenary captains.[19] The pope too had to accept defeat, and came to terms a year later, even allowing Alfonso temporary rights over the papal enclave at Benevento in the heart of southern Italy. Alfonso's illegitimate son Ferrante (Ferdinand) was recognised as heir to the throne of Naples; the tribute payable by the king of Naples to the pope was commuted into an annual gift of a white steed. Yet in a sense the pope had not done badly out of this arrangement: he had avoided the humiliation of Alfonso making peace instead with the anti-pope, Felix V; and he had asserted his formal authority over the kingdom of Naples.

Once he had installed himself permanently in southern Italy in 1442, Alfonso treated his new kingdom as a springboard for more ambitious schemes in northern Italy, the Balkans and even the eastern Mediterranean. All this cost a

18. Ryder, *Alfonso*, pp. 205–7.
19. Ibid., pp. 210–305.

fortune, which Alfonso was ruthless in raising by heavy taxation, the sale of offices, loans from bankers; he sold the city of Cefalù in Sicily to a new master even though it was supposed to be free in perpetuity, and he sold one beneficiary some lands in Sicily on the express condition that even if he sold them again to someone else they were in fact the property of the original beneficiary.[20] On the other hand, it is increasingly doubted whether such policies had the devastating effect on the local economy that was once assumed; Epstein has shown how local initiatives, for example the establishment of new fairs, generated economic growth in fifteenth-century Sicily.[21] At one point it looked as if Filippo Maria Visconti intended to bequeath him the duchy of Milan, with the result that he would have been master of the two most powerful Italian states, but rebellion broke out after Filippo Maria's death, an 'Ambrosian Republic' was declared in Milan (1447–50), and finally Francesco Sforza, head of that *condottiere* family that had supported René against Alfonso in southern Italy, achieved his great ambition and installed himself in 1450 as new duke, anchored firmly in place by the fact of his marriage (as long ago as 1441) to Filippo Maria's daughter Bianca Maria; henceforth he took care to refer to himself as 'Franciscus Sfortia Vicecomes Dux Mediolani', Francesco Sforza Visconti, duke of Milan, a rare but significant example of the husband taking the wife's surname.

Having lost Milan, Alfonso perhaps lost his dream of re-establishing something like a Roman Empire in the Mediterranean. Nevertheless, elegant medals and grandiose

20. For a very negative view, see D. Mack Smith, *Medieval Sicily* (London, 1969), pp. 94–104, based on the works of C. Trasselli, several of which are collected together in C. Trasselli, *Mediterraneo e Sicilia all'inizio dell'epoca moderna (ricerche quattrocentesche)* (Cosenza, 1977); a more positive view of Aragonese finances emerges from W. Küchler, *Die Finanzen der Krone Aragon während des 15. Jahrhunderts (Alfons V. und Johann II.)* (Münster, 1983).
21. S.R. Epstein, *An island for itself. Economic development and social change in late medieval Sicily* (Cambridge, 1992); see also E. Sakellariou, 'The Kingdom of Naples under Aragonese and Spanish rule. Population growth and economic and social evolution in the late fiteenth and early sixteenth centuries', PhD dissertation, Cambridge University, 1996, indicating that developments on the mainland were in several respects similar.

sculptures in neo-classical style, such as the beautiful triumphal arch which still exists in Naples, portrayed Alfonso as the equal of the ancient Caesars.[22] Humanist scholars and poets rubbed shoulders at court; indeed, they were often one and the same person, such as the famous Pontano.[23] Further attention will be paid to the patronage of culture by the Aragonese in Naples when the reign of his son Ferrante is examined; in Alfonso, certainly, the political uses of his patronage of classical scholarship were only one dimension to his activities as a latter-day Maecenas, for he genuinely took an interest in his scholars' endeavours as well. It is interesting to see how his reputation was cherished as far away as the court of Burgundy, where the account of his conquests and career written in 1455 by the Naples courtier Beccadelli and by Aeneas Sylvius Piccolomini of Siena (soon to become the pope) was a favourite literary entertainment, translated into French between 1469 and 1476.[24] The idea that Alfonso's achievements would still be celebrated several years after his death was itself a powerful motive behind Alfonso's grandiose ambitions.

As a major player in Italian politics, Alfonso found himself caught in the rivalry of the five dominant Italian states: his own Naples, Milan, the papacy, Florence and Venice.

22. Jerry Bentley, *Politics and Culture in Renaissance Naples* (Princeton, NJ, 1987); for the arch, completed under his successor, see G.L. Hersey, *The Aragonese arch at Naples, 1443–1475* (New Haven, CT, 1973); also F. Patroni Griffi, *Banchieri e gioielli alla corte aragonese di Napoli*, 2nd edn (Naples, 1992); A. Cole, *Art of the Italian Renaissance Courts* (London, 1995); M. Hollingsworth, *Patronage in Renaissance Italy* (London, 1994); C. Woods-Marsden, 'Art and political identity in fifteenth-century Naples: Pisanello, Cristoforo di Geremia, and King Alfonso's imperial fantasies', in C.M. Rosenberg, ed., *Art and politics in late medieval and Renaissance Italy, 1250–1500* (Notre Dame, Ind., 1990), pp. 11–37.
23. José Carlos Rovira, *Humanistas y poetas en la corte napolitana de Alfonso el Magnánimo* (Alicante, 1990); on Pontano see: C. Kidwell, *Pontano. Poet and Prime Minister* (London, 1991); G. Vitali, *Giovanni Pontano e Iacopo Sannazaro* (Milan, 1944); G. Ferraù, *Pontano Critico* (Messina, 1983).
24. 'Les actions et paroles mémorables d'Alphonse roi d'Aragon et de Naples', transl. and ed. S. Lefèvre, in D. Regnier-Bohler, ed., *Splendeurs de la cour de Bourgogne. Récits et chroniques* (Paris, 1995), pp. 630–736. A recent American study (though written in Spanish) is N. Patrone, *Príncipe y Mecenas. Alfonso V en los 'Dichos y hechos' de A. Beccadelli* (New York, 1995), though the author does not mention some important literature on Alfonso as patron, notably Ryder, *Alfonso*, pp. 306–57.

Taking Milan and Venice as allies, he focused his attention on Florence, partly in the hope of asserting his own rule over the Tuscan coast around Pisa, though his first war with Florence ended in 1448 with defeat at Piombino, and his second (1452–54) did not long outlast the abandonment of his cause by his Venetian allies. For the years after 1454 were a period in which the search for stability within the peninsula was being actively promoted not just for its own sake, but in order to fend off the Turkish threat. The fall of Constantinople to the Turk in May 1453, an unthinkable event, prompted Venice and Milan to negotiate the Peace of Lodi in 1454, to which Florence soon adhered, then the papacy, and finally, in January 1455, the king of Naples.[25] Such an agreement had the added attraction of confirming both the Sforza dominion over Milan and the Aragonese dominion over Naples. A number of minor lords and cities were drawn in as well, such as Alfonso's close ally and military commander Federigo da Montefeltro, count of Urbino; Genoa adhered as an associate of Milan, but Alfonso still reserved the right to attack this outpost of Angevin pretensions. All this seemed to have been stabilised by the election in April 1455 of Alonso Borja, a subject of Alfonso V's from Valencia, as Pope Calixtus III; the Borgia pope was an old associate of Alfonso, but his surprising decision to refuse to confirm the rights of succession of the bastard Ferrante in Naples led to a rapid breach between king and pope; the effects of this will be examined more closely later. Within the papal states, there was considerable upheaval as a result of the attempts by the mercenary captain Jacopo Piccinino to challenge the power of Sigismondo Malatesta, the much feared lord of Rimini, and to establish a power base in supposedly papal Assisi; Piccinino's associate in this enterprise, Federigo of Urbino, was one of Alfonso's closes allies, and it was clear that he did not mind making trouble for the papacy.[26] The Peace of Lodi and the Italian League that emerged from it did not guarantee the tranquillity of Italy; yet the Peace remained a fundamental point of reference in Italian politics, a principle to which allies (as they had rapidly

25. Ryder, *Alfonso*, pp. 289–90.
26. For this alliance, see C.H. Clough, 'Federico da Montefeltro and the kings of Naples: a study in fifteenth-century survival', *Renaissance Studies*, 6 (1992), pp. 113–72.

become) such as Francesco Sforza and the king of Naples could appeal in attempting to resolve such issues as the continuing Angevin claim to Naples or collective action against the Turks. But neither the Italian League nor the Congress of Mantua (1459), called by the pope to discuss a crusade, resulted in serious action against the Turkish threat.

Alfonso had his own magnificent plans for dealing with the Turks. Where the money might come from to pay for them is another question. Indeed, in 1435, on Joanna II's death, he assumed the title 'king of Hungary' in recognition of Angevin claims to a kingdom that now stood on the front line against the Turks. In 1447 an agreement was drafted according to which he would supply the Hungarian Regent John Hunyádi with troops, but he sent them to Florence instead the next year, and the Hungarians went unaided to their defeat by the Turks in 1448. In 1451 fantastic plans were aired, not in themselves alien to the political traditions of the kingdom of Naples, whereby Alfonso or the Greek prince Demetrios Palaiologos would assume the throne of Constantinople in lieu of Constantine XI, the last emperor of all, who was to die fighting the victorious Turks two years later. More substantial was the military aid Alfonso provided to the Albanian rebel Skanderbeg (George Kastriotes), who had raised the banner of revolt in Kruja across the straits from Apulia. The proximity of Albania to southern Italy, the possibility of reviving past Neapolitan influence in the western Balkans, and the usefulness of Skanderbeg as a mercenary captain in Italy when not engaged in his anti-Turkish wars all made the Aragonese kings of Naples by far the most enthusiastic supporters of the Albanian revolt. Others such as the Venetians were distinctly lukewarm towards Skanderbeg. Alfonso also took care to cultivate influence along the western coast of Greece, appointing a grandly titled 'viceroy' at Castrovillari in the Peloponnese. His relationship with the Mamluk sultans of Egypt was rather ambiguous, but he sent occasional squadrons of Aragonese ships out of Naples into Egyptian waters, to make plain his claim not merely to be king of Sicily, Hungary and much else, but also (like previous kings of Naples) king of Jerusalem.[27] All this reeks of past

---

27. A. Ryder, 'The eastern policy of Alfonso the Magnanimous', *Atti dell'Accademia Pontaniana* (1979).

Angevin policies, in the days of Charles I and his immediate successors, and the continuities in foreign policy across the centuries are certainly a distinctive feature of south Italian politics.[28] For Alfonso was not rejecting the Angevin past out of hand; he claimed to be the rightful successor to Joanna II, and he and his own successors wore the Angevin lilies of France on their elaborate coat of arms. Another, wider, recognition of the Catalan *imperium* in the Mediterranean can be found in mid- to late fifteenth-century Catalan literature; two early novels, *Curial and Guelfa* and *Tirant lo Blanc*, built their romantic plots around tales of war and conquest as far afield as Sicily and Greece, the former taking as its time frame the War of the Sicilian Vespers, the latter developing the fourteenth-century tale of Guy of Warwick into a massive evocation of Mediterranean warfare that would later move Cervantes.[29]

Alfonso's ambitions led to the neglect of Spanish affairs; Aragon, Catalonia and Valencia were governed on his behalf by viceroys, a system that worked most effectively when they were members of the royal family, such as his estranged queen.[30] His brother John, king of Navarre, became Lieutenant-General in the Spanish mainland territories for some years. On the other hand, the non-royal governor of Catalonia Galcerán de Requesens was given a hard ride by the Catalans, a point which confirmed the residual loyalty to the royal family, even when Alfonso seemed completely engaged with Italian affairs. Good claims have been made that under Alfonso a central council emerged which saw as its brief the administration of the entire Aragonese-Catalan commonwealth; but the problem became (after 1442) the difficult one of governing Spain from Naples, and it was always the Italian territories that were most fully and consistently represented on the council, while provincial councils under

28. For Alfonso and the Balkans, see also M. Spremić, *Dubrovnik e gli Aragonesi (1442–1495)* (Palermo, 1986), pp. 50–55.

29. P. Waley, transl. *Curial and Guelfa* (London, 1982); D.H. Rosenthal, transl., *Tirant lo Blanc* (London, 1984); see also P. Waley, 'Historical names and titles in *Curial e Güelfa*', in A.D. Deyermond, ed., *Medieval Hispanic Studies presented to Rita Hamilton* (London, 1976), pp. 245–56.

30. For one important aspect of Alfonso's Spanish policy, see L.M. Sánchez Aragonés, *Cortes, Monarquía y Ciudades en Aragón, durante el reinado de Alfonso el Magnánimo* (Saragossa, 1994).

211

the Lieutenant-General dealt with more local Spanish issues. Representatives of the various kingdoms could be called to Naples to attend the council when matters of general import were raised; and the council could be enlarged into a virtual parliament to discuss major Italian problems such as the peace with Milan and the plans for crusades. Naples also became the seat of a high court of appeal.[31] In all this, Alfonso took care not to irritate his Italian subjects by flooding the administration with Catalan officials; such as there were melted away on hearing news of his death in 1458. Financial administration was undoubtedly compromised by the rapid squandering of anything Alfonso had managed to raise either on armies or on magnificent display; not for nothing was he to become known as Alfonso the Magnanimous. His reception for the Holy Roman emperor Frederick III von Habsburg, who visited Alfonso in Naples in 1452, was of quite staggering splendour, though of course there were ample political dividends: this was the first occasion since Hohenstaufen times – when emperor and Sicilian king were one and the same – that an emperor had visited Naples, so that the stolid and impressionable Frederick thereby conferred a seal of approval on the kingdom's rulers.[32]

Still, Alfonso could not avoid his bankers totally. His administration in southern Italy sought to build on the ancient bureaucratic structure of the Norman, Hohenstaufen and early Angevin state, and to re-establish effective government that would meet the king's financial needs through taxation. Alan Ryder has argued that Alfonso's Naples was one of the first 'modern states', meaning that it was administered by a bureaucratic administration staffed by professionals, that the crown was dominant over the nobles and the clergy, that its income was derived from universal taxation, and that the army of the kingdom was recruited and paid directly by the

31. A. Ryder, 'The evolution of imperial government in Naples under Alfonso the Magnanimous', in J.R. Hale, J.R.L. Highfield, B. Smalley, eds, *Europe in the late Middle Ages* (London, 1965), pp. 332–57; cf. J.N. Hillgarth, *The Spanish Kingdoms, 1250–1516*, vol. 2, *1410–1516, Castilian hegemony* (Oxford, 1978), pp. 257–8.
32. Ryder, *Alfonso*, pp. 349–57. Bishop Stubbs described Frederick's reign, rather uncharitably, as 'the longest and most boring in German history'.

crown.[33] Some of these are features that are arguably visible much earlier; in 1443 the viceroy of Gaeta found himself reissuing emergency powers against robbers that had first been introduced under Charles I of Anjou. It was not always a question of new methods, but of effective ones. Particularly important, however, was a novel way of dealing with the nobility. Alfonso's fundamental problem was that he had to persuade the barons and bureaucrats who had been loyal to René of Anjou – of whom there were a great many – to accept the new order, and here he was strikingly successful. Giorgio d'Alemagna, count of Buccino, had been loyal to René to the end; but, if anything, loyalty was a virtue, and Alfonso cleverly found a place for him in the royal council as early as 1444. Barons who were prepared to accept him were confirmed in their lands, even if this meant confirming grants made in the bad days of Joanna I and Joanna II, when royal estates had been handed out right and left. Several barons had obtained jurisdiction over capital crimes, something that under the Normans and Frederick II had, at least technically, been reserved to the crown. There was thus a serious danger of the erosion of royal rights, and to hold this in check Alfonso appointed a conservator of the royal patrimony in Naples, whose job was the preservation of those royal rights that remained. (Similar officers already existed in Spain and Sicily.) And then, working within the established political traditions of Catalonia-Aragon, Alfonso sought to raise money through votes of funds in the Neapolitan parliaments. In 1455, for instance, he was able to obtain funds for the building of a flotilla of galleys which at least notionally were to serve on crusade; to achieve this, his parliament agreed to a one-fifth levy on provisions and salaries. Such bargaining was completed largely behind the scenes; but the nobles knew well enough that they could transfer much or all of the tax burden to those who lay under their authority. Alfonso thus seemed to be appeasing the barons at a time when they had become the effective rulers of the south Italian provinces; he saw no future in a challenge to those who had in the past supported his Angevin rivals precisely because the

33. A. Ryder, *The Kingdom of Naples under Alfonso the Magnanimous* (Oxford, 1975).

house of Anjou was seen as compliant towards the interest of the greater barons. 'Centralisation' could thus occur in the bureaucracy far away in the capital at Naples, but it would not involve any serious challenge to baronial power in the localities.[34]

Another important source of revenue was the taxation not of humans but of sheep. Once again, it would be a mistake to assume that this policy was completely novel; as far back as King William the Bad in the late twelfth century the kings of Sicily had legislated concerning the sheep of the Apulian plains. From 1443 onwards the kings of Naples brought the system under ever greater control. Sheep were especially lucrative now, since the population decline after the Black Death had liberated much land for grazing, and demand for pastoral products was also holding firm. The *Mena* was an organisation in some respects similar to the Castilian *Mesta* which made arrangements for the winter and summer pasturing of transhumant sheep and cattle, and collected taxes for the crown based on the number of head; the great distinction between *Mena* and *Mesta* was that the former was much more firmly under royal, the latter under noble, control. In the 1440s the *Mena* was producing about 50,000 ducats per annum for the crown, by 1450 twice that. The increase in revenue reflects a prodigious increase in the registered animal population of the kingdom, from 424,642 sheep and 9,169 cattle in 1444/5 to 1,019,821 sheep and 16,490 cattle in 1449/50.[35]

Finally, Alfonso recognised, from his stance in Naples, the useful economic role of the Jews; back home in Aragon-Catalonia as well he does not appear to have shared his father's enthusiasm for strong-arm tactics against the remaining Jews. To say that he had one eye on the economy in

34. A valuable survey of institutional developments is E. Sakellariou, 'Institutional and social continuities in the Kingdom of Naples between 1443 and 1528', in David Abulafia, ed., *The French descent into Renaissance Italy, 1494–95. Antecedents and effects* (Aldershot, 1995), pp. 327–53.

35. Ryder, *Kingdom of Naples*, pp. 359–63; J.A. Marino, *Pastoral economics in the Kingdom of Naples* (Baltimore, Md., 1988), pp. 20–4; Sakellariou, 'Kingdom of Naples'; A. Grohmann, *Le fiere del regno di Napoli in età aragonese* (Naples, 1969); also M.A. Visceglia, *Territorio feudo e potere locale. Terra d'Otranto tra Medioevo ed età moderna* (Naples, 1988), for other agrarian developments.

formulating his attitude is not to deny him more than a touch of humanity in dealing with his Jewish subjects, which sets him apart from his father Ferdinand of Antequera.

.   .   .

THE CATALAN CRISIS

There were, indeed, severe social and economic tensions within Catalonia which were in danger of being overlooked while the king was on constant campaign in Italy. Part, perhaps a quarter, of the peasantry remained unfree, subject to what were described as *mals usos*, bad usages, imposed by landlords anxious to draw on the large labour reserve the peasants offered, at a time when labour was in short supply and expensive.[36] The unfree (or *remença*) peasants agitated for release; since some were in fact fairly well off, they felt the humiliation of their status all the more, but they hoped to use their funds to pay the crown for a decree of redemption. There were about 20,000 households in early fifteenth-century Catalonia subject to these burdens, and the monarchy was keen to make money out of the decree; Alfonso at one point countered a bid of 64,000 florins from the peasantry of Girona with a demand for 100,000 florins. However, the parliament of Catalonia, the *Corts*, representing in part the noble opposition to these peasants, forced the monarchy to withdraw its support for the unfree peasants, voting the king 400,000 florins for the revocation of a decree of emancipation issued in 1455. Once the king had withdrawn his decree, the *Corts* had second thoughts and revoked its own handsome grant, leading to a reiteration of the decree in 1457. The issue was still up in the air when civil war broke out in Catalonia in 1462, and the *remences* were not surprisingly in the front line.

In the cities too there were signs of crisis. The pogroms of 1391 were not simply, as has been seen, a violent attack on the Jews, but expressed wider economic grievances too. A populist faction in Barcelona, the *Busca*, gained royal support in its attempts to unseat the old patrician *Biga*; led in part by cloth merchants, the *Busca* also offered a political home

---

36. Paul Freedman, *The origins of peasant servitude in medieval Catalonia* (Cambridge, 1991).

for the city's artisans and shopkeepers. *Busca* leaders sought to make Barcelona 'the head of the liberty of Spain'. But this was not just the florid empty jargon of politicians. The *Busca* had a radical programme of economic reform, or *redreç*, aimed at problems such as the money supply (there were serious shortages of gold bullion as a result of unrealistic official exchange rates for gold and silver in Barcelona).[37] The city banks had been in crisis since the 1380s, and even the creation of a public credit institution in 1401, the *Taula de Canvi* (pronounced 'Cambi'; meaning 'Table of Exchange'), had not restored faith in public finances, though it was given control over the city budget.[38] Indeed, there was a trend away from direct investment in trade towards the purchase of bonds and insurance contracts, which some have seen as harmful to the economic infrastructure. The governor Galcerán de Requesens was sympathetic to the *Busca*, bringing with him the support of the crown in the 1450s. But *Busca* policies proved unworkable, at least in the amount of time they were allowed to operate, and the more moderate elements became deeply concerned at the radicalisation of the movement by an extreme wing. The moderates joined forces with their former foes, and by 1460 the *Biga* was once again dominant, resentful at the failure of the monarchy to lend support to the Barcelona establishment. In the mid-fifteenth century social conflicts also affected another major centre of Aragonese economic power, the City of Majorca.[39] There the despoliation of the Jews had generated economic difficulties. During the early 1450s, there was violent conflict on the island between the rural peasantry and the citizens of Majorca City; this rebellion was handled badly by Alfonso, who took too long to crush it, at vast economic cost to the island. Of the major cities of the Spanish lands of Alfonso, only Valencia continued to experience the economic boom that had started in the 1380s, if not earlier.

The traditional picture is a rather gloomy one of the once great Catalan trading network now in steep decline. Yet it is

37. C. Batlle Gallart, *La crisis social y económica de Barcelona a mediados del siglo XV*, 2 vols (Barcelona, 1973).
38. A.P. Usher, *The early history of deposit banking in Mediterranean Europe* (Cambridge, MA, 1943), pp. 269–77.
39. Hillgarth, *Spanish Kingdoms*, vol. 2, p. 80.

also obvious that the picture is one of light and shade, the lightest part by far being the success story that was fifteenth-century Valencia, of which more presently. Barcelona's population plummeted in the late fifteenth century, to about 75,000 in 1483, but this was at the end of a trying period of civil war. Until the 1470s the keynote of Catalan economic life was crisis rather than decline. When Alfonso of Aragon conquered Naples in the 1440s he did so in the face of tough Florentine opposition; the Florentines had a strong hold on the economy of Naples. They were mostly kicked out, and it is striking how rapidly and successfully the Catalans filled the gap, becoming within very few years the largest group of foreign merchants in the city, and completely dominating its textile trade; they also traded intensively to Palermo, in Sicily, Alghero, in Sardinia, and to areas outside the Aragonese political orbit such as Rhodes. Out of 1,981 voyages recorded in Barcelona between 1428 and 1493, Sicily attracted 459 visits for trade purposes, about one-quarter of the grand total, with Palermo attracting just under half (220) of the Sicilian voyages. Sardinia attracted 334 visits, of which over half (186) were to the Catalan base at Alghero or L'Alguer. The kingdom of Naples scores 212, of which 137 were directed at Naples itself; the island of Rhodes, an important base for the Levant trade, scored 129. Some historians, such as the eminent Italian scholar Mario del Treppo, have argued that Alfonso was seeking to create a western Mediterranean 'Common Market' in the lands he ruled.[40]

The fifteenth century was a period of massive readjustment rather than of headlong economic decline. Old trading centres, including some of the great Flemish cities, had to change or die. So too in the Catalan world it was sometimes new areas that rose to prominence, areas that could, for example, respond rapidly to the fundamental changes in the pattern of demand that followed the population losses

40. M. del Treppo, *I mercanti catalani e l'espansione della Corona d'Aragona nel secolo XV* (Naples, 1972); cf. C. Carrère, *Barcelone centre économique à l'époque des difficultés 1380–1462*, 2 vols (Paris/The Hague, 1967), which points part of the way in the same direction. The old approach of P. Vilar, 'Le déclin catalan au bas Moyen Âge', *Estudios de Historia moderna*, 6 (1956–59), pp. 1–68, dominates that of J.H. Elliott, *Imperial Spain 1469–1716* (London, 1963), pp. 24–30, but cannot now be accepted.

generated by plague from 1347 onwards. Thus Minorca, long a pastoral backwater, became a major wool exporter by 1400, supplying the famous Tuscan merchant Francesco Datini, the 'merchant of Prato', with large amounts of wool; and Majorcan cloths made from Minorcan and other wools were in sound demand. It was only with the civil war of 1462–72 that a sharp decline set in, as Barcelona was incapacitated; even so, recent studies suggest that the merchants bounced back once the war was over.[41] Barcelona did not collapse; maybe it did not even decline; but it experienced lengthy crises and, during the civil war, severe recession.

The question of the 'decline' of Catalonia can be addressed from another angle. It is true that the once frequent sailings of Catalan and Majorcan ships to Flanders and England came to an effective end by the mid-fifteenth century. The other side of the coin is the increasing interest of Catalan cloth makers in English wool, brought in mainly on Italian ships. This new supply did much to stimulate the city's economy in the mid-fifteenth century. While the Italians and other foreign merchants now dominated the long-distance sailings into the Atlantic, the ships that passed through Aragonese waters were now visiting a more conveniently situated port than Barcelona: Valencia. Here there was a veritable economic boom in the fifteenth century.[42] In 1483 it may have had four times the population of Barcelona, though this is clearly an extreme contrast taken from Barcelona's worst years. Valencia was itself a source of rice, dried fruits and other luxuries typical of the Islamic world, many of which were less easily accessible elsewhere than they had been before because of the Turkish advances in the eastern Mediterranean. Their availability in Spain brought Flemish, German, Milanese, Venetian and other merchants to Valencia.[43] Another attraction was the magnificent 'Hispano-Moresque' pottery made to order in the area around Valencia for the nobility of Europe. The excellent

---

41. M. Peláez, *Catalunya després de la guerra civil del segle XV* (Barcelona, 1981).

42. J. Guiral-Hadziiossif, *Valence, port méditerranéen au XVe siècle (1410–1525)* (Paris, 1986); A. Furió (ed.), *València, un mercat medieval* (Valencia, 1985).

43. P. Mainoni, *Mercanti lombardi fra Barcellona e Valenza nel basso medioevo* (Milan, 1983), partially reprinted in Furió, *València*, pp. 81–156.

quality of the gold currency of Valencia in the mid-fifteenth century provides a curious contrast to the position in Barcelona, for different currencies continued to serve different parts of the Crown of Aragon.[44] The pogroms of 1391 apart, Valencia was a more tranquil setting than either Barcelona or Majorca, showing few of the bitter social conflicts that blighted those two rivals. The frequent residence of the royal court in Valencia, especially under Ferdinand I, stimulated local business and also helped strengthen ties to Flanders and other distant lands, visible in the increasing fondness for Flemish styles of painting.

It would also be a mistake not to take into account the evidence that in Aragonese-controlled Sicily there were vigorous attempts to stimulate economic activity, for instance by the patronage of fairs, with the result that a flourishing internal market was able to develop. Historians disagree on the extent to which Sicily was dominated by outside interests, that is, Catalan, Genoese and Tuscan merchants; the great landlords had plenty of opportunity to impose heavy burdens on their peasants, but local industries developed well in parts of the island, and the creation of a durable peace between Sicily and Naples ensured the renewed prosperity of the area around Messina. Alfonso's rapaciousness did not after all take the wind out of the sails of the reviving economy. As population recovered, both in Sicily and in Spain, the boom became more obvious: demand for Sicilian grain on the overseas market also picked up.

Yet the lack of resources of the monarchs made them increasingly reliant on votes of funds from the parliaments; the 'pactist' view of royal power grew in potency, according to which the king was in a contractual relationship with his subjects, and if he failed to respect their rights they could have recourse to their last and greatest right, that of denying the authority of the crown.[45] But it was not Alfonso who had to pay the price. After he died in 1458 his brother King John of Navarre succeeded him in his Spanish lands and in the Italian islands; Alfonso's illegitimate son Ferrante succeeded him in Naples. (Navarre itself reverted to the

44. E. Hamilton, *Money, prices and wages in Valencia, Aragon and Navarre, 1351–1500* (Cambridge, MA, 1936).
45. Hillgarth, *Spanish Kingdoms*, vol. 2, pp. 203–5, 247–8.

house of Foix and was not united to the rest of Spain until the early sixteenth century.) He had no legitimate heirs of his own. John II's own son Charles of Viana became the focus for opposition within Catalonia against a new king who seemed far more interested in bolstering his already powerful position in Castile than in addressing the region's problems. The dangers to the crown were seen in the civil war of 1462–72, a messy series of conflicts that involved the peasants, the towns, the *Corts* and even the king of France, Louis XI, who invaded the Catalan counties on the French side of the Pyrenees and supported the claims of René of Anjou to the throne of Aragon.[46] Although Valencia, Sardinia and Sicily supported John II, this was small consolation: it was in Catalonia that the conflict was really waged, with the *Diputació* of the *Corts* leading the struggle against the crown, itself supported by many of the nobility. There were no winners: Charles of Viana died even before conflict broke out, in 1461, and was said to have been poisoned. René of Anjou, elected king in 1466, was as short of funds as poor John, now sick and poor of sight. Barcelona, occupied for a time by the Angevins, suffered loss of population and loss of trade, to the distinct benefit of Valencia, which perhaps was the one real winner. In the midst of these events, at a time when the king of Aragon was desperate to clutch at any straw he could find, there took place the marriage of John's son Ferdinand to Isabella of Castile (1469); this came at a time when the ruling house of Aragon needed all the allies it could find against powerful external and internal foes. And even Isabella was not likely to be much help, sucked as she was into the bitter conflicts that dominated Castile at this time. The marriage united two royal figures who had aspirations to a crown, but little certainty of one.

.   .   .

CONCLUSION

The struggle for the crown of Naples between René of Anjou and Alfonso of Aragon was itself largely the product of the internal difficulties which were tearing the kingdom apart in

---

46. J. Calmette, *Louis XI, Jean II et la révolution catalane (1461–1473)* (Toulouse, 1903); Hillgarth, *Spanish Kingdoms*, vol. 2, pp. 267–99.

the early fifteenth century: to the indecisiveness of the highly susceptible Queen Joanna II was added the fractiousness of a baronage that saw in the weakness of the monarchy an opportunity to strengthen its own power in the localities. (A further ingredient was, of course, the unbridled ambition of King Alfonso, who at one time hoped to dominate all of Italy.) Such barons as the Prince of Taranto, of the family del Balzo-Orsini, partly Provençal and partly Italian in descent, established a degree of authority in their lands which fell not far short of that of a king. The trend towards regional statelets is in many ways reminiscent of that in northern Italy, where warlords taking employment as *condottieri* or mercenaries were able to establish regional states around Milan, Urbino, Mantua and other centres great and small, gaining the title of duke or count, and, despite often illegitimate origins, creating lasting dynasties. Such war captains were by no means absent in southern Italy as well, where the family of Muzio Attendolo, the Sforzas, earned their formidable reputation as skilled leaders of men, and were rewarded with grants of lands and favours, before going on to capture Milan in 1450. Although this may be overstating the contrast, René could be seen as the hero of those in southern Italy who believed that their interests were best served by a compliant monarch, willing to give due weight to the baronage, while the Aragonese were regarded as interlopers who would wish to favour their own followers. In the event, Alfonso was extremely careful to show regard for the baronage, and his solution to the problem of finding adequate sources of income was to leave the greater nobles in charge in the provinces, while relying on votes of funds through parliaments. Since his major concerns included projects outside the *Regno* – notably his over-ambitious plans to establish himself as ruler in the Balkans, Constantinople and, ultimately, Jerusalem – it was always the search for money rather than the internal affairs of his kingdoms that appeared to be uppermost in his mind. He was a ruler in the south Italian tradition, reminiscent of Frederick II in his appeal to the Roman past as a source of royal authority; and of Charles I of Anjou in his campaigns in Albania, Achaia and north Africa, and in his attempt to secure the kingdom of Hungary for his house. Though his rival René seems at times the very paradigm of fifteenth-century chivalry, Alfonso too was exposed as much to the cult of Arthur and the medieval heroes as he was to the classical humanism expounded by his brilliant staff of Italian advisers, men such as Beccadelli and Lorenzo Valla.

That this involvement in Italy and even further afield led to a neglect of Spanish affairs seems obvious. And yet the tradition of ruling the separate kingdoms of the Crown of Aragon through viceroys, generally close relatives, was already established. Still, Alfonso was unable to achieve within his Spanish lands the economic improvements that he desired: the policies of the *Busca* remained unenforced, and the unfree Catalan peasants remained unenfranchised. Conventionally, this is regarded as a period of severe economic crisis in Catalonia, but it is also plain that Alfonso's conquests had a regenerating effect on the economy of the Crown of Aragon, enabling Barcelona to forge newly intense links to conquered Naples, and generally stimulating trans-Mediterranean traffic in primary materials such as foodstuffs and in luxury goods. As, gradually, the population of Europe began to recover from the worst ravages of plague, the territories he ruled, notably Sicily and southern Italy, were well placed to experience economic revival; and one of the great success stories of his reign, and indeed of the fifteenth-century European economy, was the expansion of the sheep flocks of the Italian South. Here too the crown was able to benefit, by taxing the movement of sheep and creating for itself a constantly growing and very substantial source of income. The question that remained open was how these successes would be affected when the Kingdom of Naples was transferred by Alfonso's will to his illegitimate son Ferrante, while the rest of his lands went to Alfonso's younger brother John.

Chapter 10

ARAGON IN ITALY AND SPAIN, 1458–94

. . .

FERRANTE OF NAPLES

King Ferrante or Ferdinand of Naples, whose long reign stretched from 1458 to 1494, seems almost the embodiment of the Renaissance prince, sharing with his contemporaries in Milan, Ferrara and elsewhere a reputation for subtle diplomacy, duplicity and cruelty that has been vividly perpetuated in Jacob Burckhardt's characterisation of him in *The Civilisation of the Renaissance in Italy*: 'it is certain that he was equalled in ferocity by none among the princes of his time', and yet he was 'recognised as one of the most powerful political minds of the day', who avoided all other vices in order to concentrate on the destruction of his political opponents. He enjoyed above all having his enemies near him, 'either in well-guarded prisons, or dead and embalmed, dressed in the costume which they wore in their lifetime. He would chuckle in talking of the captives with his friends, and made no secret whatever of his museum of mummies'.[1] To this day, shrivelled corpses preserved in the vaults of the Castelnuovo at Naples are pointed out, rightly or wrongly, as Ferrante's victims. John Addington Symonds summed this attitude up by describing Ferrante as 'a demon for dissimulation, treachery and avarice', only moderating the force of his words by remarking that his son Alfonso II was even worse.[2]

1. J. Burckhardt, *The Civilisation of the Renaissance in Italy*, ed. P. Burke (Harmondsworth, 1990), pp. 40–1.
2. There is no proper biography of Ferrante in any language, despite his agreed importance in Italian fifteenth-century politics, and despite the existence of biographies of his father, daughter, cousin, grandson, etc.

This appalling reputation has its origins in the violent controversies that raged over the legitimacy of Ferrante's claim to the throne, and in the constant attempts of French princes to assert their own right to the kingdom of Naples, culminating in the descent into Italy by Charles VIII of France in 1494. The French chronicler Philippe de Commynes, who served Charles VIII as an ambassador in Italy, established for all time Ferrante's evil reputation, writing of Ferrante's son Alfonso, duke of Calabria, 'never was any prince more bloody, inhuman, lascivious or gluttonous, but his father was more dangerous still, since no one knew when he was angry or pleased'. Such images of the Neapolitan royal family served their purpose in justifying the French invasions of Italy.

Ferrante was born in Valencia around 1425, but raised in southern Italy and recognised as duke of Calabria, that is, royal heir, by the south Italian barons.[3] But the crown of Naples was not really in their gift, and Alfonso turned to the papacy for approval of Ferrante's claim to the throne. It has been seen that Pope Calixtus III ignored two of his predecessors' acceptance of Ferrante as heir to the throne and obstinately refused to accept him as king of Naples;[4] it was only with the unexpected death of Calixtus late in 1458 and the election as pope of the great scholar Aeneas Sylvius Piccolomini as Pope Pius II that Ferrante received the recognition he craved, largely because Pius was anxious to maintain the peace of Italy while planning a great crusade against the Turks.[5] It has been seen too that René of Anjou

The Neapolitan historian Ernesto Pontieri produced several editions of a volume of studies *Per la storia di Ferrante I re di Napoli* (Naples, 1947 etc.), but this is no more than a collection of valuable articles on specific aspects of the reign, and the projected *vita* was never written. A good introduction to the period is Jerry H. Bentley, *Politics and Culture in Renaissance Naples* (Princeton, 1987). There are studies of several key cultural figures by Carol Kidwell, notably her *Pontano. Poet and Prime Minister* (London, 1991); see also her *Marullus. Soldier poet of the Renaissance* (London, 1989); and *Sannazaro and Arcadia* (London, 1993).

3. E. Pontieri, 'La giovinezza di Ferrante I d'Aragona', *Studi in onore di Riccardo Filangieri*, 2 vols (Naples, 1959), pp. 531–601; see also Antonius Panhormita, *Liber rerum gestarum Ferdinandi regis*, ed. G. Resta (Palermo, 1968), which in fact only deals with his career before his accession.

4. M. Mallett, *The Borgias. The rise and fall of a Renaissance dynasty*, 2nd edn (London, 1971), pp. 60–78.

5. C.M. Ady, *Pius II* (London, 1913) and R.J. Mitchell, *The laurels and the tiara* (London, 1962) have rather little to say about the pope's relations

seized the chance of Alfonso's death to relaunch an invasion of Naples, by way of Genoa, but Angevin interference
there pushed Francesco Sforza, duke of Milan, even more
decisively into cooperation with Ferrante.[6]

As well as facing an external enemy, Ferrante faced internal
foes who were only too glad to seize the opportunity offered
by the renewed Angevin challenge to the house of Aragon.
Since the reign of Joanna I the south Italian baronage had
been able to claim for itself ever increasing autonomy, a
trend which was recognised by Alfonso the Magnanimous
when he reformed the tax system and the military organisation of the kingdom of Naples. In south-eastern Italy,
Giovanni del Balzo Orsini, prince of Taranto, exercised quasi-
regal authority over a vast swathe of lands, and Alfonso sought
to tie him to the crown by a marriage alliance between his
daughter Isabella and the young Ferrante; despite noticeable
differences of character, the couple remained devoted to
one another. And yet several key barons, most importantly
the prince of Taranto, were reluctant from the start to recognise Ferrante as king. An Angevin revival was seen as an even
surer guarantee of baronial autonomy than an Aragonese
succession. René's son Jean arrived in Italy and fostered
revolt among the south Italian barons; René tried to exercise
influence at the Congress of Mantua of 1459, summoned by
the pope to discuss plans for a new crusade; he presented
his cause as one that would also serve the crusade. Ferrante
worked hard to contain this first baronial revolt, building
close ties to the most important Italian princes, such as
Sforza, to whose daughter Ippolita his own son Alfonso was
betrothed; Ferrante's persistent message was that he had no
ambitions within Italy beyond the maintenance of the peace
of the peninsula. Ferrante keenly realised that his major
task was simply that of imposing order in southern Italy;
unlike his father, Alfonso, he possessed no great empire in
Spain and the Mediterranean which could offer him the

---

with Ferrante; see my contribution to *Montjoie*, ed. J. Riley-Smith and
B.Z. Kedar (Aldershot, 1997); and J.G. Russell, *Diplomats at work. Three
Renaissance Studies* (Stroud, Glos., 1992), pp. 60–7.

6. David Abulafia, 'The inception of the reign of King Ferrante I of
Naples: the events of summer 1458 in the light of documentation
from Milan', in Abulafia, *The French descent into Renaissance Italy. Antecedents and effects* (Aldershot, 1995), pp. 71–89.

means to dominate all of Italy. Several times Ferrante was on the verge of being destroyed; the battle of Sarno in July 1460 resulted in devastating defeat, from which Ferrante only recovered because the Angevins failed to follow up their advantage.[7] Moreover, the great Albanian military commander Skanderbeg, who spent much of his career fighting the Turks in his homeland, at the start of Ferrante's reign saved the king from almost certain defeat at the hands of Jean d'Anjou, using his Albanian *stradiot* soldiers to wear away the opposition by constant attrition.[8] The longer the war lasted, the less funds Jean could find to meet his needs; and the tables were turned at the battle of Troia in August 1462, but all the same Jean d'Anjou was not seen off until 1465, after a joint Neapolitan and Aragonese fleet destroyed the Angevin navy.

Revolt spelled treachery, and Ferrante was merciless to those who had stabbed him in the back. The mercenary captain Jacopo Piccinino had been seeking to carve out a principality for himself around Assisi, in the papal state, a position perilously close not merely to the borders of the kingdom of Naples but to other influential lordships, such as that of Sigismondo Malatesta, lord of Rimini and that of Federigo da Montefeltro, count of Urbino, a very close ally of King Ferrante. Frustrated in his ambition (partly because Ferrante himself failed to lend support for fear of damaging relations with the papacy), Piccinino served with his mercenaries in the Angevin armies. At the end of the war, in 1465, the victorious Ferrante invited Piccinino to his court in what was assumed to be an act of magnanimity. When the war was over, the mercenary captains traditionally had no special reason to fear recriminations; they were essentially apolitical, selling their services to the highest bidder. Besides, Ferrante offered Piccinino a safe conduct to attend his court. Nearly a month of feasting in honour of Piccinino, who had just married an illegitimate daughter of the duke of Milan, ended abruptly with the arrest of Piccinino, who then fell in suspicious circumstances out of a high window and died of his injuries. What aroused horror was the king's cynical

7. E. Nunziante, 'I primi anni di Ferrante I d'Aragona e l'invasione di Giovanni d'Angiò', *Archivio storico per le province napoletane*, 17–23 (1892–98).
8. F. Noli, *George Castrioti Skanderbeg* (New York, 1947) is still the best life of this figure.

behaviour, toasting the health of someone he had resolved to kill; yet this was also a message to those south Italian barons who contemplated further resistance; if a mercenary captain from outside the kingdom was dispensable, how much more so were they?[9]

The ambition of maintaining the peace of Italy was more easily proclaimed than achieved. Ferrante's persistent professions of friendship towards the other major powers within Italy, Sforza Milan, Venice, Medicean Florence and the papacy, were thrown off balance in 1478 when the enemies of Lorenzo de'Medici sought by assassination to put to an end the ascendancy of the Medici within Florence. The Pazzi conspiracy against the Medici, from which Lorenzo himself escaped, culminated in a joint papal-Neapolitan campaign against Florence; under pressure from the Neapolitan armies, the Florentine government allowed Lorenzo de'Medici to travel to see Ferrante in Naples and to negotiate a peace. This was portrayed at the time, in a letter from Lorenzo to the government of Florence, as a heroic gesture by a private citizen of Florence who was well aware how capricious the king of Naples could be, and who could easily find himself sharing the fate of Jacopo Piccinino: 'if our adversaries aim only at me, they will have me in their power'. Indeed, Machiavelli recounts that some of Lorenzo's enemies within Florence were hoping Ferrante would treat him as he had treated Piccinino. Yet it is also plain that Lorenzo and Ferrante knew the time had come for peace; Ferrante drew honour from his generous treatment of so mighty a foe as Lorenzo, while Florence was granted an equitable peace which also confirmed the Medicean ascendancy in the city. Ferrante began to regard Lorenzo as one of the chief guarantors of stability within Italy, constantly protesting his friendship and admiration for Lorenzo, even elevating him to the high office of Grand Chamberlain of the kingdom in 1483; Ferrante mourned Lorenzo's death in 1492, seeing it as a sign that the old order was dissolving.[10]

9. C.M. Ady, *A history of Milan under the Sforzas* (London, 1907), pp. 78–9.
10. R. Fubini, *Italia Quattrocentesca* (Milan, 1994); H. Butters, 'Lorenzo and Naples', in G.C. Garfagnani, ed., *Lorenzo il Magnifico e il suo mondo. Convegno internazionale di studi (Firenze, 9–13 giugno 1992)* (Florence, 1994), pp. 143–51; H. Butters, 'Florence, Milan and the Barons' War (1485–1486)', in G.C. Garfagnani, ed., *Lorenzo de'Medici. Studi* (Florence, 1992), pp. 281–308.

Yet the price of friendship for Florence was open papal enmity after years of tension beneath the surface; this break culminated in 1482–84 in an ugly war between Naples, Florence and Milan on the one hand and Venice and the papacy on the other over control of Ferrara, a territory that had long been a focus of disagreement between the north Italian states. The conflict further generated discord within the Neapolitan kingdom, resulting in the outbreak of a second baronial revolt in 1485–86, directed in large measure against royal attempts to rein in the power of the nobility.[11] Duke Alfonso of Calabria, the heir to the throne, was credited with plans to break the power of the nobility by establishing direct royal control over a great swathe of territory around Naples. Ferrante and his son had broken with the policy of King Alfonso, who had accepted the need to compromise with baronial aspirations to local autonomy, partly so as to raise funds for his ambitious adventures elsewhere in Italy and the Mediterranean; Ferrante, whose resource base extended no further than the shores of his Neapolitan kingdom, saw in the development of the towns and the creation of new alliances with the merchant elite an alternative support for the crown's authority. Indeed, the experience of his first years as king suggested that the barons could never be a reliable source of political support. The barons looked in vain for a new king; but René was dead and the French monarchy as yet uninterested. Yet there were still Angevin shadows over the *Regno*: the father of the new pope, Innocent VIII, had actually fought for René of Anjou against the Aragonese; Innocent now eagerly supported the rebels.[12] Ferrante had been right that the stability of his own lands depended on the wider stability of the Italian peninsula. It was the papacy

11. C. Porzio, *La congiura dei Baroni* (various editions since 1586: Naples, 1964, Milan, 1965, Venosa, 1989, etc.). For external effects, see Butters, 'Florence, Milan and the Barons' War (1485–1486)', pp. 281–308; H. Butters, 'Politics and diplomacy in late Quattrocento Italy: the case of the Barons' War (1485–1486)', in P. Denley, C. Elam, eds., *Florence and Italy. Renaissance Studies in honour of Nicolai Rubinstein* (London, 1988), pp. 13–31; see also P.C. Clarke, *The Soderini and the Medici. Power and patronage in fifteenth-century Florence* (Oxford, 1991).

12. E. Pontieri, *Venezia e il conflitto tra Ferrante I d'Aragona e Innocenzo VIII* (Naples, 1969), reprinting material published in the *Archivio storico per le province napoletane* in 1966–67.

that had sanctioned his succession to the throne; and disputes with the Holy See, over border territories and over the payment of annual tribute by the king of Naples, had particularly serious consequences in a kingdom whose barons were suspicious of attempts at royal centralisation and of the king's fiscal policy. Yet what is particularly striking about the revolt is that the ringleaders included new men who had risen to prominence from very modest backgrounds only as a result of royal favour, notably the millionaire Francesco Coppola, count of Sarno; Ferrante and his son had thus succeeded in alienating even some of those whom they had sought to elevate into a new, dependent nobility.

Apart from the pope, then, the rebels lacked really decisive external support, and 'how many legions has the pope?', as the famous question goes. Unable to crack royal power, the rebels decided to come to terms. They hoped that they had taught the king a lesson, and that government policy would be tailored to their needs. Ferrante appeared compliant. But in time-honoured fashion, he destroyed the opposition by inviting his leading foes, supposedly forgiven, to a conciliatory marriage feast in honour of the son of the leading rebel, the count of Sarno, and Ferrante's own grand-daughter. In the midst of the feasting he arrested the count and his allies, later also arresting many other powerful noblemen who had resisted him. Apparently those of his enemies who were not tried and publicly executed were murdered in prison, along with their families, whose bodies were supposedly dumped in the sea in sacks; 'to make people think that they were all still alive, the king continued to have food sent to them in gaol', the sixteenth-century historian Camillo Porzio reports. But one day the chief executioner was seen wearing a gold chain that belonged to the count of Bisignano. The secret was out.

Ferrante's wish for stabilisation within Italy reflected wider Mediterranean concerns; there was simply no time for the luxury of internal squabbles when a powerful external threat to all Italy existed in the east. A few years before the second baronial rebellion, the arrival of a Turkish fleet at Otranto in 1480–81 served as a bitter reminder that the kingdom of Naples now lay on the edge of the Ottoman world. The capture of Otranto was followed by the massacre of many of its inhabitants; twelve thousand out of its population of twenty thousand (including all the males in the town) were reported to have been put to death.[13] But the fall of Otranto also meant that the Turks were within a whisker of being able to shut the vital sea lanes down the Adriatic. The death of the sultan meant that the Turks suddenly lost interest in their Italian campaign; they were chased away by Alfonso of Calabria with the naval help of Ferrante's cousin Ferdinand king of Aragon, and Italy (including even the irate Pope Sixtus IV) united for once in support of Ferrante; but the strategic issue of control of the Adriatic ports of the kingdom of Naples remained an important one throughout the late fifteenth and the sixteenth centuries. Ferrante's close political and cultural links to Matthias Corvinus, king of Hungary, who married his daughter Beatrice, must also be seen as part of a far-sighted wider strategy of building a vast barrier against the Ottomans in the Balkans and the Adriatic.[14]

It was natural that, as an Aragonese prince, Ferrante should seek good relations with his Spanish cousins, who in any case controlled the neighbouring island of Sicily, which might also suffer badly if the Turks gained a stranglehold on the southern Adriatic and the Ionian Sea. Relations with Aragon were generally smooth, and there was little sense that Ferrante was in any way subordinate to his father's successors in Spain; King John II of Aragon had even helped resist the Angevin invaders at the start of Ferrante's reign. Yet Ferrante was immune to one major feature of Spanish policy in these years. In 1492 Ferdinand and Isabella expelled the Jews from all their lands in Spain and Italy; there was a massive influx of Sicilian and Spanish Jews into the kingdom of Naples which Ferrante openly welcomed. He saw the Jews as a valuable source of artisan skills, for many Spanish and Sicilian Jews were active in such crafts as cloth production; he also reveals, in his public documents, a genuine desire to protect the Jews in southern Italy from increasing persecution at the hands of their Christian neighbours. Such attitudes were rather rare by this time. In 1493 he protected the Jews against the accusation that they had brought pestilence with them

---

13. F. Babinger, *Mehmed the Conqueror and his time* (Princeton, NJ, 1978), pp. 390–2.
14. M. Spremić, *Dubrovnik e gli Aragonesi (1442–1495)* (Palermo, 1986), pp. 26–34, 55–8, etc.

from Spain and Sicily, at a time when Naples was struggling with an outbreak of plague.[15]

Certainly Ferrante was keen to establish manufacturing industries in southern Italy, notably the silk industry; and he aimed to fit out a royal fleet whose galleys could reach as far afield as England, entering into a treaty with Edward IV in 1468. He attempted to limit the sale of the Catalan and Majorcan cloths which were flooding into southern Italy, to give breathing space to local producers. Peace with Florence in 1479 brought with it handsome privileges for Florentine merchants, who offered invaluable financial help in the struggle against the Turks encamped at Otranto. There may be some validity in the suggestion that Ferrante was conducting an 'anti-feudal policy', that he saw the cities and their potential wealth as a powerful counterweight against the barons; he was, in a sense, a *roi bourgeois* anxious to create an alternative power base that did not depend on noble approval, a policy that would mark a break from his father's ready acceptance of the nobles as partners in government. Ferrante's close adviser Diomede Carafa (himself a great Neapolitan nobleman) wrote a tract on economic policy advising Ferrante to moderate taxes so that business could flourish unhampered, 'for a king cannot be poor to whose power wealthy men are subject'; Carafa insisted that 'where one just rule flourishes, there the cities flower and the riches of the citizens grow'. Moreover, 'money is struck not for the profit of the prince, but for ease of buying and selling, and for the advantage of the people'. Carafa thus moves beyond the straightforward fiscalism of earlier south Italian governments towards the enunciation of a liberal economic policy based on the principle that the crown will reap more benefits the less it intervenes through heavy taxation in the economic life of the kingdom, an outlook Ferrante shared with contemporary rulers in France and Spain. There are signs that Carafa's ideals were put into practice under Ferrante, who also had the chance to benefit from growing population, expansion of the massive sheep flocks (a major source of revenue to the crown), and commercial recovery in the western Mediterranean. The fair of Salerno in 1478 is particularly well

15. P. Lopez, *Napoli e la Peste 1464–1530. Politica, istituzioni, problemi sanitari* (Naples, 1989), pp. 91–122.

documented; there, north Italian businessmen congregated in sizeable numbers, and, although few southerners could compete with them in scale of business (except for Francesco Coppola, future count of Sarno), the fair provided a base for over two hundred south Italian merchants, and was a centre of exchange for cloths from Majorca, Languedoc, Florence and elsewhere. Even though Ferrante's hopes of reviving manufactures within the *Regno* proved difficult to achieve, some significant progress was made, and in economic terms this reign does not deserve the bad press it has traditionally received.[16] Royal initiatives alone do not explain the growing prosperity of southern Italy in the late fifteenth century: population growth after a century of demographic depression stimulated local cloth industries, the exploitation of minerals and metals and the further expansion of the *mena delle pecore*. Similar trends are visible on the island of Sicily, where fairs, established under royal and baronial licence, offered a framework for the exchange of locally produced agrarian and industrial goods, so that the island may have become less dependent on foreign imports of textiles than has sometimes been assumed.[17]

Ferrante's economic adviser Diomede Carafa was one of a group of distinguished men of letters who gathered at the king's court. Alfonso the Magnanimous had already established a lively court in Naples, and under Ferrante the emphasis shifted slightly; Ferrante himself had been trained to a high pitch in law, and there was a shift towards what might be called more practical learning and away from the patronage of lyric poetry and the fine arts. But this was a movement of degree only; Naples continued to attract artists of the stature of the painter Antonello da Messina and the

16. David Abulafia, 'The Crown and the economy under Ferrante I of Naples (1458–1494)', in T. Dean, C. Wickham, eds, *City and Countryside in late medieval and Renaissance Italy. Essays presented to Philip Jones* (London, 1990), pp. 125–46; E. Sakellariou, 'The Kingdom of Naples under Aragonese and Spanish rule', PhD dissertation, Cambridge University, 1996.
17. S.R. Epstein, *An island for itself. Economic development and social change in late medieval Sicily* (Cambridge, 1992) should be taken against H. Bresc, *Un monde méditerranéen. Économie et société en Sicile, 1300–1450*, 2 vols (Rome/Palermo, 1986); the years around 1450 may perhaps be seen as the period of transition towards greater economic autonomy within Sicily.

sculptor Guido Mazzoni, whose life-size terracotta depiction of the entombment of Christ in the church of Monteoliveto in Naples incorporates portraits of the royal family.[18] The sculptured triumphal gateway to the Castelnuovo in Naples was completed under Ferrante, who commissioned portrayals in this complex of his own escape from the rebellious barons and of his coronation; Duke Alfonso of Calabria initiated plans for the rebuilding of Naples which promised to make the town into a model city, furnished with fountains, streams and straight streets, which 'would, besides giving the city beautiful proportions, have turned it into the cleanest and most elegant in Europe', to cite the Neapolitan humanist Summonte, a figure who gave the Aragonese kings of Naples an unusually good press.[19] Important innovations in court music resulted from the arrival in Naples of Flemish composers such as the royal cantor Johannes Tinctoris, who spent twenty years at Ferrante's court, and whose influence lay not merely in his compositions and his performances, but also in his treatises on the art of music. Tinctoris, according to the major authority on Neapolitan Renaissance music, 'put Naples in the centre of the musical mainstream'; he was 'one of the seminal figures in Renaissance music theory'. Ferrante's policy was to offer salaries to the best musicians he could find in Europe.[20]

Distinguished literary figures at court included the eminent poet and administrator Giovanni Gioviano Pontano, who was active in the literary circle that still persists as the Accademia Pontaniana of Naples;[21] Antonio Beccadelli, or Panormita, a reformed pornographer, wrote an elegant history of Ferrante's life up to his assumption of the crown;[22] the royal

18. On Antonello see: S. Tramontana, *Antonello e la sua città* (Palermo, 1981); L. Arbace, *Antonello da Messina. Catalogo completo dei dipinti* (Florence, 1993); D. Thiébaut, *Le Christ à la colonne d'Antonello de Messine* (Paris, 1993).

19. G.L. Hersey, *Alfonso II and the artistic renewal of Naples, 1485–95* (New Haven, Conn., 1969).

20. A. Atlas, *Music at the Aragonese court of Naples* (Cambridge, 1985); Guglielmo Ebreo di Pesaro, *De pratica seu arte tripudii. On the practice or art of dancing*, ed. and transl. B. Sparti (Oxford, 1993).

21. Kidwell, *Pontano*, passim, and the items mentioned in Chapter 9, note 23.

22. Antonius Panhormita, *Liber rerum gestarum Ferdinandi regis*; A. Ryder, 'Antonio Beccadelli: a humanist in government', in C.H. Clough, ed.,

librarian Giovanni Brancati built up a splendid collection of books, including fine illuminated manuscripts, and was himself the author of several political tracts and translations of key classical works.[23] Ferrante took an interest in the new craft of printing, extending his protection to such figures as the immigrant German printer Sixtus Rießinger, and Naples became one of the major centres not merely for the printing of Latin and Italian works, but also for Hebrew printing.[24] Given his legal interests, it is not surprising that Ferrante stimulated the dormant university of Naples into new life, a policy which had a knock-on effect on demand for printed books. One of the early printed books to survive from Naples is Rießinger's edition, dated 1475, of the famous law-book of 1231 composed for Ferrante's predecessor as ruler and as patron of Naples University, Emperor Frederick II. In intellectual circles considerable thought was given to the problem how to adapt the predominantly civic republican ideals expressed in the political tracts of early fifteenth-century Florentine humanists to the political structure of a large Italian kingdom. Indeed, Naples became a magnet for Florentine intellectuals, with Ferrante himself earning elegant praise from Francesco Bandini in the 1470s on the grounds that he had brought justice, stability and prosperity to his kingdom at a time when Florence was lacking all three.[25]

Ferrante I died early in 1494 as the sound of French war drums began to be heard from across the Alps. Egged on by the ruler of Milan, Ludovico il Moro, King Charles VIII proposed to enter Italy, as rightful heir to the house of Anjou,

Cultural aspects of the Italian Renaissance. Essays in honour of Paul Oskar Kristeller (Manchester, 1976), pp. 123–40.

23. Bentley, *Politics and culture*, pp. 66–7, 69–71, 169–71, 181–2, 214–15. On manuscripts, see also J.J.G. Alexander, *The Painted Page. Italian Renaissance book illumination, 1450–1550* (London/New York, 1994). An example of a manuscript of Dante's Paradiso prepared for Ferrante's father has been published in facsimile by J. Pope-Hennessy, *Paradiso. The illuminations to Dante's Divine Comedy by Giovanni di Paolo* (London, 1993).

24. D. Maffei, *Un epitome in volgare del Liber Augustalis* (Bari, 1995) reprints in facsimile a handsome manuscript version of Frederick II's lawbook from this period; H. Dilcher, *Constitutiones regni Siciliae 'Liber Augustalis' Neapel 1475* (Glashütten/Taunus, 1973) reprints the Rießinger *incunabulum* in facsimile.

25. P.A. de Lisio, *Studi sull'umanesimo meridionale* (Naples, 1973).

to recover Naples and to launch from there a crusade for the recovery of Constantinople and Jerusalem. The history of the French invasion and of the fall of the Neapolitan house of Aragon will be examined in a moment. What needs to be asserted here is that the destruction of the Aragonese dynasty resulted in a propaganda victory for Ferrante's enemies. He was illegitimate by birth; but so were many contemporary Italian rulers, and he had the benefit of papal sanction as they generally did not. He was duplicitous and cruel; but his enemies gave in equal kind; he was, after all, a contemporary of Louis XI and Richard III. Yet he also had ideals which were not simply self-centred: the preservation of peace within Italy, which only occasionally proved achievable; the stabilisation of his kingdom in the face of baronial power; the prosperity of his subjects. He was conscious enough of the precarious nature of south Italian politics not to allow himself, in imitation of his father, to be bewitched by vainglory and grandiose ambition. However, the high price Ferrante paid was to have an altogether nastier reputation, as the antithesis of the knightly virtues Alfonso had supposedly sustained.

· · ·

RECOVERY IN ARAGON

The intention in the following section is to look at the restoration of royal authority in Aragon-Catalonia at the end of the fifteenth century, before examining in the final chapter the last phase of Aragonese involvement in Italy and the incorporation of the kingdom of Naples into the Spanish empire, at the start of the sixteenth century. It is not easy to write about Ferdinand II of Aragon without also writing about his formidable wife Isabel or Isabella, queen of Castile, whom he married in 1469 when they were both hoping to succeed to crowns which they could not be certain of winning.[26] It is not simply a question of disentangling the history of Castile and Aragon at this stage: one problem in the existing literature on the Spain of Ferdinand and Isabella is the sheer assumption that Spain's destiny lay with Castile, an assumption based

26. P. Liss, *Isabel the Queen* (New York/Oxford, 1992) is one of several recent biographies of Isabella.

on a foreknowledge of the relationship between Spain's two main parts in the sixteenth and seventeenth centuries. Certainly, there were striking contrasts between the two entities: Castile had few centres of industry, though Segovia possessed some importance as a textile producer; the major resource of Castile was the wool of its millions of sheep, and there was an active export trade in iron and other raw materials. Despite the years of crisis, the Catalan cities, and the rising commercial centre of Valencia, had no obvious competitors within Castile; even Seville, the great entrepôt linking the Atlantic and Mediterranean trade routes, was dominated by Genoese rather than local business interests. Although the monarchy in Castile was unfettered by the pactist constitutional theories in vogue in Catalonia and Aragon, exceptionally powerful noble families dominated large tracts of the countryside in a manner foreign to Catalonia. Thus the marriage was not one of natural partners, nor even one of newly reconciled competitors, but of unlike with unlike.

Politics, not economics, dominated discussion of the marriage. The terms of the marriage alliance between Ferdinand and Isabella are still seen by many historians as humiliating to Aragon, as in some sense they were; but they reflect a state of affairs where neither party to the marriage was universally recognised as future monarch, and where it was important for Isabella to be able to call on the resources of Aragon to defend her against her rival Juana, and for Ferdinand to have support against the French pretender René of Anjou; even King Henry IV of Castile was unhappy about the Aragonese marriage. Thus under the agreement Ferdinand was to spend his time mainly in Castile and he was only to reign as co-ruler in Isabella's lifetime.[27] Another side to these stipulations was surely the fear that Aragon would lord it over Castile, rather than, as commonly supposed, the other way round. No one was in a position to say that Catalonia's once strong economy was in irredeemable decline; its Mediterranean empire remained intact, and the social tensions that afflicted Barcelona, Majorca, Sicily were not completely absent in Castile, which, after years of inter-noble conflict, was also wracked by tension in the towns between Jews, converted

27. J.H. Elliott, *Imperial Spain 1469–1716* (London, 1963), pp. 6–12, 30–2; H. Kamen, *Spain 1469–1714. A society of conflict*, 2nd edn (London, 1991), pp. 1, 9–10.

Jews (or 'New Christians') and Old Christians. Ferdinand was of Castilian descent, and the memory of the Antequera hegemony in Castile in the early fifteenth century was still fresh; the brother of Alfonso of Aragon had acquired the crown of Navarre, thereby boxing in Castile on its Pyrenean frontier. (Admittedly he did little to serve Aragon's wider interests thereafter, until he became king of Aragon and surrendered Navarre.) The conclusion seems to be that the marriage was a good proposition for Aragon, even though it perpetuated the tendency of the Aragonese kings to reside outside their core territories; for Castile, or rather the would-be heiress Isabella, it was a straw at which to clutch in the hope of making real a claim to the crown that, in 1469, not all the nobles of Castile were prepared to countenance. Even after King Henry died in 1474, at the end of a tumultuous reign in which the authority of the monarchy had been derided, it took some years to convince the Castilian grandees that Isabella's claims were irresistible.

Isabella's message was one of unstinting moral reform; it was on the firm basis of the rechristianisation of Castilian society that her kingdom would be rebuilt; both kingdoms were evidently in need of reconstruction after Ferdinand and Isabella saw off their enemies in the 1470s. What is note-worthy is the great conservatism of Ferdinand's policies in Aragon-Catalonia. To restore himself as king, he must restore the monarchy as it had always been. He was not aiming to establish a 'modern', absolutist form of government, but to re-establish a medieval, consensual form of rule that was the only basis for legitimacy in Catalonia and Aragon. In 1480–81 he confirmed the traditional powers of the Catalan *Corts* and its permanent committees; even when, in 1494, he put together a Council of Aragon for the whole group of kingdoms that made up the Crown of Aragon, he was only returning to methods that had been laid down by Alfonso the Magnanimous in the 1440s; the lands of the Crown of Aragon remained, as they were long to do, an assortment of five kingdoms and one principality.[28] In freeing the *remença* peasants of Catalonia, with the *Sentencia de Guadalupe* of

28. A. Ryder, 'The evolution of imperial government in Naples under Alfonso the Magnanimous', in J.R. Hale, J.R.L. Highfield, B. Smalley, eds, *Europe in the late Middle Ages* (London, 1965), a point not suffi-ciently appreciated by Elliott, *Imperial Spain*, pp. 71–2.

1486, he was merely doing what earlier kings had promised to do. Ferdinand had no intention whatsoever of suppressing the traditional liberties of the Catalans and of imposing Castilian hegemony over Aragon.[29] Union with Castile went little further than the appearance of the effigies of both king and queen on the coinage of their various realms; on the other hand, Ferdinand took care to strengthen his influence in Castile by taking control of the major Military Orders, and by involving himself directly in such prestigious operations as the conquest of Muslim Granada (1492) and the extension of Castilian (but not Aragonese) authority in the New World.

There is little reason to doubt that Ferdinand shared with his wife the formulation of the policies that resulted in the expulsion of the Jews from Spain in 1492. The expulsion followed a century of erosion of the Jewish communities, which had greatly accelerated after the pogroms of 1391 and the mass conversions that followed; the Catholic Monarchs took the view that the time had come to tell the Jews to convert, leave or die. The order of expulsion, signed at conquered Granada in 1492, was extended to the Italian islands as well. Behind the wish to rid Spain of its productive communities of Jews, who had played so significant a role in the transmission of Islamic learning to the west, was the view propounded by the Inquisition that observant Jews were leading astray those of their brethren who had earlier converted to Christianity. Indeed, the primary function of the Inquistion, which began to operate in the 1480s throughout Spain under royal patronage, was the suppression of 'judaising' tendencies among the *converso* population (or, equally, 'islamising' ones among those of Muslim descent); that some *conversos* continued to practise their faith in secret is certain, but there is considerable disagreement about the scale of crypto-Judaism in Spain. So too are the numbers of those who left in 1492 uncertain, with estimates of 100,000 not uncommon; it is evident, however, that Castile suffered a greater population loss than Aragon, whose Jewish communities had withered away more rapidly in the years after 1391, though the expulsion of Jews from Aragonese Sicily

---

29. Elliott, *Imperial Spain*, p. 70; P. Freedman, *The origins of peasant servitude in medieval Catalonia* (Cambridge, 1991), pp. 188–94.

certainly displaced a substantial population of artisans.[30] Southern Italy and eventually the Balkans became the target for the Spanish Jewish refugees or *Sephardim* (the Hebrew word for 'Spaniards'), and these communities persisted in the Turkish empire, aware of their ancestry and intellectual heritage, for many centuries.[31]

Purged of Jews, Spain was not at once purged of Muslims; the fall of Granada in January 1492 signalled the submission but not the extinction of Islam, and the right of Muslims to continue to worship according to their rites was guaranteed in the surrender treaty that ended the Granadan crusade. Aggressive attempts at conversion and rebellion within Granada led to the loss of the right to practise Islam in all the Castilian lands by 1502; but what is astonishing is the lack of application of similar legislation in Aragon and Valencia. A fundamental study of the Valencian Muslims by Mark Meyerson explains why. He distinguishes between the outlook of Isabella (advised by Archbishop Cisneros of Toledo), always more fanatical on the question of religious uniformity, and the more pragmatic Ferdinand II, who saw the Muslims as financial assets in the same way as his predecessors on the Aragonese throne had done. For Isabella, the conversion of a scattering of isolated Muslim communities in Castile was a viable project. For Ferdinand, the conversion of perhaps a quarter of his subjects in Aragon and Valencia was a different proposition: there was the danger of mass resistance in areas still heavily populated by Muslims, and the fear of loss of revenue from a productive element in the population; this was a time when the monarchy needed to foster economic recovery in the Aragonese realms after a period of civil war and uneven economic performance. The result was that Islam was quite simply allowed to survive for another generation.[32] In 1525 political trouble, compounded by the renewed fear

30. For an outline of the issues, see David Abulafia, *Spain and 1492. Unity and uniformity under Ferdinand and Isabella* (Headstart History Papers, Bangor, 1992), pp. 33–53. Recent attempts by Benzion Netanyahu and Norman Roth to insist that the *conversos* were virtually all sincere Christians are based on a seriously flawed reading of the evidence.

31. N. Ferorelli, *Gli Ebrei nell'Italia meridionale dall'età romana al secolo XVIII*, new edition by F. Patroni Griffi (Naples, 1990).

32. M. Meyerson, *Muslims of Valencia in the age of Fernando and Isabel* (Berkeley/Los Angeles, 1991); Abulafia, *Spain and 1492*, pp. 21–33.

that Muslims were interfering with new conversions, prompted Charles V (Carlos I of Spain) to order the mass baptism of the *mudéjares* of Valencia and Aragon. Even then the practice of Islam continued in secret until the early seventeenth century, when renewed rebellion resulted in a mass expulsion of the people who were now known as the Moriscos.[33]

The Christianisation of Spain was, to Isabella at least, a moral issue. Attempts were also made to enforce draconian legislation against homosexuals, who in the most severe cases might face castration and execution. Since Henry IV of Castile was strongly suspected of sodomy, this policy had a political message also: the recovery of her kingdom from the chaos of Henry's reign could be achieved by the purification of Spain, with the Inquisition as the single tool which could reach into the furthest corners of Castile, Aragon and even the as yet unconquered Navarre, which expelled its own Jews in 1498. It remains an open question whether Ferdinand, who certainly liked to take credit for expelling Spain's Jews, had the same priorities. When he conquered Naples he allowed the richer Jews to remain behind, a reminder that (as with the Valencian Muslims) there were always financial dimensions to Ferdinand's approach to moral questions.

The imponderable question was where the marriage of the two monarchs would actually lead. The failure of Ferdinand and Isabella to provide a surviving male heir to their crowns resulted in a succession of expedients to find a future king: the Infante John died in 1497. A contemporary Jewish view was that these problems were the judgement of God against two rulers who were seen as persecutors of Israel. For a brief moment new hopes of a male succession arose out of the decision to create warmer ties with Portugal, whose king married Isabella's daughter; in 1498 she gave birth to a son who was therefore heir to all of Castile, Aragon and Portugal. The personal union achieved by Ferdinand and Isabella was surely about to be deepened and extended with the eventual succession of a single ruler. But the infant soon died. It now seemed likely that the succession would devolve on another

33. S. Haliczer, *Inquisition and society in the Kingdom of Valencia, 1478–1834* (Berkeley/Los Angeles, 1990); W. Monter, *Frontiers of heresy. The Spanish Inquisition from the Basque lands to Sicily* (Cambridge, 1990); A. Chejne, *Islam and the West: the Moriscos. A cultural and social history* (Albany, NY, 1983).

daughter of the Catholic Monarchs, Juana, about whose sanity there were increasing doubts, and on her husband, the Flemish archduke Philip, whose knowledge of Spanish affairs was very limited. These difficulties were accentuated when Isabella died in 1504, leaving Ferdinand's status in Castile highly uncertain; he had ruled in right of his wife, and it had been agreed in advance that were she to predecease him, her death would mark also the end of his reign over Castile. Moreover, he had made enough enemies at the Castilian court to make it unlikely that the nobility would support any attempt on his part to hold on to the crown of Castile.

Ferdinand tried to make up for the loss of Castile by withdrawing to Aragon, and awaiting the arrival from Flanders of Philip and Juana, who were set to become rulers of Castile. Ferdinand accordingly tried to ensure that his own patrimony, the lands of the Crown of Aragon, would have a separate, native-born, ruler once again. Ferdinand was, as ever, highly pragmatic in his approach to political problems, choosing a new bride, Germaine of Foix, who would, he hoped, produce a male heir to Aragon as well as some diplomatic advantages in his relations with France and Navarre. Once again a son was born, but lived only a short time. However, in the summer of 1506 the Treaty of Villafáfila between Philip and Ferdinand marked an attempt to secure a few remaining rights in Castile to Ferdinand, such as the mastership of the Military Orders and a half share in royal income from Caribbean trade, from which the Catalan merchants were largely excluded. At least Ferdinand was able to show that he could not be kept out of Castilian politics; and the unexpected death of Philip later the same year, while Ferdinand was away in Naples, prompted the archbishop of Toledo to summon Ferdinand back as regent. The alternative seemed to be a relapse into the divisiveness that had been rampant half a century before under Henry IV. The rights of Juana were easily set aside by making public her mental state. Castile thus fell into Ferdinand's hands by chance; and even so he had to reconcile himself to the eventual succession of yet another Flemish prince, Philip's son Charles of Habsburg (the future Emperor Charles V).[34]

---

34. Elliott, *Imperial Spain*, pp. 125-33; J.F. Ramsey, *Spain: the rise of the first world power* (Alabama, 1973), pp. 290-318.

Further evidence of Ferdinand's attitude to relations between Aragon and Castile can be found in his policy towards Navarre. This kingdom had for centuries been coveted by its Aragonese neighbour; Ferdinand's own father had ruled Navarre before succeeding Alfonso V on the throne of Aragon, and Navarre had then passed into the hands of the powerful and autonomous counts of Foix. By marrying into the house of Foix after the death of Isabella, Ferdinand acquired a contested claim to Navarre. Castilian influence in Navarre was certainly strong: the suppression of the Navarrese Jews in 1498 was achieved under pressure from Castile; but it was only in 1512 that Ferdinand was sufficiently free of outside distractions to seize nearly all the mountain state, followed a few months later by papal recognition of his claims. Like any Aragonese king, he respected ancient autonomies, and Navarre retained its own *Cortes*, as well as possessing a *Diputación* (a permanent committee of the *Cortes*) on the Catalan model. Indeed, the sixteenth-century chronicler Zurita believed that Ferdinand was afraid union with Aragon would prompt the Navarrese to claim further liberties similar to those of the Aragonese, so in the end he placed Navarre under Castilian law instead.[35]

The Catholic Monarchs (*reyes católicos*, a title granted by the papacy in recognition of their Christian achievements) pursued a vigorous African policy, bringing together here longstanding priorities of the Iberian kingdoms. The conquest of Ceuta by Portugal, in 1415, stimulated debate about which Iberian power was entitled to which part of a reconquered north Africa. Castilian hopes of setting foot in Africa were strengthened by the conquest of the last Muslim state in Spain; it was no new idea to argue that the reconquest of Spain must be followed by that of north Africa. The distraction of wars in Italy slowed the African campaigns, but a significant start was made in 1496–97 when the duke of Medina Sidonia sent an army to take Melilla, which effectively marked the western edge of a Castilian sphere in Africa, with Portuguese rights assigned to the area beyond. Melilla has remained part of Spain ever since. From 1505 onwards renewed campaigns resulted in the acquisition of the important commercial centre of Oran (1509), of Bougie (1510), and of a line of cities extending as far east as Tripoli (captured

35. Elliott, *Imperial Spain*, pp. 131–2; Ramsey, *Spain*, pp. 315–17.

in 1511). Most of these places were placed under the Castilian flag, and seized with Castilian resources, but Tripoli was not unreasonably attached to the nearby Sicilian kingdom.[36] Ferdinand forced the Jews out of these territories, acting consistently in the wake of his expulsion of Jews from Spain. The problem was that conquering the outer edge of the limitless expanse of Africa was not like conquering Spain: for one thing, the population consisted only of Muslims and Jews; for another, the further east the Spanish fleets moved, the nearer they came to the advancing Turkish armies which were shortly (1517) to overwhelm Egypt.

The Catholic Monarchs saw the expeditions as crusades, and Pope Alexander VI was generous with grants of crusade taxes. Yet the African conquests must also be seen as the fruit of centuries of Catalan-Aragonese ambition in the western Mediterranean, of which Ferdinand II of Aragon was now the standard bearer, even if it now proved easier to achieve results with Castilian armies. The basic conception of securing control of the prosperous ports of Morocco, Algeria and Tunisia, which had long served as termini for the gold caravans crossing the Sahara, went back centuries. It is possible too that the African conquests were thought necessary to secure the safety of the sea routes bringing Sicilian grain and other produce of the island kingdoms of the Crown of Aragon to the Spanish mainland.[37]

The other major concern of fifteenth-century Aragonese kings in the western Mediterranean was, of course, southern Italy. But to explain Aragonese intentions there it is necessary first to see how they reacted to the fall of the kingdom of Naples, held by their cousins, to the kings of France, successors to the Angevins.

· · ·

CONCLUSION

Ferrante of Naples makes an interesting contrast with his father Alfonso. Alfonso, as the epithet 'Magnanimous'

36. A.C. Hess, *The forgotten frontier: a history of the sixteenth-century Ibero-African frontier* (Chicago, 1978); Elliott, *Imperial Spain*, pp. 41–4; Ramsey, *Spain*, pp. 232–7.

37. F. Braudel, *The Mediterranean and the Mediterranean world in the age of Philip II*, transl. S. Reynolds, 2 vols (London, 1972–73), vol. 1, pp. 117–18.

suggests, was known for his affable generosity; and his policies in Naples showed a statesmanlike willingness to accommodate the baronage, despite a long history of disruption and of preference for Anjou over Aragon. At the same time, he brought to his court at Naples many Catalan advisers, and looked beyond southern Italy towards the creation of a new Roman Empire in the Mediterranean. Ferrante's objectives were, as he confessed in the first days of his reign, far more modest; his claim to the crown of Hungary was to all intents forgotten, and, far from saving Skanderbeg's Albanians from the Turk, it was the Albanians who came to southern Italy to save him from his enemies. In restricting himself to Italian politics, he naturally became entangled in bitter rivalries within the peninsula, and his ability to make friends with Florence after long years of hostility is testimony to his political sense as well as to his consistent pursuit of the goal of a wider Italian peace. But this was impossible to achieve without the acquiescence of the south Italian barons, whose continual sympathy for the Angevin cause threatened his power at the start of his reign, and again during the baronial rebellion of 1485, in which other Italian powers were also soon implicated. Seeking to strengthen the crown's finances, he initiated an imaginative economic policy, not unlike the policies adopted by his ally the duke of Milan; but the more he leaned towards the cities and merchants for support, the more he was seen by the barons as hostile to their interests. At the end of his reign, this atmosphere of suspicion between crown and nobles proved a dangerous legacy to his cruel and much disliked heir Alfonso II.

The contrast between Ferrante of Naples and Ferdinand of Aragon is also instructive. There is not simply the difference of character that enabled Ferrante to show sympathy for the plight of the Jews his cousin had expelled from Spain; it also seems that Ferdinand the Catholic was the one who completed several of Alfonso's own projects, emancipating the unfree serfs in Catalonia, and helping further to stimulate the trade of Barcelona and Valencia. There was a degree of pragmatism that he shared with Ferrante: he expelled the Jews from his lands, while allowing the Muslims to stay put in Aragon and Valencia, aware as he was of the financial loss that would ensue from their expulsion. Ferdinand's Mediterranean policies were aimed, in the ancient Aragonese tradition, at north Africa and the supply lines bringing grain from Sicily, though such plans were delayed by the great project in which he joined his wife, Isabella of Castile: the extinction of the last Muslim state in Spain, Nasrid Granada. After 1492, however, he could look eastwards out of Aragon, and, as events were to prove, westwards out of Castile towards the New World. And yet in many respects it was the Mediterranean rather than the Americas that had to be the main focus of his policies; his own claim to authority in Castile would lapse were Isabella to predecease him, as she did. His difficulties were compounded by the succession problem that faced the Catholic Monarchs, and which seemed to make it likely that the personal union of Castile and Aragon would not persist. In the last analysis, Ferdinand was indeed an Aragonese and not simply a Spanish monarch, looking towards the Mediterranean kingdoms that lay under the rule of the kings of Aragon. (Sicily was, in fact the first territory over which the young Ferdinand had become king.) As will be seen in the next chapter, it was Naples that finally became the focus of his ambitions.

Chapter 11

THE FRENCH INVASION OF ITALY, 1494–95

. . .

TENSIONS IN ITALY

It has been seen that Ferrante's son Alfonso, duke of Calabria, was already exceedingly unpopular with some of the barons in the 1480s, so that he rather than his father appears to have been the primary focus of complaint during the Second Barons' War. His accession in 1494 was therefore less smooth than appearances suggested: the papal chronicler Burchard offers a glittering description of Alfonso's coronation in May at the hand of the pope's nephew.[1] The alliance between the papacy and Naples seemed still to have some meaning; marriage alliances linked the Borgia family with the house of Aragon, and attached to them were assignments of grand titles and lands in the deep south of Italy. In reality, however, Pope Alexander VI was constantly wavering between the desirability of showing some friendship to France and the advantages of maintaining close influence over his vassal and neighbour the king of Naples.

So too in recent years had other props of the Italian League been seriously weakened. The death of Lorenzo de'Medici in 1492 had already been recognised by Ferrante as a blow to the peace of Italy; more serious still was the erosion of Neapolitan influence at the court of Milan. Duke Giangaleazzo Sforza had married Alfonso's daughter Ippolita,

---

1. Johann Burchard, *At the Court of the Borgia, being an account of the reign of Pope Alexander VI written by his Master of Ceremonies*, transl. G. Parker (London, 1963), pp. 70–81; original edn: *Liber Notarum ab anno 1483 usque ad anno 1506*, ed. E. Celani, Rerum italicarum scriptores, 2 vols (Città di Castello, 1906).

and this should have further confirmed the warmth of relations between Milan and Naples.[2] The reality was, however, that power in Milan was exercised by Giangaleazzo's uncle, Lodovico il Moro. And it was Ludovico who saw in the arrival of French armies a chance to bolster his position in Milan, and to counter Neapolitan influence in the peninsula, and, no less urgently, to fend off Venice's attempts to secure its influence in the cities of the Lombard plain.[3]

The moment was a propitious one for the French. The death of King Louis XI (1461–83) marked the end of a reign in which a firm emphasis had been placed on the consolidation of royal authority within France and along its immediate borders: the ending of the hundred-year-long conflict with England; the resolution of difficulties with the Valois dukes of Burgundy, past arbiters of Anglo-French relations; the assertion of French interests in Provence and Roussillon – all were sizeable objectives in themselves, whether or not Louis 'always loathed everything Italian', as the great sixteenth-century Florentine historian Francesco Guicciardini asserted.[4] Louis did, however, mediate when appropriate in the affairs of Italy, helping to broker peace between Naples, Florence and Milan in 1479.[5] Despite shocking Italians with his earthy allusions to the doubtful parentage of King Ferrante, and supporting Florence when it was threatened by Ferrante, Louis had the political acuteness to realise that he would gain nothing from further instability in the peninsula. He was even prepared to lease the city of Genoa to Milan, putting an end by an imaginative compromise to the bitter dispute, itself largely fuelled by factionalism within Genoa, that had soured relations between Milan and France. Louis was

2. C.M. Ady, *A history of Milan under the Sforzas* (London, 1907), p. 126.
3. F. Catalano, *Ludovico il Moro* (Milan, 1985). He was also duke of Bari in southern Italy: L. Pepe, *Storia della successione degli Sforzeschi negli stati di Puglia e di Calabria* (Bari, 1900); N. Ferorelli, 'Il ducato di Bari sotto Sforza Maria Sforza e Ludovico il Moro', *Archivio storico lombardo*, 41 (1914), pp. 389–468 [also the critique of Pepe's book, *Archivio storico lombardo*, 29, 1902, pp. 412–22]; V.A. Melchiorre, *Il ducato sforzesco di Bari* (Bari, 1990).
4. F. Guicciardini, *History of Italy*, Book 1, cap. 4 (citations are from the translation by C. Grayson, *History of Italy and History of Florence* (Chalfont St Giles, 1964; there is also a very good translation of the *History of Italy* by S. Alexander, 2nd edn, Princeton, NJ, 1984).
5. P.M. Kendall, *Louis XI* (London, 1971), pp. 417–18.

certainly not prepared to let René of Anjou mould his Italian policies.

By contrast, Louis's son Charles VIII was an enthusiastic devourer of historical romances, who shared with his father a direct and passionate piety, but who looked beyond France to redeem Christendom as the new Charlemagne; dreaming of the recovery of Constantinople and Jerusalem, Charles VIII well knew that Naples was traditionally seen as the base from which a massive eastern crusade could best be launched. Though mocked in his own lifetime for his dwarfish stature and his large head with its massive nose atop a skinny body, Charles was not the idiot king who is often portrayed; his concerns were traditional ones that had occupied generations of Capetian kings of France and of Angevin kings of Naples, and which seemed to have gained rather than lessened in urgency now that the Turk was knocking on the gates of western Europe.[6] The absorption of most of René of Anjou's claims brought Charles the title to Jerusalem and Sicily (i.e. Naples), and so his plans for the conquest of southern Italy were not an end in themselves, but part of a fantastic strategy aiming to wrest the Mediterranean from the Turks and the Mamluks. Lord already of Brittany, through his marriage to the heiress to this previously autonomous territory, Charles seemed to have all France in his grasp. His father had created a French realm that stretched across the whole landmass between the Atlantic, the Pyrenees, the Alps and the western Rhineland; it was to be his task to create a French empire that stretched across all Christendom. As Guicciardini says:

> Charles was not at all unwilling to attempt to acquire by force the Kingdom of Naples as his own rightful property. The idea had been with him almost instinctively since childhood, and had been nourished by the encouragement of certain people who were very close to him. They filled him up with vain ideas and made him believe this was an opportunity to surpass the glory of his predecessors, as, once he had conquered the kingdom of Naples, he could easily defeat the empire of the Turks.[7]

6. Y. Labande-Maillfert, *Charles VIII. La jeunesse au pouvoir (1470–1495)* (Paris, 1975); more briefly, Y. Labande-Maillfert, *Charles VIII. Le vouloir et la destinée* (Paris, 1986); I. Cloulas, *Charles VIII et le mirage italien* (Paris, 1986); A. Denis, *Charles VIII et les italiens. Histoire et mythe* (Geneva, 1979).
7. *History of Italy*, Book 1, cap. 4.

It was on these sentiments that Ludovico Sforza could play, in trying to defend himself against the imagined threat to his authority posed by the Aragonese in Naples. Yet it is a moot point whether Ludovico had in mind the massive expedition that actually reached Italy in 1494. Attuned to subtle diplomatic bargaining, Ludovico was in the first place seeking to use Charles as a mighty counterweight against his enemies in Italy, to secure his dubious claims to authority over Milan, and to enable Milan to withstand regional threats. There is no reason to suppose that he sought to make France the true master of Italy.

There is some reflection of these priorities in a grandiloquent speech that Guicciardini put into the mouth of Ludovico's ambassador to Charles; all the emphasis is placed on the glory that will accrue to Charles from a war against Naples, which will surely be far easier to accomplish than the wars of René of Anjou and Jean de Calabre, who had lacked resources and yet always came perilously near to destroying the Aragonese dynasty in Naples. But now 'it is God who leads you with such wonderful opportunities', while it is a matter of law that the house of France, as successor to that of Anjou, has a just claim to Naples, and a duty to remove from it the Catalan tyrants who oppress Charles's south Italian subjects.[8] This is thus a just war of liberation, whether of the victims of despotism in southern Italy or of the Church itself which has lost control of the holy places in the East. Yet the subtext is plain: 'Ludovico would gain nothing but a just revenge against the intrigues and offenses of the Catalans.' By insisting how little direct benefit this campaign would supposedly bring to the master of Milan, Ludovico's ambassador was attempting to by-pass Ludovico's real concern to establish himself more securely in Milan. And not surprisingly opinion at the French court was sharply divided. The longstanding presence of south Italian exiles at court helped stimulate belief in the justice of the enterprise. Was Ludovico any more to be trusted than the other Italian princes? The reality was that the rulers of Milan had shifted back and forth in and out of friendship with Naples, while the expedition would undoubtedly cost a vast fortune. How would the conquered

8. *History of Italy*, Book 1, cap. 4.

area be secured in the long term? To opponents of the scheme, the risks were overriding.

Nor were Ludovico's protestations of friendship towards France fully supported by his actions. In his dealings with Naples and Florence, Ludovico tried to present himself as yet another potential victim of French aggression, arguing that he had little choice but to appear to cooperate with Charles VIII, in the light of the ancient alliance binding France and Milan, and in view of his wish to hold on to Genoa. At this time Ludovico's primary aim seems to have been to secure his investiture as duke of Milan, setting his nephew to one side, and this meant careful negotiation not with the French king but with the Holy Roman Emperor Maximilian. In other words, Ludovico's aims were not the resolution of an Italian issue, the claim to Naples, but of his own status as lord of Milan.

The pope too sought to play off the different sides, negotiating with France and Naples, offering tentative promises, though agreeing in secret that he would defend Naples if Ferrante would defend the papal states. Having sanctioned Alfonso's coronation, Alexander insisted that he would not grant the kingdom of Naples to Charles until the legal rights of the French king and his rivals had been properly investigated, which was a neat way of evading the whole issue: since Charles claimed the kingdom by right of inheritance, and Alexander claimed the right to dispose of the kingdom as its overlord, the pope had clearly resolved to wait to see what the outcome of a French invasion would be. Still, it is hard to escape from a sense of *déjà vu*: there was a strong similarity between what was happening in 1492–94 and what had happened on many an occasion earlier in the fifteenth century. Italy once again faced a French army, though this time it was to be a royal army backed by substantially greater resources than the Angevins had ever been able to mobilise. Yet for Guicciardini, the arrival of French armies was the start of a series of calamities that transformed Italy from its 'happy state' of peace under Lorenzo and his contemporaries, into a battleground of foreign armies.[9] The breakdown of this peace made 1494 'a most unhappy year for Italy, and truly the beginning of years of wretchedness, because it opened

9. *History of Italy*, Book 1, cap. 1.

the way for innumerable horrible calamities which later for various reasons affected a great part of the rest of the world'.[10] Most dramatically, new forms of warfare and new attitudes to the fighting of war reached the peninsula; whereas in past times wars had cost little in blood, and had mainly consisted of tactical manoeuvres by *condottiere* captains, now horrible instruments arrived in Italy for the extermination of whole armies. Guicciardini romanticises the nature of combat before 1494, just as he exaggerates the degree of peace achieved in the aftermath of the Peace of Lodi of 1454.

News of French invasion plans posed a quandary for Florence; Piero de'Medici, whose hand was much less firm than that of Lorenzo, had to balance the interests of Florentine trade in France against Neapolitan demands for active support against the French. Venice too had to think hard about its stance, and, not untypically, refused to take sides despite being bombarded with pleading messages from both France and Naples; the argument for neutrality was the unsurprising one that the Turk was so serious a threat in the Balkans and in the Mediterranean (raiding, in fact, as far as Venetian territories in north-eastern Italy) that Venice could not allow herself to be sucked into peninsular rivalries.[11]

The obvious first step in resistance against the French had to be a naval victory off Genoa which would block French access into the peninsula and prevent the French from landing their field and siege artillery, much of it reportedly of types as yet unknown in Italy. Two attempts by Alfonso's brother Federigo to gain a foothold on the Genoese coast met with failure. The way was thus clear for a French army to move south; the French were at Asti in early September 1494, and nothing seemed to stand in their way as they steadily progressed southwards.[12] It was a large army, containing many of the feared Swiss infantrymen, as well as impressive machines, and yet 'it was not the number but the calibre' of the troops

10. *History of Italy*, Book 1, cap. 6.
11. M. Jacoviello, *Venezia e Napoli nel Quattrocento* (Naples, 1992); C. Kidwell, 'Venice, the French invasion and the Apulian ports', in D. Abulafia, *The French descent into Renaissance Italy. Antecedents and effects* (Aldershot, 1995), pp. 295–308.
12. C.H. Clough, 'The Romagna campaign of 1494: a significant military encounter', in Abulafia, *French descent*, pp. 191–215, for action on one front.

that made the army so fearsome, according to Guicciardini.[13] Close discipline and effective battle tactics compounded the threat, whereas Italian troops led by mercenary captains were famed rather for their fickleness and lack of commitment to a great cause. Military might was bolstered by political successes: the French king made a courtesy call on Duke Giangaleazzo of Milan who was lying grievously ill at Pavia; Giangaleazzo's wife, the Neapolitan princess Isabella, threw herself in tears at the French king's feet, imploring him to show mercy to the house of Aragon; Charles was apparently much moved by the young princess's pleas, but insisted that work begun must be brought to an end.[14] In the next few days, news came that Giangaleazzo had died, and Ludovico il Moro persuaded the ducal council to recognise himself as duke in view of the current emergency, rather than the late duke's infant son. So Ludovico had secured what he sought. In a sense, he now had little need of the French king, though his investiture by Charles with the lordship of Genoa a few weeks later was a welcome boost to his power. Ludovico began to fall out with Charles over small territorial questions arising from control of the small coastal towns of southern Liguria and northern Tuscany, and this growing unease, or rather sense that Charles was not an agent of Milan but a power in his own right, made Ludovico well aware that he had unleashed in Italy forces that were beyond his own control. Even greater were the difficulties of Piero de'Medici in Florence; tension over French aims led to a coup d'état and his fall from power.[15]

Unable to hold the French back from Rome, Alfonso's son Ferrante duke of Calabria (generally known as Ferrandino) fell back with his troops, while Pope Alexander VI also recognised that he could not withstand Charles's might.[16] When the French king entered Rome, Alexander had to promise

13. *History of Italy*, Book 1, cap. 11; F.L. Taylor, *The art of war in Italy 1494–1529* (Cambridge, 1921, repr. London, 1993); S. Pepper, 'Castles and cannon in the Naples campaign of 1494–5', in Abulafia, *French descent*, pp. 263–93.
14. Cloulas, *Charles VIII*, pp. 68–71.
15. M. Mallett, 'Personalities and pressures: Italian involvement in the French invasion of 1494', in Abulafia, *French descent*, pp. 151–63.
16. C. Shaw, 'The Roman barons and the French descent into Italy', in Abulafia, *French descent*, pp. 249–61.

that the kingdom of Naples would eventually be his; he also handed over to him the Ottoman prince Jem, long held in detention in the west, thereby signifying that Charles must pursue the war against the Turk as soon as the affair of Naples had been settled. Once the depths of winter had passed, all was ready for the final assault on Naples. Indeed, Alfonso II of Naples seemed to recognise the futility of resistance; obsessed with his past sins, he abdicated the crown before the year was out, passing it on to Ferrandino (Ferrante II), and hurried in despair to Sicily, where he lived out his few remaining days behind the walls of a convent. This once famous military commander, whose experience of government stretched far back to his teens, when his father had appointed him his lieutenant during the war against Jean de Calabre, threw himself with pious passion into a life of deep religious devotion. He was well aware that he commanded fear rather than respect, and in abdicating he aimed not to hand his kingdom over to Charles but to grant his able and vigorous son a chance to win back the goodwill of his subjects, barons and townspeople alike.

Ferrandino's influence was whittled away by the mile as the French worked their way into the kingdom of Naples during February 1494. Retreating to Naples, Ferrandino recognised that he had no hope of withstanding the French, not just because of their might, but because of the defections which occurred day by day. He and his family, including his uncle Federigo, took ship for Ischia, hoping only that the Neapolitans would recognise before long that 'the natural arrogance of the French' (the words are Guicciardini's) would lead them some day to recall the house of Aragon.

．　．　．

THE FALL OF NAPLES TO THE FRENCH

So on 24 February 1495 Charles VIII solemnly entered Naples. Violence was largely contained, with an important exception: the Jews became the scapegoats for the misfortunes of the *Regno*, and even before the French reached Naples the Jewish quarter was sacked by local Christians. Overall, to judge from his surviving administrative acts, Charles tried to ensure that local methods of government, which had been so successful in ensuring both central control and the collection of handsome revenues, were perpetuated without major changes. Guicciardini is surely very unfair when he says that Charles was content to leave the government of the south of Italy entirely to his advisers, 'who partly out of inability and partly out of avarice made a muddle of everything'.[17]

At the time of the conquest, at any rate, such problems were not yet visible. With Charles in Naples and Ferrandino in Ischia, most of the country fell away from the house of Aragon, though some remote coastal towns held out against the French. Yet Charles's position was not as secure as his triumphal entry into Naples perhaps suggested; this was by far the biggest Italian state, and control of its further reaches had eluded many of his predecessors. A long stay would be necessary were the king to bond his new kingdom to the house of France. Attempts to persuade Ferrandino and his uncle (and heir apparent) Federigo to resign their claims to royal status and to hand over their extensive estates, in return for vast tracts of land in France, were met with firm but polite refusal: if God and the people of the kingdom had handed their kingdom to Charles, it was not for Ferrandino to stand in the way.[18] Charles assumed that he could solve the problems of his new kingdom by appointing a lieutenant (Gilbert de Montpensier), granting lands and office to faithful Italian allies, and then taking his leave. This was to underestimate first of all the residual if localised loyalty to Ferrandino, and second the growing concern of the north Italian powers that Charles's presence was generating more trouble than peace. The pope was strangely forgetful of his declared willingness to confer the kingdom of Naples on Charles. The fall of Naples had not after all won Charles a vast number of powerful friends.

On 20 May 1495, shortly after a formal coronation in Naples, Charles left the *Regno* never to return. The return journey was to prove more dangerous than his descent into Italy. Old allies ganged up against him; the result of his victory had been to regenerate the Italian league, with Venice, Milan and minor Italian powers attempting to block the king's passage out of Italy. Whether this was entirely wise is

17. *History of Italy*, Book 2, cap. 4.
18. *History of Italy*, Book 2, cap. 3. This statement may, rather, reflect Guicciardini's views on the ability of men to alter their fate.

a moot point. Some were then of the opinion that it was best simply to let him go over a 'silver bridge' out of Italy. When confronted by the Italian confederates at Fornovo close to the Apennines, on 6 July 1495, Charles's army acquitted itself well, but both sides believed they had won a victory. Indeed, this was the signal for a return by the Aragonese to their south Italian lands, and Ferrandino was able to win some support from his relative and namesake Ferdinand the Catholic, king of Aragon, who supplied him with a few ships and men under the redoubtable Gonzalo Fernández de Córdoba (though Ferdinand had his own ambitions in the region, and hoped at least to obtain Calabria for himself, if necessary from the French). Out of loyal bases in Calabria and Apulia, Aragonese power began to expand northwards through the kingdom once again. Several Apulian towns were drawn under Venetian rule after Ferrandino pledged several Apulian coastal towns to Venice, which was anxious to create a line of defence against the Turks. Such concessions were worthwhile if the result was an Aragonese restoration. Ferrandino's career peaked in 1496 with his victorious return to Naples, after which he died still young, having won a reputation for bravery in battle. He was succeeded by Alfonso's brother, Federigo, the last Aragonese king of Naples.

Like Ferrandino, Charles VIII only lived a few more years, dying prematurely in 1498 when he cracked his large head against a low door jamb in one of his palaces. And, like Ferrandino, he had no direct male heir, and was succeeded instead by the duke of Orleans, as King Louis XII. In many ways, it was with the succession of Louis, rather than with the invasion by Charles VIII, that the fortunes of Italy began to change decisively. In some respects, though not of course its massive scale, Charles VIII's invasion bears closer comparison with those of René of Anjou than historians have allowed for; the ephemeral nature of the conquest and the lack of long-term impact on the institutional, social and economic structure of southern Italy distinguish Charles VIII's brief period of rule from the long-lasting Spanish domination of the south that began in 1502. In particular, historians have laid too much emphasis on the first French invasion of 1494–95, too little on the second which began with Louis XII's attack on Milan in 1499, in vindication of claims by the house of Orleans to the duchy which Ludovico (by 1500 a captive in French hands) had won for himself by means of his subtle political skills.[19] It has been seen that these skills were in a sense so subtle that he nearly brought disaster on himself in 1494–95.

The king of Aragon had an eye open for his own opportunities too, seeking in the longer term to draw southern Italy more closely under his influence. One complication was that Charles VIII of France agreed to return to Aragon the lost Catalan counties of Roussillon and Cerdagne, which had been occupied by Louis XI of France in 1463, during the Catalan civil war; it would obviously be improper for Ferdinand to repay his French neighbour by taking a prominent role in the defence of Italy against the French hordes. Clever diplomatic manoeuvres, such as an Anglo-Aragonese alliance which sent Ferdinand's daughter Catherine to England as wife to the heir to the throne, made the French aware that the return of Roussillon was a small price to pay for an improvement in relations with both Aragon and Castile.[20] Ferdinand the Catholic kept his eyes open, anxious to protect his interests in the island of Sicily; by 1497, when an agreement was signed at Alcalá de Henares between the French and the Spaniards, Ferdinand had manoeuvred Charles VIII into a position where the French agreed to the partition of southern Italy. At first Ferdinand of Aragon was to receive only Calabria, the toe of Italy adjoining his existing possession of Sicily; but the Treaty of Granada with King Louis XII of France (1500) promised the valuable south-east of Italy, Apulia, as well. When in the next few years the French attempted to assert their claims, the Aragonese literally stood in their way; by the end of 1503 southern Italy was in Catalan-Aragonese hands, that is, the hands of Ferdinand and not of the local Aragonese dynasty, whose ruler, Federigo, had been pensioned off.[21] Among the victims of the war were the south Italian Jews, many of whom who were ordered to leave

19. F. Baumgartner, *Louis XII* (Stroud, Glos./New York, 1994); B. Quilliet, *Louis XII, père du peuple* (Paris, 1986).
20. J. Calmette, *La question des Pyrénées et la Marche d'Espagne au Moyen Âge* (9th edn, Paris, 1947).
21. For the last members of the house of Aragon-Naples, see A. Chastel, *Le cardinal Louis d'Aragon. Un voyageur princier de la Renaissance* (Paris, 1986); D. Chiomenti Vassalli, *Giovanna d'Aragona tra baroni, principi e sovrani del Rinascimento* (Milan, 1987).

the kingdom in 1510, though a final expulsion did not occur for another thirty years; the protective cover offered by the old Aragonese dynasty of Naples was thus blown away. 1503 marked not a restoration of the native dynasty but its replacement by Spanish cousins who were still unsure what priority needed to be placed on Italian affairs. Would the French return? Would the Turks return? Would the south Italian barons enjoy the absence of their monarch, and build ever more powerful statelets? Would Ferdinand of Aragon become so marginalised in Castile that he would decide to follow in his uncle Alfonso's footsteps, abandoning his Spanish lands and concerns for Italy? These were all possibilities. The Italian wars tended in future to be fought further north, with Milan as a major focus; the Turks never quite managed their return, and Ferdinand was not in the end excluded from Spanish affairs. The two kingdoms of Sicily thus remained provinces of a larger Spanish empire.

· · ·

CONCLUSION

The French invasion of Italy represented a reversion, after the pragmatic policies of Louis XI, to the Angevin dream of acquiring control not merely of southern Italy but of the title to Jerusalem as well; quite apart from its romantic connotations, recalling both the legends of Charlemagne and the career of Charles of Anjou, the crusade was seen, not without some justice, as a matter of urgency; and southern Italy, in the best Angevin tradition, was regarded as an ideal launching pad for a war in the East by the third Charles, Charles VIII of Valois. Charles's expedition was, however, substantially facilitated by the appeal of Ludovico il Moro for the French to intervene, an appeal which the Milanese ruler soon regretted, and which was largely intended to help Ludovico consolidate his own position in Milan. As it was, the French invasion coincided with a period of weakness in Italy, following the death of both Lorenzo de'Medici and Ferrante d'Aragona; old alliances had fallen to pieces, and the champions of the peace of Italy had been replaced by heirs who seemed less certain of their ability to retain power by the combination of charm and ruthlessness their predecessors had managed so well. Neither Alfonso II of Naples

257

nor Piero de'Medici had the backbone to withstand the French armies, while the pope was boxed into a corner, and discovered, not for the first time, that the crown of Naples was in theory his to dispose of, but in practice belonged to the invader with the most fearful army.

And yet Charles VIII himself retained power in the south of Italy only briefly, and proved far less able to secure the peace and cooperation of the other Italian powers than had his Aragonese predecessors in Naples. By creating further instability, he only succeeded in preparing the way for the final destruction of the house of Aragon-Naples by that of Aragon-Catalonia. Thus a third force, already present in the Italian islands, now took charge of southern Italy, which was to remain for centuries a Spanish dominion.

GENERAL CONCLUSION

The history of the 'Sicilian Question' is one of early successes, as a small group of conquerors from far away in Normandy created and briefly sustained one of the richest and most intensively governed kingdoms within the Roman obedience. The seeds of crisis can be seen in these early successes; the wealth of the kingdom attracted new conquerors, with claims of varying validity, from Germany and from France, while the German claim itself generated that of the house of Barcelona, whose queen was of Hohenstaufen descent. Intensive government, or 'over-government', bred resentment within the kingdom, especially among those who had never been conquered, notably the settlers, often of Italian origin, who had arrived to replace the old Muslim population of the island of Sicily. The Mediterranean frontier was an area in which expectations of light taxation and moderate obligations to one's lord were widespread; indeed, the franchises offered to settlers were a major incentive, attracting newcomers who still had to face the perils of long journeys and the pain of leaving their original homes and families to seek their fortune elsewhere.

The newcomers into Sicily also included increasing numbers of Catalan merchants, and even if it was not they but their king who made the decision to take Sicily from the house of Anjou, the creation of a complex networks of trade routes linking Sicily to Spain, north Africa and the other Mediterranean islands brought prosperity to Barcelona and kept the Catalan capital as well as Majorca well supplied with essential foodstuffs. Catalans, Genoese and Tuscans vied to supply Sicily and southern Italy with high quality textiles required at princely courts. The importance of the region was thus not simply that it had become by 1300 the battle-ground of the rival dynasties of Anjou and Aragon, but that it was also the field of competition (and very often of coop-eration) for Florentines, Genoese, Catalans and other mer-chants; on the other hand, its own merchants, from Messina, Amalfi, Bari and other centres, played a more localised role in trade, keeping mainly by this time within the waters of the Tyrrhenian Sea, the Adriatic Sea and the straits dividing Sicily from Africa; despite occasional visits by traders of Messina to the Near East, the days were gone when southern Italian merchants dominated the trade of the Mediterranean. More-over, the middle of the fourteenth century saw the region immersed in wars and plague, and the ability of Sicily and southern Italy to supply the needs of their neighbours was reduced; but so too was demand, as population throughout Europe plummeted in the wake of the Black Death. Recovery did come; but it took time in southern Italy and Sicily, and it was perhaps impeded by the political strife which, particu-larly on the mainland, led to the deliberate destruction of sheepfolds and the exclusion of enemy merchants.

On the horizon, always after 1282, loomed the king of Aragon. Yet it is clear that in the thirteenth century the Aragonese had no clearly focused programme of empire-building. What Sir John Seeley said of the British Empire applies almost as well to the Catalan-Aragonese Common-wealth, whose rulers only in the mid-fourteenth century began to appreciate what they had acquired: 'we seem, as it were, to have conquered and peopled half the world in a fit of absence of mind'. Catalan settlement in the Mediter-ranean took off after the fall of Majorca in 1229, and had a similar character to the resettlement of Sicily that was taking place in the same period: the island was latinised, and the Muslim population gradually disappeared. This was the 'middle' solution to a problem that the rulers of Aragon-Catalonia and Sicily faced: how to reconcile Christian king-ship with the fact of ruling over large numbers of Muslims and Jews. The 'strong' solution was to expel the Muslims, and the 'extra-strong' solution was to sell them as slaves, as occurred in Minorca in 1287 and at Lucera in 1300. The 'weak' solution, revealed in Valencia, was to permit Muslims to practise their own religion, subject to certain limitations; here the model was the traditional way of permitting Jews to practise their faith under Christian rule. Yet both Jews and Muslims found themselves being targeted, with increasing persistency, by those who sought their conversion, making them attend missionary sermons and studying their holy books in order to be able to challenge rabbis and imams on their own religious territory. In the lands of the Crown of Aragon, the condition of both Jews and Muslims gradually worsened, though the decline was not continuous.[1] Nor were their fates so closely bound together that the expulsion of the Jews from Spain, in 1492, entailed the expulsion also of the Muslims, who within the Crown of Aragon continued to maintain public worship until 1525.

The western Mediterranean was thus a battleground of dynasties, of merchants and of religions; its political history in the late Middle Ages was dominated by the two hundred years' war for control of the Sicilian kingdom. This war ended in a final loss of independence. The territories brought under a single rule by Roger II of Sicily in the early twelfth century had, by the beginning of the sixteenth century, become once again the possession of a single king, even if he wore separate crowns in what would become known as the 'Two Sicilies'. But, whereas the Normans had established a kingdom in the face of outside threats, from German and Greek emperors and from African emirs, the king of Aragon would henceforth rule Naples and Sicily as far flung, though very important, provinces of an empire which would soon extend to Flanders, Milan and vast tracts of the New World. Aragon itself would become increasingly subordinated, in political, cultural and economic life, to Castile; the succession of Charles of Habsburg to both kingdoms and their dependencies guaranteed that Naples would not resume its position as effective capital of an Aragonese Mediterranean

1. J. Boswell, *The Royal Treasure. Muslim communities under the Crown of Aragon in the fourteenth century* (New Haven, Conn., 1977) assumed a linear decline in the fortunes of the Muslims, a view challenged in important respects by the work of Mark Meyerson, *Muslims of Valencia in the age of Fernando and Isabel* (Berkeley/Los Angeles, 1991). See also the perceptive assessment of the early fourteenth century in D. Nirenberg, *Communities of Violence. Persecution of minorities in the Middle Ages* (Princeton, NJ, 1996), which, despite its title, concentrates on events c.1320 in southern France and Aragon-Catalonia, and makes telling comparisons between the treatment of Jews and that of Muslims.

empire. The island of Sicily had already, in the years around 1400, become an overseas possession of Spanish kings who rarely thereafter visited what was in fact a valuable possession, strategically as well as economically. The south Italian mainland was granted by the will of Alfonso V a chance to flourish as an independent kingdom with a significant role in the wider politics of the Italian peninsula; but the continuing tension between the crown and the baronage weakened the ability of the ruling family to resist foreign pretenders, whether from France or from Spain. Ironically, the monarchy was pursuing at this time a promising economic policy which coincided with population growth and general recovery.[2] This recovery would not be brought to a halt by the wars of conquest between 1494 and 1503, but the independent Neapolitan monarchy would not be in place ready to reap the benefits. The command centre now lay in Spain. After the brief period of Alfonso the Magnanimous's rule in Naples, the south Italian lands would no longer be the fulcrum of Empire.

2. Epstein, *Island for itself*; Sakellariou, 'Kingdom of Naples'. Even those who accept Bresc's strictures about the Sicilian economy in his *Monde méditerranéen* must bear in mind that his discussion reaches only 1450, while Epstein's more positive view encompasses the late fifteenth century as well, a point which actually helps explain their radically different results. On social conditions in Sicily proper, see A. Ryder, 'The incidence of crime in Sicily in the mid-fifteenth century: the evidence from composition records', in T. Dean, K. Lowe, eds, *Crime, society and the law in Renaissance Italy* (Cambridge, 1994), pp. 59–73.

FURTHER READING

The footnotes to this book provide a running bibliography topic by topic: the aim here is to identify a group of studies that are of basic importance for the themes treated in this book. Entries have been organised so that the reader can move from more general items to those that deal with specific aspects of the period; they thus appear neither in alphabetical nor chronological order.

PRIMARY SOURCES

The Catalan sources are the most accessible, and have much to say not merely about the house of Barcelona but also about that of Anjou. Partly because several were originally written in Catalan, there exist translations into other languages; the four Catalan chronicles exist in English translation, as does the multilingual, semi-official, chronicle of San Juan de la Peña:

Chronicle of James I king of Aragon, transl. J. Forster, 2 vols (London, 1883).
Chronicle of the reign of King Pedro III, transl. F.L. Critchlow, 2 vols (Princeton, NJ, 1928–34).
The Chronicle of Muntaner, transl. Lady Goodenough, 2 vols (Hakluyt Society, London, 1921).
Chronicle of San Juan de la Peña, transl. L. Nelson (Philadelphia, 1991).
Pere III of Catalonia (IV of Aragon), *Chronicle*, ed. J. Hillgarth and transl. M. Hillgarth, 2 vols (Toronto, 1980).

Other sources for Catalan history include:

D. Kagay, ed. and transl., *The Usatges of Barcelona. The fundamental law of Catalonia* (Philadelphia, 1994).

S. Jados, *The Consulate of the Sea and other documents* (University, Alabama, 1975).

T.N. Bisson, *Fiscal accounts of Catalonia under the early Count-Kings (1151–1213)*, 2 vols (Berkeley/Los Angeles, 1984).

On relations between different religions see:

H. Maccoby, *Judaism on Trial. Jewish-Christian disputations in the Middle Ages* (London/Toronto, 1982).

A. Bonner, *Select Works of Ramon Llull*, 2 vols (Princeton, NJ, 1985; condensed version: *Doctor illuminatus. A Ramon Llull reader*, Princeton, NJ, 1993).

Ramón Lull, *Blanquerna*, transl. E.A. Peers (London, 1923).

Sources for the Angevins in Italy are not widely available in English. See:

Villani's Chronicle, transl. Rose E. Selfe and ed. P.H. Wicksteed (London, 1906), which is only a series of oddly chosen selections. The *Decameron* of Boccaccio (available in several editions and translations) is rich in tales of Angevin Naples.

The voices of the rulers themselves may be heard in:

Robert d'Anjou, *La vision bienheureuse. Traité envoyé au pape Jean XXII*, ed. M. Dykmans (Miscellanea Historiae Pontificiae, Rome, 1970).

René d'Anjou, *Le Livre du Cueur d'Amours Espris*, illustrations from the Vienna manuscript with commentary by F. Unterkircher (London, etc., 1975); for the text, S. Wharton, ed., *Le Livre du Cuer d'Amours Espris* (Paris, 1980).

Other valuable sources for this period include:

'Les actions et paroles mémorables d'Alphonse roi d'Aragon et de Naples', transl. and ed. S. Lefèvre, in D. Regnier-Bohler, ed., *Splendeurs de la cour de Bourgogne. Récits et chroniques* (Paris, 1995), pp. 630–736.

Antonius Panhormita, *Liber rerum gestarum Ferdinandi regis*, ed. G. Resta (Palermo, 1968).

Pius II (Aeneas Sylvius Piccolomini), *Memoirs of a Renaissance Pope. The Commentaries of Pope Pius II*, transl. F.A. Gragg and ed. L.C. Gabel (New York, 1959), republished as *Secret Memoirs of a Renaissance Pope* (London, 1988). [This is an abridgement from a full translation published previously in parts in *Smith College Studies in History*.]

C. Porzio, *La congiura dei Baroni* (various editions since 1586: Naples, 1964; Milan, 1965; Venosa, 1989; etc.)

Several texts of interest from a cultural perspective are:

Guglielmo Ebreo of Pesaro, *De pratica seu arte tripudii. On the practice or art of dancing*, ed. and transl. B. Sparti (Oxford, 1993).

P. Waley, transl. *Curial and Guelfa* (London, 1982).

D.H. Rosenthal, transl., *Tirant lo Blanc* (London, 1984).

On the Italian invasions, see:

Johann Burchard, *At the Court of the Borgia, being an account of the reign of Pope Alexander VI written by his Master of Ceremonies*, transl. G. Parker (London, 1963).

F. Guicciardini, *History of Italy*, translation by C. Grayson, *History of Italy and History of Florence* (Chalfont St Giles, 1964), and by S. Alexander, *History of Italy*, 2nd ed. (Princeton, NJ, 1984).

. . .

SECONDARY SOURCES

Many of the articles by the author of this book can be found in one or another of two collections of reprinted essays:

David Abulafia, *Italy, Sicily and the Mediterranean, 1100–1400* (London, 1987), and:

David Abulafia, *Commerce and Conquest in the Mediterranean, 1100–1500* (Aldershot, 1993). The letters ISM and CCM have been placed in square brackets after the titles of items in this Further Reading list which are reprinted in those volumes.

The Kingdom of Sicily under the Normans and the Hohenstaufen

R.H.C. Davis, *The Normans and their myth* (London, 1976).
D.C. Douglas, *The Norman achievement* (London, 1969), and *The Norman Fate* (London, 1976).
John Julius Norwich, *The Kingdom in the Sun* (London, 1970); repr. as part 2 of *The Normans in Sicily* (London, 1992).
E. Borsook, *Messages in Mosaic. The royal programmes of Norman Sicily, 1130–1187* (Oxford, 1990).
C.M. Brand, *Byzantium confronts the West, 1180–1204* (Cambridge, MA, 1968).
David Abulafia, *The Two Italies. Economic relations between the Norman Kingdom of Sicily and the northern communes* (Cambridge, 1977).
D. Matthew, *The Norman kingdom of Sicily* (Cambridge, 1992) has some rather quirky views.
H. Takayama, *The administration of the Norman Kingdom of Sicily* (Leiden, 1993).
E. Jamison, *Admiral Eugenius of Sicily. His life and work* (London, 1958) is one of the substantial contributions to the study of Norman Sicily by a British scholar whose career spanned much of the twentieth century.
David Abulafia, 'The Norman Kingdom of Africa', *Anglo-Norman Studies*, 7 (1985), pp. 26–49.
David Abulafia, 'The end of Muslim Sicily', in James M. Powell, *Muslims under Latin rule, 1100–1300* (Princeton, 1990), pp. 101–33 [CCM].
P. Csendes, *Heinrich VI.* (Darmstadt, 1993).
A. Kantorowicz, *Frederick the Second, 1194–1250*, transl. E.O. Lorimer (London, 1931), on which see David Abulafia, 'Kantorowicz and Frederick II', *History*, 62 (1977), pp. 193–210 [ISM].
David Abulafia, *Frederick II. A medieval emperor* (London, 1988), for a revisionist viewpoint.
W. Stürner, *Friedrich II.*, vol. 1, *Die Königsherrschadt in Sizilien und Deutschland, 1194–1220* (Darmstadt, 1992).
T.C. Van Cleve, *The Emperor Frederick II of Hohenstaufen* (Oxford, 1972) was out-of-date before it was published.
David Abulafia, 'Henry Count of Malta and his Mediterranean activities', in *Medieval Malta*, ed. A.T. Luttrell (London, 1975), pp. 104–25 [ISM].

David Abulafia, 'Ethnic variety and its implications. Frederick II's relations with Jews and Muslims', in W. Tronzo, ed., *Intellectual life at the court of Frederick II Hohenstaufen* (Washington, DC, 1994), pp. 213–24.

H.J. Pybus, 'The Emperor Frederick II and the Sicilian Church', *Cambridge Historical Journal*, 3 (1929/30), pp. 134–63; see also J.M. Powell, 'Frederick II and the Church in the Kingdom of Sicily, 1220–40', *Church History*, 30 (1961), pp. 28–34 and 'Frederick II and the Church. A revisionist view', *Catholic Historical Review*, 44 (1962/3), pp. 487–97.

David Abulafia, 'La politica economica di Federico II', *Federico II e il mondo mediterraneo*, ed. P. Toubert and A. Paravicini Bagliani (Palermo, 1994), pp. 165–87.

David Abulafia, 'The Kingdom of Sicily and the origins of the political crusades', *Società, istituzioni, spiritualità. Studi in onore di Cinzio Violante*, 2 vols (Spoleto, 1994), vol. 1, pp. 65–77.

P. Herde, 'Literary activities of the imperial and papal chanceries during the struggle between Frederick II and the papacy', in *Intellectual life at the court of Frederick II*, pp. 227–39.

E. Pispisa, *Il regno di Manfredi. Proposte di interpretazione* (Messina, 1991).

The Catalans

J.N. Hillgarth, *The problem of a Catalan Mediterranean Empire, 1229–1324* (English Historical Review Supplement no. 8, 1975).

J.N. Hillgarth, *The Spanish Kingdoms*, vol. 1, *1250–1410, Precarious balance* (Oxford, 1975).

F. Fernández-Armesto, *Before Columbus. Exploration and colonisation from the Mediterranean to the Atlantic, 1229–1492* (London, 1987) is very agreeable.

F. Fernández-Armesto, *Barcelona. 1000 years of a city's past* (London, 1991).

T.N. Bisson, *The Medieval Crown of Aragon. A short history* (Oxford, 1986).

S. Bensch, *Barcelona and its rulers, 1096–1291* (Cambridge, 1995).

E. Lourie, *Crusade and Colonisation. Muslims, Christians and Jews in medieval Aragon* (Aldershot, 1990).

T.N. Bisson, *Medieval France and its Pyrenean neighbours. Studies in early institutional history* (London, 1989).

David Abulafia, *A Mediterranean Emporium. The Catalan Kingdom of Majorca* (Cambridge, 1994).

T. Glick, *From Muslim fortress to Christian castle. Social and cultural change in medieval Spain* (Manchester, 1995).

P. Guichard, *Les musulmans de Valence et la reconquête, XIe–XIIIe siècles*, 2 vols (Damascus, 1990–91).

R.I. Burns, 'Muslims in the thirteenth-century realms of Aragon: interaction and reaction', in J.M. Powell, ed., *Muslims under Latin rule* (Princeton, NJ, 1990), pp. 57–102; *Medieval Colonialism. Postcrusade exploitation of Islamic Valencia* (Princeton, NJ, 1975); *Muslims, Christians and Jews in the Crusader Kingdom of Valencia. Societies in symbiosis* (Cambridge, 1984); *Diplomatarium of the Crusader Kingdom of Valencia*, vol. 1, *Society and Documentation in Crusader Valencia* (Princeton, NJ, 1985), among the many distinguished works of Fr Burns.

R.I. Burns, *Jews in the Notarial Culture. Latinate wills in Mediterranean Spain 1250–1350* (Berkeley/Los Angeles, 1996).

L.P. Harvey, *Islamic Spain, 1250 to 1500* (Chicago, 1991).

J. Cohen, *The friars and the Jews* (Ithaca, NY, 1982), to be complemented by:

R. Chazan, *Daggers of Faith. Thirteenth-century Christian missionizing and Jewish response* (Berkeley/Los Angeles, 1989), and by R. Chazan, *Barcelona and Beyond. The disputation of 1263 and its aftermath* (Berkeley/Los Angeles, 1992).

David Abulafia, 'Catalan merchants and the western Mediterranean, 1236–1300: studies in the notarial acts of Barcelona and Sicily', *Viator: medieval and Renaissance Studies*, 16 (1985), pp. 209–42 [ISM].

A.B. Hibbert, 'Catalan Consulates in the thirteenth century', *Cambridge Historical Journal*, 9 (1949), pp. 352–8.

M. Riu, 'The woollen industry in Catalonia in the later Middle Ages', in N.G. Harte, K.G. Ponting, eds, *Cloth and clothing in medieval Europe. Essays in memory of E.M. Carus-Wilson* (London, 1983), pp. 205–29.

M. Riu, 'Banking and society in late medieval and early modern Aragon', *The Dawn of Modern Banking*, ed. by Center for Medieval and Renaissance Studies, University of California, Los Angeles (New Haven, Conn., 1979), pp. 131–67.

C.E. Dufourcq, *L'Ibérie chrétienne et le Maghreb, XIIe–XVe siècles* (London, 1990), for a selection of the research of a notable scholar.

C.E. Dufourcq, *La vie quotidienne dans les ports méditerranéens au Moyen Âge* (Paris, 1975), for an overview based on a close reading of the sources.

David Abulafia and Blanca Garí, eds, *En las costas del Mediterráneo occidental* (Barcelona, 1997), for studies of Barcelona, Perpignan, Valencia, Almería, etc.

The rise of the Angevins, 1266–1309

S. Runciman, *The Sicilian Vespers. A history of the Mediterranean world in the thirteenth century* (Cambridge, 1958).

P. Herde, *Karl I. von Anjou* (Stuttgart, 1979).

G. Galasso, *Il Regno di Napoli. Il Mezzogiorno angioino e aragonese (1266–1494)* (UTET Storia d'Italia, Turin, 1992) is a massive survey of all aspects of the history of southern Italy, political, social and economic.

L. Cadier, *Essai sur l'administration du Royaume angevin de Sicile* (Paris, 1891); new Italian ed. prepared by F. Giunta, *L'amministrazione della Sicilia angioina* (Palermo, 1974).

N. Housley, *The Italian Crusades. The papal-Angevin alliance and the Crusades against Christian lay powers, 1254–1343* (Oxford, 1982).

É. Jordan, *Les origines de la domination angevine en Italie* (Paris, 1909; repr. in 2 vols, New York, 1960).

É. Léonard, *Les Angevins de Naples* (Paris, 1954); Italian edition, *Gli Angioini di Napoli* (Milan, 1967).

D.M. Nicol, 'The relations of Charles of Anjou with Nikephoros of Epiros', *Byzantinische Forschungen*, 4 (1972) is invaluable.

A. Ducellier, *La façade maritime de l'Albanie au Moyen Âge. Durazzo et Valona du XIe au XVe siècle* (Thessalonika, 1981) is invaluable.

D.J. Geanakoplos, *Michael VIII Palaeologus and the West, 1258–1282* (Cambridge, MA, 1959).

H. Wieruszowski, *Politics and Culture in medieval Spain and Italy* (Rome, 1971).

L. Catalioto, *Terre, baroni e città in Sicilia nell'età di Carlo I d'Angiò* (Messina, 1995).

W. Percy, *The revenues of the Kingdom of Sicily under Charles I of Anjou, 1266–1285, and their relationship to the Vespers* (repr. from Princeton doctoral dissertation, 1964, by University Microfilms).

H. Bresc, *Politique et société en Sicile, XIIe–XVe siècles* (Aldershot, 1990).

H. Bresc, *Un monde méditerranéen. Économie et société en Sicile, 1300–1450*, 2 vols (Rome/Palermo, 1986).

G. Yver, *Le commerce et les marchands dans l'Italie méridionale* (Paris, 1903).

David Abulafia, 'Southern Italy and the Florentine economy, 1265–1370', *Economic History Review*, ser. 2, vol. 33 (1981), pp. 377–88 [ISM].

S.R. Epstein, *An island for itself. Economic development and social change in late medieval Sicily* (Cambridge, 1992).

T.S.R. Boase, *Boniface VIII* (London, 1933).

David Abulafia, 'Monarchs and minorities in the medieval Mediterranean c.1300: Lucera and its analogues', in P. Diehl and S. Waugh, eds, *Christendom and its discontents. Exclusion, persecution and rebellion, 1000–1500* (Cambridge, 1996), pp. 234–63.

David Abulafia, 'The merchants of Messina: Levant trade and domestic economy', *Papers of the British School at Rome*, 54 (1986), pp. 196–212 [CCM].

M.R. Toynbee, *St Louis of Toulouse* (Manchester, 1929).

Catalonia-Aragon in the fourteenth century

In addition to the general works by Bisson and Hillgarth already cited, see:

M. McVaugh, *Medicine before the plague. Practitioners and their patients in the Crown of Aragon 1285–1345* (Cambridge, 1993).

C. Backman, *The decline and fall of medieval Sicily. Politics, religion and economy in the reign of Frederick III, 1296–1337* (Cambridge, 1995).

David Abulafia, 'The Aragonese kingdom of Albania. An Angevin project of 1311–16', *Mediterranean Historical Review*, vol. 10 (1995), repr. as *Intercultural contacts in the medieval*

Mediterranean. Studies in honour of David Jacoby (London, 1996), pp. 1–13.

On Sardinia see mainly literature in Italian:

F.C. Casula, *La Sardegna aragonese*, 2 vols (Cagliari, 1990), and other works by the same author.

J. Day, *Sardegna sotto la dominazione pisano-genovese* (Turin, 1986), originally published as part of the UTET *Storia d'Italia*, ed. G. Galasso.

M. Tangheroni, *La città dell'argento* (Naples, 1985).

C. Manca, *Aspetti dell'espansione economica catalano-aragonese nel Mediterraneo occidentale. Il commercio internazionale del sale* (Milan, 1966).

An important study of social conditions within Catalonia is:

P. Freedman, *The origins of peasant servitude in medieval Catalonia* (Cambridge, 1991).

On cultural developments in the era of Llull see:

J. Hillgarth, *Lull and Lullism in fourteenth-century France* (Oxford, 1971). See also:

M.D. Johnston, *The spiritual logic of Ramon Llull* (Oxford, 1987).

M.D. Johnston, *The evangelical rhetoric of Ramon Llull* (New York/Oxford, 1995).

D. Urvoy, *Penser l'Islam. Les présupposés islamiques de l''art' de Lull* (Paris, 1980).

F. Yates, *Lull and Bruno*, ed. J.B. Trapp and J.N. Hillgarth (London, 1982), pp. 9–125.

G. Scholem, *Major Trends in Jewish Mysticism* (New York, 1946).

M. Idel, *The mystical experience in Abraham Abulafia* (Albany, NY, 1988); *Studies in ecstatic Kabbalah* (Albany, NY, 1988); *Language, Torah and Hermeneutics in Abraham Abulafia* (Albany, NY, 1989).

Naples, Sicily and Aragon in the fourteenth century

G. Galasso, *Il Regno di Napoli. Il Mezzogiorno angioino e aragonese (1266–1494)* (UTET Storia d'Italia, Turin, 1992).

G. Mollat, *Les Papes d'Avignon, 1305–1378*, 10th edn (Paris,

1965); English transl. of earlier edn as *The Popes at Avignon* (London, 1963).

W. Bowsky, *Henry VII in Italy* (Lincoln, Nebraska, 1960).

N. Housley, *The Avignon papacy and the Crusades, 1305–1378* (Oxford, 1986).

David Abulafia, 'Venice and the Kingdom of Naples in the last years of King Robert the Wise', *Papers of the British School at Rome*, 48 (1980), pp. 187–8 [ISM].

E.H. Hunt, *The Medieval Super-Companies. A study of the Peruzzi Company of Florence* (Cambridge, 1994).

N.J. Housley, 'Pope Clement V and the crusades of 1309–10', *Journal of Medieval History*, 8 (1982), pp. 29–43.

L. Green, *Castruccio Castracani. A study on the origins and character of a fourteenth-century Italian despotism* (Oxford, 1986).

David Abulafia, 'Genova Angioina, 1318–35: gli inizi della Signoria di Roberto re di Napoli', *La storia dei Genovesi*, vol. 12. *Atti del Convegno internazionale di studi sui Ceti Dirigenti nelle Istituzioni della Repubblica di Genova, 12a Tornata, Genova, 11–14 giugno, 1991*, part 1 (Genoa, 1994), pp. 15–24.

D. Wood, *Clement VI. The pontificate and ideas of an Avignon pope* (Cambridge, 1989).

É. Léonard, *Histoire de Jeanne Ière reine de Naples, comtesse de Provence*, vol. 3, *Le règne de Louis de Tarente* (Monaco/Paris, 1936).

J. Pryor, 'Foreign policy and economic policy: the Angevins of Sicily and the economic decline of southern Italy', in L.O. Frappell, *Principalities, Powers and Estates. Studies in medieval and early modern government and society* (Adelaide, 1980), pp. 43–55.

E.R. Labande, 'La politique méditerranéenne de Louis Ier d'Anjou et le rôle qu'y joua la Sardaigne', *Atti del VI Congresso internazionale di studi sardi* (Cagliari, 1957), pp. 3–23; repr. in E.R. Labande, *Histoire de l'Europe occidentale, XIe–XIVe s.* (London, 1973).

D'A.J.D. Boulton, *The Knights of the Crown. The monarchical orders of Knighthood in later medieval Europe, 1325–1520* (Woodbridge, 1987).

On intellectual developments see:

V. Branca, *Boccaccio. The man and his works* (Hassocks, Sussex, 1976).

R. Weiss, *Medieval and Humanist Greek* (Padua, 1977).

K. Pennington, *The Prince and the Law, 1200–1600. Sovereignty and rights in the western legal tradition* (Berkeley/Los Angeles, 1993).

W. Ullmann, *The medieval idea of law as represented by Lucas de Penna* (London, 1946).

On Sicily see:

D. Mack Smith, *Medieval Sicily* (London, 1968).

C. Backman, *The decline and fall of medieval Sicily. Politics, religion and economy in the reign of Frederick III, 1296–1337* (Cambridge, 1995).

S.R. Epstein, *An island for itself. Economic development and social change in late medieval Sicily* (Cambridge, 1992).

V. d'Alessandro, *Politica e Società nella Sicilia aragonese* (Palermo, 1963).

V. d'Alessandro, *Terra, nobili e borghesi nella Sicilia medievale* (Palermo, 1994).

C. Mirto, *Il regno di Sicilia e delle isole adiacenti dalla sua nascita alla peste del 1347–9* (Messina, 1986).

C. Fisber Polizzi, *Amministrazione della contea di Ventimiglia nella Sicilia aragonese* (Supplement to vol. 6 of Atti del l'Accademia Agrigentina di scienze lettere e arti, Padua, 1979).

E. Mazzarese Fardella, *I Feudi comitali di Sicilia dai Normanni agli Aragonesi* (Milan/Palermo, 1974).

L. Sciascia, *Le donne e i cavalier, gli affanni e gli agi. Famiglia e potere in Sicilia tra XII e XIV secolo* (Messina, 1993).

A. Romano, ed., *Istituzioni politiche e giuridiche e strutture del potere politico ed economico nelle città dell'Europa mediterranea medievale e moderna. La Sicilia* (Messina, 1992).

I. Peri, *La Sicilia dopo il Vespro. Uomini, città e campagne, 1282–1376* (Bari, 1981; the middle volume of a series of three by Peri, on the society and economy of medieval Sicily).

I. Peri, *Villani e cavalieri nella Sicilia medievale* (Bari, 1993).

F. Benigno and C. Torrisi, eds, *Élites e potere in Sicilia dal medioevo ad oggi* (Catanzaro, 1995).

P. Corrao, *Governare un regno. Potere, società e istituzioni in Sicilia fra Trecento e Quattrocento* (Naples, 1991).

S. Correnti, *La Sicilia del Quattrocento. L'umanesimo mediterraneo* (Catania, 1992).

Malta was also part of the Sicilian realm, on which see:

A.T. Luttrell, ed., *Medieval Malta. Studies on Malta before the Knights* (London, 1975).

On Aragon-Catalonia see, above all, the introduction to the Hillgarth translation of Peter the Ceremonious's chronicle [listed above under Primary Sources].

J.A. Robson, 'The Catalan fleet and Moorish sea-power (1337–1344)', *English Historical Review*, 74 (1959), pp. 386–408.

R. Tasis, *La vida del rei En Pere III* (Barcelona, 1954).

R. d'Abadal, *Pere el Ceremonió i els inicis de la decadència política de Catalunya* (Barcelona, 1972).

P. Cateura Bennàsser, *Política y finanzas del reino de Mallorca bajo Pedro IV de Aragón* (Palma de Mallorca, 1982).

R. Giesey, *If Not, Not. The oath of the Aragonese and the legendary laws of Sobrarbe* (Princeton, NJ, 1968).

P. Wolff, 'The 1391 pogrom in Spain. Social crisis or not?', *Past and Present*, 50 (1971).

S. Sobrequés i Vidal, *El Compromís de Casp i la noblesa catalana* (Barcelona, 1973; originally published in article form in the *Anuario de Estudios medievales*, 7, 1970–1); F. Soldevila, *El Compromís de Casp* (3rd edn, Barcelona, 1994).

On the end of the Angevin period in Naples see:

N.F. Faraglia, *Studii intorno al regno di Giovanna II d'Angiò* (Naples, 1895; repr. Cosenza 1990).

L. Boccia, *Giovanna II. Una regina di paglia* (Naples, 1980).

J. Levron, *Le bon roi René* (Paris, 1972).

M. Miquel, *Quand le bon roi René était en Provence (1447–1480)* (Paris, 1979).

R. Duchêne, *La Provence devient française, 536–1789* (Paris, 1976).

A. Ryder, 'The Angevin bid for Naples, 1380–1480', in David Abulafia, ed., *The French descent into Renaissance Italy, 1494–5. Antecedents and effects* (Aldershot, 1995), pp. 55–69.

A. Peyronnet, 'The distant origin of the Italian wars: political relations between France and Italy in the fourteenth and fifteenth centuries', in Abulafia, *French descent.*

C. de Mérindol, *Les fêtes de chevalerie à la cour du roi René* (Paris, 1993).

F. Piponnier, *Costume et vie sociale. La cour d'Anjou, XIVe–XVe siècle* (Paris/The Hague, 1970).

M. Reynolds, 'René of Anjou, king of Sicily, and the Order of the *Croissant*', *Journal of Medieval History*, 19 (1993), pp. 125–61.

The Aragonese in the fifteenth century

A. Ryder, *Alfonso the Magnanimous King of Aragon, Naples, and Sicily 1396–1458* (Oxford, 1990).

J.N. Hillgarth, *The Spanish Kingdoms, 1250–1516*, vol. 2, *1410–1516, Castilian hegemony* (Oxford, 1978).

C.M. Ady, *A history of Milan under the Sforzas* (London, 1907).

D. Mack Smith, *Medieval Sicily* (London, 1968).

C. Trasselli, *Mediterraneo e Sicilia all'inizio dell'epoca moderna (ricerche quattrocentesche)* (Cosenza, 1977).

W. Küchler, *Die Finanzen der Krone Aragon während des 15. Jahrhunderts (Alfons V. und Johann II.)* (Münster, 1983).

Jerry Bentley, *Politics and Culture in Renaissance Naples* (Princeton, NJ, 1987).

C.H. Clough, 'Federico da Montefeltro and the kings of Naples: a study in fifteenth-century survival', *Renaissance Studies*, 6 (1992), pp. 113–72.

A. Ryder, 'The eastern policy of Alfonso the Magnanimous', *Atti dell'Accademia Pontaniana* (1979). A. Ryder, 'The evolution of imperial government in Naples under Alfonso the Magnanimous', in J.R. Hale, J.R.L. Highfield, B. Smalley, eds, *Europe in the late Middle Ages* (London, 1965), pp. 332–57.

A. Ryder, *The Kingdom of Naples under Alfonso the Magnanimous* (Oxford, 1975).

E. Sakellariou, 'Institutional and social continuities in the Kingdom of Naples between 1443 and 1528', in David Abulafia, ed., *The French descent into Renaissance Italy, 1494–95. Antecedents and effects* (Aldershot, 1995), pp. 327–53.

G. Galasso, *Il Regno di Napoli. Il Mezzogiorno angioino e aragonese (1266–1494)* (UTET Storia d'Italia, Turin, 1992).

Carol Kidwell, *Pontano. Poet and Prime Minister* (London, 1991); *Marullus. Soldier poet of the Renaissance* (London, 1989); *Sannazaro and Arcadia* (London, 1993).

M. Mallett, *The Borgias. The rise and fall of a Renaissance dynasty*, 2nd edn (London, 1971).

David Abulafia, 'The inception of the reign of King Ferrante I of Naples: the events of summer 1458 in the light of documentation from Milan', in Abulafia, *French descent*, pp. 71–89.

J.G. Russell, *Diplomats at work. Three Renaissance Studies* (Stroud, Glos., 1992).

David Abulafia, 'Ferrante I of Naples, Pope Pius II and the Congress of Mantua (1459)', in B.Z. Kedar and J. Riley-Smith, eds, *Montjoie. Studies on the crusades presented to Hans Meyer* (Aldershot, 1997).

R. Fubini, *Italia Quattrocentesca* (Milan, 1994).

H. Butters, 'Lorenzo and Naples', in G.C. Garfagnani, ed., *Lorenzo il Magnifico e il suo mondo. Convegno internazionale di studi (Firenze, 9–13 giugno 1992)* (Florence, 1994), pp. 143–51; H. Butters, 'Florence, Milan and the Barons' War (1485–1486), in G.C. Garfagnani, ed., *Lorenzo de'Medici. Studi* (Florence, 1992), pp. 281–308; H. Butters, 'Politics and diplomacy in late Quattrocento Italy: the case of the Barons' War (1485–1486)', in P. Denley, C. Elam, eds, *Florence and Italy. Renaissance Studies in honour of Nicolai Rubinstein* (London, 1988), pp. 13–31.

E. Pontieri, *Venezia e il conflitto tra Ferrante I d'Aragona e Innocenzo VIII* (Naples, 1969), reprinting material published in the *Archivio storico per le province napoletane* in 1966–67.

P. Lopez, *Napoli e la Peste 1464–1530. Politica, istituzioni, problemi sanitari* (Naples, 1989).

Works on cultural developments include:

G.L. Hersey, *The Aragonese arch at Naples, 1443–1475* (New Haven, Conn., 1973).

F. Patroni Griffi, *Banchieri e gioielli alla corte aragonese di Napoli*, 2nd edn (Naples, 1992).

José Carlos Rovira, *Humanistas y poetas en la corte napolitana de Alfonso el Magnánimo* (Alicante, 1990).

A. Atlas, *Music at the Aragonese court of Naples* (Cambridge, 1985).

A. Ryder, 'Antonio Beccadelli: a humanist in government', in C.H. Clough, ed., *Cultural aspects of the Italian Renaissance. Essays in honour of Paul Oskar Kristeller* (Manchester, 1976), pp. 123–40.

J.J.G. Alexander, *The Painted Page. Italian Renaissance book illumination, 1450–1550* (London/New York, 1994).

A. Cole, *Art of the Italian Renaissance Courts* (London, 1995).

M. Hollingsworth, *Patronage in Renaissance Italy* (London, 1994).

C. Woods-Marsden, 'Art and political identity in fifteenth-century Naples: Pisanello, Cristoforo di Geremia, and King Alfonso's imperial fantasies', in C.M. Rosenberg, ed., *Art and politics in late medieval and Renaissance Italy, 1250–1500* (Notre Dame, Ind., 1990), pp. 11–37.

P.A. de Lisio, *Studi sull'umanesimo meridionale* (Naples, 1973).

On the economy see:

David Abulafia, 'The Crown and the economy under Ferrante I of Naples (1458–1494)', in T. Dean, C. Wickham, eds, *City and Countryside in late medieval and Renaissance Italy. Essays presented to Philip Jones* (London, 1990) [CCM].

J.A. Marino, *Pastoral economics in the Kingdom of Naples* (Baltimore, Md., 1988).

A. Grohmann, *Le fiere del regno di Napoli in età aragonese* (Naples, 1969).

M.A. Visceglia, *Territorio feudo e potere locale. Terra d'Otranto tra Medioevo ed età moderna* (Naples, 1988).

M. del Treppo, *I mercanti catalani e l'espansione della Corona d'Aragona nel secolo XV* (Naples, 1972).

C. Carrère, *Barcelone centre économique à l'époque des difficultés 1380–1462*, 2 vols (Paris/The Hague, 1967).

A. Garcia i Sanz and N. Coll i Julia, *Galeres mercants catalanes dels segles XIV i XV* (Barcelona, 1994).

M. Peláez, *Catalunya després de la guerra civil del segle XV* (Barcelona, 1981).

J. Guiral-Hadziiossif, *Valence, port méditerranéen au XVe siècle (1410–1525)* (Paris, 1986).

A. Furió (ed.), *València, un mercat medieval* (Valencia, 1985).

P. Mainoni, *Mercanti lombardi fra Barcellona e Valenza nel basso medioevo* (Milan, 1983).

P. Iradiel, ed., *València i la Mediterrània medieval* [= vol. 2 of *Revista d'Història Medieval*] (Valencia, 1992).

E. Hamilton, *Money, prices and wages in Valencia, Aragon and Navarre, 1351–1500* (Cambridge, MA, 1936).

On Spain in this period there is a vast literature. Starting points include:

J.H. Elliott, *Imperial Spain 1469–1716* (London, 1963).

H. Kamen, *Spain 1469–1714. A society of conflict*, 2nd edn (London, 1991).

David Abulafia, *Spain and 1492. Unity and uniformity under Ferdinand and Isabella* (Headstart History Papers, Bangor, 1992), offering a guide also to literature on the Jews and Muslims in Spain.

P. Liss, *Isabel the Queen* (New York/Oxford, 1992).

M. Meyerson, *Muslims of Valencia in the age of Fernando and Isabel* (Berkeley/Los Angeles, 1991).

The French invasion of Italy

David Abulafia, ed., *The French descent into Renaissance Italy. Antecedents and effects* (Aldershot, 1995); several individual items from this collection are cited below.

F. Catalano, *Ludovico il Moro* (Milan, 1985).

Y. Labande-Maillfert, *Charles VIII. La jeunesse au pouvoir (1470–1495)* (Paris, 1975).

Y. Labande-Maillfert, *Charles VIII. Le vouloir et la destiné* (Paris, 1986).

I. Cloulas, *Charles VIII et le mirage italien* (Paris, 1986).

A. Denis, *Charles VIII et les italiens. Histoire et mythe* (Geneva, 1979).

M. Jacoviello, *Venezia e Napoli nel Quattrocento* (Naples, 1992).

C. Kidwell, 'Venice, the French invasion and the Apulian ports', in Abulafia, *The French descent*, pp. 295–308.

C.H. Clough, 'The Romagna campaign of 1494: a significant military encounter', in Abulafia, *The French descent*, pp. 191–215.

F.L. Taylor, *The art of war in Italy 1494–1529* (Cambridge, 1921, repr. London, 1993).

S. Pepper, 'Castles and cannon in the Naples campaign of 1494–5', in Abulafia, *The French descent*, pp. 263–93.

M. Mallett, 'Personalities and pressures: Italian involvement in the French invasion of 1494', in Abulafia, *The French descent*, pp. 151–63.

C. Shaw, 'The Roman barons and the French descent into Italy', in Abulafia, *The French descent*, pp. 249–61.

F. Baumgartner, *Louis XII* (Stroud, Glos./New York, 1994).

B. Quilliet, *Louis XII, père du peuple* (Paris, 1986).

Christine Shaw, *Julius II. The warrior pope* (Oxford, 1993).

R.J. Knecht, *The rise and fall of Renaissance France* (London, 1996).

J. Kirshner, ed., *The origins of the state in Italy 1300–1600* (Chicago, 1996; repr. from *Journal of Modern History*, vol. 67, 1995).

MAPS

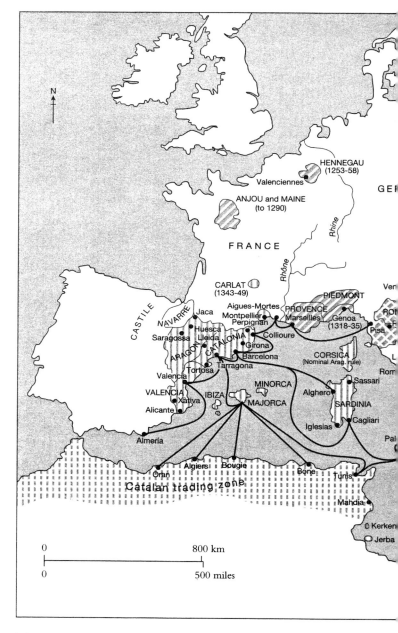

Map 1: Anjou and Aragon *c*.1380

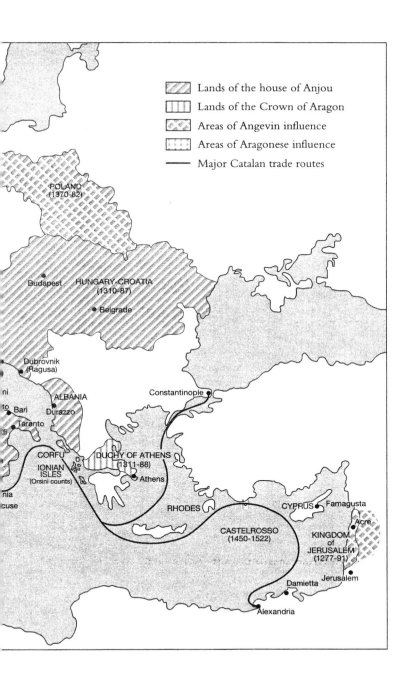

Lands of the house of Anjou

Lands of the Crown of Aragon

Areas of Angevin influence

Areas of Aragonese influence

Major Catalan trade routes

POLAND
(1370-82)

Budapest   HUNGARY-CROATIA
(1310-87)

● Belgrade

Dubrovnik
(Ragusa)

ni

to Bari   ALBANIA
● Durazzo

 fi   Taranto

CORFU

IONIAN   DUCHY OF ATHENS
ISLES   (1311-88)
(Orsini counts)   ● Athens

nia

cuse   RHODES   CYPRUS ● Famagusta

Constantinople

● Acre

CASTELROSSO   KINGDOM
(1450-1522)   of
JERUSALEM
(1277-91)

● Jerusalem

Damietta

● Alexandria

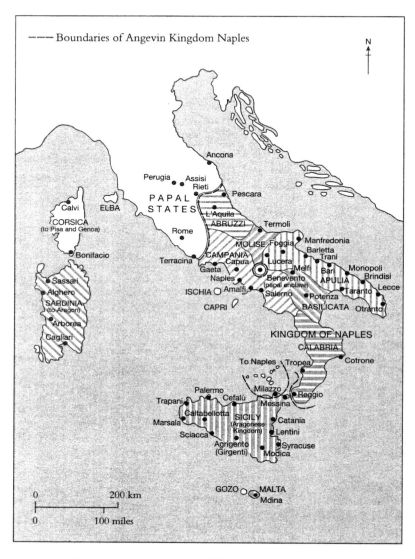

Map 2: The Italian South *c.*1350

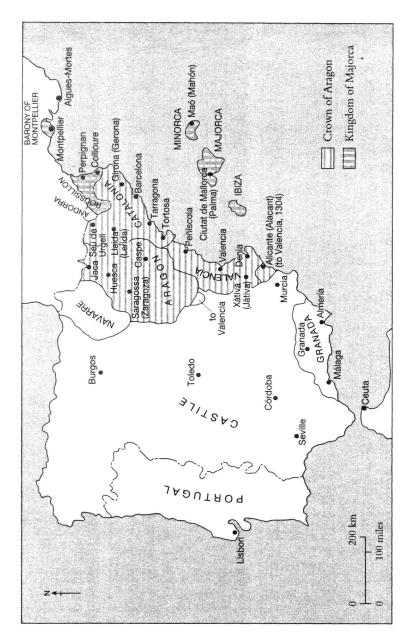

Map 3: The Spanish Kingdoms c.1320

Crown of Aragon

Kingdom of Majorca

BARONY OF MONTPELLIER
Montpellier
Aigues-Mortes
Perpignan
Collioure
Girona (Gerona)
ANDORRA
ROUSSILLON
CATALONIA
Barcelona
Tarragona
Tortosa
MINORCA
Maó (Mahón)
MAJORCA
Ciutat de Mallorca (Palma)
IBIZA
Peñiscola
Valencia
VALENCIA
Alicante (Alacant) (to Valencia, 1304)
Dénia
Xátiva (Játiva)
Murcia
NAVARRE
Jaca
Seu de Urgell
Huesca
Lleida (Lérida)
Saragossa (Zaragoza)
Caspe
ARAGON
to Valencia
Almería
Granada
GRANADA
Málaga
Burgos
Toledo
CASTILE
Córdoba
Seville
Ceuta
PORTUGAL
Lisbon

N

0   200 km
0   100 miles

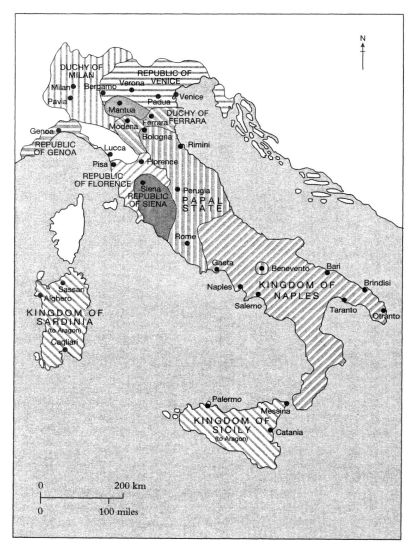

Map 4: Italy in 1494

GENEALOGICAL TABLES

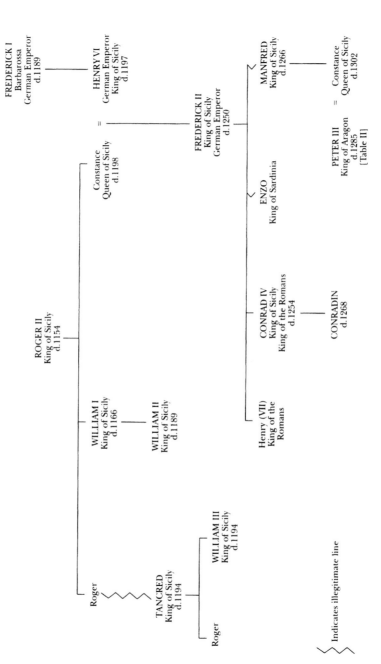

GENEALOGICAL TABLE I: THE NORMAN KINGS OF SICILY AND THE HOUSE OF HOHENSTAUFEN

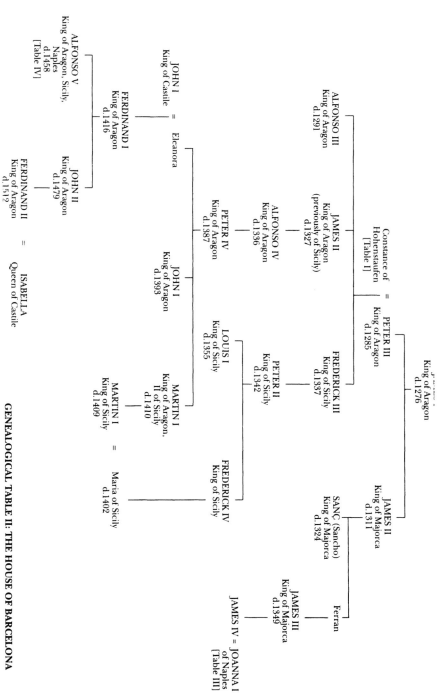

GENEALOGICAL TABLE II: THE HOUSE OF BARCELONA

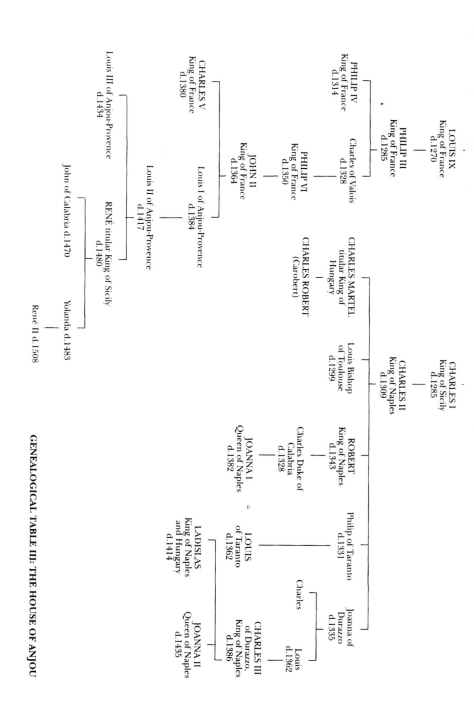

GENEALOGICAL TABLE III: THE HOUSE OF ANJOU

GENEALOGICAL TABLE IV: THE HOUSE OF ARAGON-NAPLES

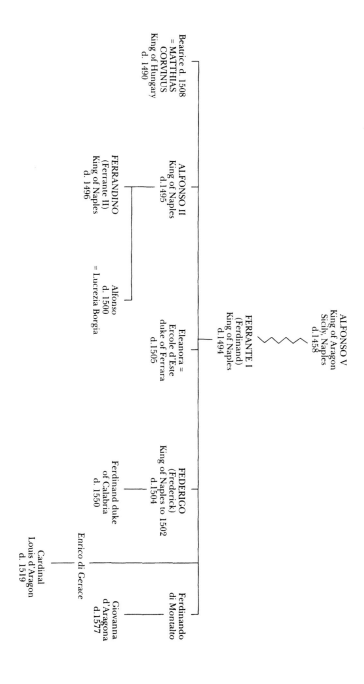

INDEX

Note: Certain terms that recur throughout the text, such as *Sicily*, *Italy* or *Catalonia*, have not been included. Pre-1450 names are given with the first name first, post-1450 names with the surname first. Popes are further identified by giving their original name in brackets. Catalan spelling has been adopted for place-names in Catalonia and Valencia, in accordance with current usage (*Lleida*, not *Lérida*); however, for the Balearic islands English, and for Catalan territories in France French, usage has been followed. English name forms ('Peter', 'John') are generally confined to rulers only.